I0131312

ABOVE THE GROUND
AND BENEATH THE CLOUDS

ABOVE THE GROUND AND BENEATH THE CLOUDS

Schizophrenia in Lacanian Psychoanalysis

Yannis Grammatopoulos

Routledge
Taylor & Francis Group

LONDON AND NEW YORK

First published 2017 by
Karnac Books Ltd.

Published 2018 by Routledge
2 Park Square, Milton Park, Abingdon, Oxon OX14 4RN
711 Third Avenue, New York, NY 10017, USA

Routledge is an imprint of the Taylor & Francis Group, an informa business

Copyright © 2017 by Yannis Grammatopoulos

The right of Yannis Grammatopoulos to be identified as the author of this work has been asserted in accordance with §§ 77 and 78 of the Copyright Design and Patents Act 1988.

All rights reserved. No part of this book may be reprinted or reproduced or utilised in any form or by any electronic, mechanical, or other means, now known or hereafter invented, including photocopying and recording, or in any information storage or retrieval system, without permission in writing from the publishers.

Notice:
Product or corporate names may be trademarks or registered trademarks, and are used only for identification and explanation without intent to infringe.

British Library Cataloguing in Publication Data

A C.I.P. for this book is available from the British Library

ISBN-13: 9781782205166 (pbk)

Typeset by Medlar Publishing Solutions Pvt Ltd, India

CONTENTS

ACKNOWLEDGMENTS

A few words of gratitude are owed to the following people and institutions for their contribution to the realisation of the present as a doctoral thesis and as a book: to Julia Borossa, for welcoming the idea for this research project at the Centre for Psychoanalysis of Middlesex University no matter how distant it might have sounded at a sunny central Athens café in October 2010; to Werner Prall and Anne Worthington, who undertook the task of supervising its realisation for five entire years in a matchless way: being always there when I needed their guidance and withdrawing discreetly when I felt I wanted to walk the tangled and lonely paths of doctoral research on my own; to George Constantinou, for his omnipresent willingness and support at the research office of Middlesex University; to Nassia Linardou and Réginald Blanchet, laborious workers of the World Association of Psychoanalysis, and outstanding teachers of the Lacanian theory and clinic; to Charalampos Orfanidis, young and talented graphic designer who bore patiently with my excruciatingly trivial demands on the topological depiction of the case of Vizyenos and of Lacanian theory, and not only; to the Greek State Scholarships Foundation (IKY), for funding generously the second part of my academic studies thanks to the bequest "in the memory of

Maria Zaousi"; last but not least, to Karnac Books who, unquestionably devoted to the proliferation of the psychoanalytic cause as they are, were more eager and generous than I could have imagined in undertaking the publication and circulation of my approach to the encounter between psychosis and Lacanian psychoanalysis.

ABOUT THE AUTHOR

Yannis Grammatopoulos is a psychologist and a psychoanalytic therapist. He was born in the border city of Didymoteicho, in north-eastern Greece. His academic and psychoanalytic studies have taken place in Greece and in the UK. He studied psychology at the Panteion University of Social & Political Sciences in Athens and applied psychology (MSc) at Brunel University in London. In 2016 he received his PhD in psychoanalysis from Middlesex University in London. He was sponsored for it with a bequest from the Greek State Scholarships Foundation (IKY) offered to research subjects that fall within the interests of psychiatry.

For the past years, he has been teaching psychology in higher and professional education. He is a Lecturer at Athens colleges partnered with British and Irish academic institutions. During the past year Yannis has also been running theoretical and clinical seminars for professionals from a variety of backgrounds with an emphasis on psychosis and its psychoanalytic approach.

He was trained as a psychoanalyst at the College of Clinical Studies of Athens, an institution under the auspices of the Institute of the Freudian Field—Lacanian orientation, the training scheme of the World

Association of Psychoanalysis. Since 2011 he has been a member of the Hellenic Society of the New Lacanian School (NLS).

As an active member of the Lacanian community he has attended and participated in relevant conferences with paper presentations and he has contributed original articles on the theory and clinic of psychoanalysis in Greek, English, and French. He has also translated a book and papers from the three languages, which were published in *Hurly-Burly* (now the *Lacanian Review*), the *Psychoanalytical Notebooks*, the electronic version of *Lacan Quotidien*, and others.

For the past decade, he has been seeing patients in a variety of public institutions and in private practice, in both Athens and London. He has worked with adult mental health patients, children with ASD and special educational needs, military personnel, and detained refugees and immigrants.

Above the Ground and Beneath the Clouds is his first book, which began as his doctoral thesis in psychoanalysis, where he investigated the Lacanian—theoretical and clinical—approach to schizophrenia. His other theoretical and clinical interests are the psychoanalytic approach to art and literature, the relation between the first and the later Lacan, and the concept of the psychoanalytic act.

PREFACE

I still remember the first time I met people diagnosed with schizo-phrenia; people whose bodies lay "above the ground and beneath the clouds". The encounter took place many years ago in my native Greece. It happened at a public mental health centre in the southern suburbs of Athens, during my placement as an undergraduate psychology student.

It was the first days of March, a beautiful time of the year in the Greek capital. Making my way to that institution through an alley of poplars, I recall being over the moon for having been allocated to a clinical set-ting instead of a business or a primary school, like some of my peers. I had wanted to meet and work with psychotic patients. My wish was certainly fulfilled thanks to that placement: I met those people, and I was intrigued by the way they spoke and the way they treated their bodies. I remember Peter, diagnosed with catatonic schizophrenia, sit-ting in a peculiar posture and pointing to his throat while declaring that there lay his mother's genitalia (making use of less "proper" terminol-ogy needless to say).

It took more than a decade of clinical work, psychoanalytic training, but mostly the labour of doctoral studies, in order to transform the early fascination by statements like these into a number of suggestions on the status of language and the body in the clinic of schizophrenia. In effect, the encounter between the two areas featuring in this book's sub-title, schizophrenia and Lacanian psychoanalysis, had to take place under the auspices of academia for the reader to hold the present volume in their hands today.

In this respect, the year that the aforementioned encounter took place seems quite topical. Although my meeting with schizophrenics and Lacanian psychoanalysis had taken place a few years before the present research commenced, it seems that this could not have happened at a more appropriate time than in 2011. This is because 2011 marked two anniversaries related to the fields whose junction appears in the sub-title: first, the centenary of the earliest citations of schizophrenia in the psychiatric domain; second, the thirtieth anniversary of Jacques Lacan's death.

Many might think that the links between the two anniversaries are either too few or too indirect—and this may be partly true. On my part, I was certainly led to an impression like this after a preliminary bibliographical investigation that took place between my having taken up psychoanalytic training and beginning my doctoral studies.

Lacan, as we know, initially trained as a psychiatrist. It is therefore to be expected that the term "schizophrenia" would have been of use to him both during and shortly after his training. Yet this was not the case concerning his teaching on psychoanalysis, which started in the 1950s. If, indeed, "schizophrenia" was a term used by Lacan the young psychiatrist, Lacan the psychoanalyst, who taught a "return to Freud", rarely made use of it. He did use this term when discussing Freud's restricted approach to the psychotic types (paranoia and dementia praecox/paraphrenia/schizophrenia), but schizophrenia certainly did not occupy a pivotal position in his yearly round of seminars, as had also been the case with Freud. In fact, the founder of psychoanalysis was not even happy with the name introduced in the early twentieth century to describe this psychotic type.

Indeed, the artificial term "schizophrenia" seems to carry a relatively awkward meaning. Its first element is the Greek verb σχίζω (schizo), which means "to split", and the second is one of many ancient Greek nouns meaning "mind": φρην (phrene)—another one, νους (nous), is the second element of "paranoia". The idea of the split mind had been introduced to describe an aspect of the behaviour of patients suffering from schizophrenia, but that was not the aforementioned peculiar relation to their bodies. One may hear a schizophrenic claim that their brain has been split in two parts, yet the psychiatrist who coined the term, Eugen Bleuler, did not intend to describe a mind actually cut in half.

He wanted to describe deficits in the observed functions of the patient's mind, such as in their association and affectivity.

On their part, Freud and other psychoanalysts' initial interest in schizophrenia seemed to serve the purpose of describing unconscious mechanisms rather than the condition in question. In fact, Freud did not refer to psychosis extensively after the mid-1910s, having found that people who suffered from it could not benefit from a proper psychoanalysis. This is the Freud that Lacan was commenting on in the first period of his teaching. As for Lacan, who took greater interest in the psychoses, he only left a handful of remarks on schizophrenia, the most indicative of which about the schizophrenic's relation to language and the body is probably found as late as the early 1970s, in his influential paper "L'Étourdit". Beyond that, there isn't very much.

In fact, another conclusion I was led to following my preliminary bibliographical investigation was our relative lack of familiarity with Lacan's teaching on psychosis *in its totality*. Sixty years after Lacan's teaching of the 1950s, and thirty years after his death, we may, indeed, have come to grips with the Lacan of the symbolic and the "return to Freud". We may already have started putting our finger on the Lacan of the 1960s, the Lacan of the shift to jouissance. Yet Lacan's teaching on psychosis is not limited to the 1950s and 1960s. There is also Lacan's later teaching, which did not leave psychosis or his views on subjectivity, language, and the body untouched. Our familiarity with that final stage of Lacan's teaching seems restricted—and this has had enduring consequences. We may have been to some extent capable of summarising what Lacan thought about schizophrenia in the context of his early theories of the "paternal metaphor" and the "question prior to any possible treatment of psychosis", but what the later Lacan thought of it seemed—and still seems—relatively obscure. In fact, without the later Lacan I felt that any attempt to conceive of and attempt to treat via the help of language the schizophrenic body's lying "above the ground and beneath the clouds" was bound to remain incomplete.

Here is therefore an attempt to investigate the status of the schizophrenic's relation to language and the body, which will, I hope, bear some theoretical and clinical value for Lacanian psychoanalysis. This attempt takes place in three steps, corresponding to three parts. The first part takes the form of review of the literature; the second, of a psychoanalytic case history; the third, of a discussion of the theoretical and clinical implications of the first two parts. Examples drawn from my clinical experience are also used all the way through in an attempt to highlight the clinical impact of the discussed Lacanian conceptualisation and treatment of schizophrenia. More specifically:

In Part I, the reader will find an analysis of the history and theoretical foundations of the conceptualisation and treatment of schizophrenia in Freud and Lacan's original writing and teaching. The psychiatric origins of this term are presented first. Then I discuss Freud's view of schizophrenia, which changed throughout the years, alongside his theoretical and clinical approach to psychosis (Chapter One). After Freud and a short reference to current psychoanalysts who attempted to treat schizophrenia through a mechanism more suited to paranoia, the reader will find an examination of the theoretical formulations and teachings of Jacques Lacan on psychosis to the extent that this is feasible. The conceptions of the ego and the subject, significant for the imaginary and the symbolic respectively, come first (Chapter Two), and then comes the speaking being, lalangue, the sinthome, and the stepladder, all concepts closer to the third register, the real, which characterises the later Lacan and focuses on the subject's relation to its body (Chapter Three). Thus, a more comprehensive illustration than usual of Lacan's views on schizophrenia is attempted.

Part II employs the paradigm of the case history, which is the usual approach in psychoanalytic research and practice, and which always focuses on the subject's singularity. One of the advantage of the case history is that, like the discourse of the psychoanalyst, it focuses on the subject's singular relation to the real of their jouissance.

The case employed is that of a late-nineteenth-century Greek writer, Georgios Vizyenos, who resided for a few years in Germany, Paris, and London, and died in a psychiatric hospital a few years before the end of that century. The instruments from Freud and Lacan's writing and teaching presented in Part I are used in a reading of Vizyenos' life and work (Chapters Four, Five, & Six), as derived from contemporary testimonies in the press and in various memoirs, from his biographies and his psychiatric records, and from his correspondence and his written works. My aim is to use this man as an example for treating the body by means of an invention through language, which did not depend on otherness, the pathway taken by those who are not schizophrenic. It is suggested that Vizyenos managed to knot for a considerable amount of time the three registers—imaginary, symbolic, and real—that localised his body and organs thanks to such an invention (Chapter Seven).

Finally, in Part III, the theoretical and clinical implications from studying cases like Vizyenos's for the contemporary Lacanian approach to schizophrenia are discussed. Two practical aspects of the psycho-analytic approach to schizophrenic subjects are presented: diagnosis (Chapter Eight) and treatment (Chapter Nine). The vital role played by investigating the subject's relation to the real for both aspects is dis-cussed based on the case example of Vizyenos, whose achievement was based on an elaboration of jouissance related to a concept of particular value. It is suggested that this can be one of the orientations in working with schizophrenic subjects, one that does not lean on processing other-ness, which leans on the imaginary (ego) and/or the symbolic (subject of the signifier), but on their interrelation with the real (jouissance) inherent in the One.

My core aspiration—apart from the obvious popularisation of the fascinating case of Georgios Vizyenos, which has already been hap-pening through presentations and publications in the UK, France, and Greece—was for the present volume to be of assistance to clinicians see-ing schizophrenic subjects. More than a hundred years after the creation of the signifier "schizophrenia" and more than thirty years after Jacques Lacan's death, I hoped that bringing the two together could yield use-ful suggestions for the clinical—as well as theoretical—approach to the schizophrenic subject. The clinician who sees schizophrenic subjects in the consulting room or in the hospital ward will probably be the best judge of that. He or she is wholeheartedly invited to judge the present by borrowing the schizophrenic's rigour for literalism, which, as the reader will find out, is what gave its title to the present book.

And one final warning. In the nine following chapters I make, to my knowledge, the frequent use of the etymology of clinical terms as schizophrenia, paranoia, etc. Surprise, surprise, their etymology is always—like myself—of Greek origin. I am also aware of the danger of this tendency of mine to remind the reader of a fictional character in the popular early-2000s film *My Big Fat Greek Wedding*: Gus Portokalos. Gus Portokalos is a Greek-American man who takes great pride in his Greek roots and is very confident about his capacity to trace the origin of every foreign word in the Greek language, with rather bizarre and always inaccurate outcomes. On the one hand, I would like to ensure the reader that even if the frequent reference to the Greek vocabulary in support of my argumentation becomes at times as irritating as that of Gus Portokalos, none of it is made-up. On the other, if a chapter with no reference at all to Greek etymology is expected, I would like to warn ye, who enter here, to abandon any hope …

PART I

THE "POOR RELATION'S" STORY: SCHIZOPHRENIA IN FREUD AND LACAN

Introduction to Part I

In 1908, a prominent Swiss psychiatrist named Eugen Bleuler gave a speech to an association of German psychiatrists. In that speech, he suggested the replacement of the designation "dementia praecox" with a term of his own invention: "schizophrenia". Dementia praecox had been an earlier psychiatric term that described the same "mental disease". Three years later, in 1911, Bleuler published an influential monograph that introduced the term formally to the psychiatric domain.

Psychoanalysis, a psychological theory and therapeutic technique that had already been developing for a few years, soon caught up with psychiatry. It was also in 1911 that its founder, Sigmund Freud, published one of his five famous case studies: "President Schreber". Freud had been discussing schizophrenia with one of Bleuler's hospital subordinates, Carl Gustav Jung, since Bleuler first suggested it. In his study of 1911, Freud analysed the new-fangled concept in light of a dysfunction in the establishment of narcissism, which, in contrast, happens in paranoia, which was the paper's original focus. In another paper, published four years later, he would refer to a therapeutic orientation for schizophrenia different from the one he had suggested in his study of paranoia. Yet somehow both views relate to what Lacanian psychoanalysis places at the centre of the schizophrenic being: the challenge to relate to one's body and organs through language. Freud's thinking is examined below, following the history of the psychiatric configuration of schizophrenia.

In spite of the present volume focusing on the psychoanalytic rather than the psychiatric approach to psychosis, references to the psychiatric origins of schizophrenia will not be avoided. This is not only due to this concept having been configured by late-nineteenth and early-twentieth-century psychiatric classifiers. It is also due to those scholars having described, from an early stage and with precision, what Freud and other psychoanalysts who came after him would designate as a field that treatment with schizophrenics cannot ignore: the particular status of their discourse, which, itself, is responsible for structural problems in the schizophrenic's relation to his or her body.

Of course, like current psychiatry, psychoanalysis did not claim to be able to cure schizophrenia. Although a number of Freud's first disciples aspired quite optimistically to treat schizophrenia through the application of psychoanalysis, this objective soon proved pointless. No one was able to treat schizophrenia by applying the standard talking cure that Freud developed when treating hysterical patients in the late nineteenth century.

Nevertheless, thanks to the work of another outstanding—and relatively controversial—figure in psychoanalysis, the second half of the twentieth century saw a change in the way psychosis and its treatment were viewed. That man was the French psychoanalyst and psychiatrist Jacques Lacan. His thirty-year-long teaching seems to indicate a designation for treatment with schizophrenic subjects by use of psychoanalytic instruments.

Of course, as was highlighted above, psychoanalysis does not claim to be able to cure schizophrenia. What we therefore find in Lacan's teaching is the logic behind a treatment that can take place in the clinic of schizophrenia, that is, with subjects who are schizophrenic; a logic stemming from his continuously evolving conceptualisation of subjectivity and its coordinates.

This designation, however, does not appear clear-cut in Lacan's work. When his teaching labelled as a "return to Freud" began, Lacan was not even talking about psychosis in particular. He was interested in reformulating the concepts of speech and subject as he believed he had encountered them in Freud. His theoretical preoccupation with psychosis came in the third year of his yearly seminar and was summarised in a paper written a couple of years later; even then the schizophrenic body does not occupy a central place.

Therefore, the Lacanian orientation for the treatment of the schizophrenic body through language is not mainly found there. We had to wait longer for a number of more explicit, but always rare and ambiguous, references to schizophrenia by Lacan—references that form the coordinates of its conceptualisation and treatment suggested in the present book. A final theoretical formulation, which marked the last step in Lacan's thirty-year-long teaching, still remains to be linked to the status of schizophrenia. To link it to the schizophrenic body is one of the main objectives of this, first, part of the book. This attempt is carried forward in the other two parts, assisted by examples from the clinic, art and literature, and even cinematography.

CHAPTER ONE

From the splitting of the mind to the unity of the ego

In spite of this chapter investigating the *psychoanalytic* conceptualisation and treatment of an originally *psychiatric* concept, its discussion cannot avoid referring to a third discipline studying the human mind, one whose name also includes the element "psyche". This discipline is *psychology*, thanks to my undergraduate studies in which I first came into contact with patients deemed schizophrenic and I was intrigued by their discourse and by their relation to their bodies and organs.

Yet the need to refer to psychology at this point does not concern my academic background. It stems from this scientific discipline having affected the original configuration of schizophrenia, which obscured the significance of the schizophrenic's particular relation to their body. This happened concerning both the form in which it first appeared in psychiatric textbooks, as dementia praecox, as well as its later reformulation by a prominent psychiatric scholar and one of Freud's first disciples. All these take place in the work of the German psychiatrist Emil Kraepelin and the Swiss psychiatrists Eugen Bleuler and Carl Gustav Jung, discussed below.

Before Freud

Kraepelin

The concept that Eugen Bleuler suggested replacing in his 1908 speech to the Association of German Psychiatrists with "schizophrenia" was "dementia praecox" (Küchenhoff, 2008). The latter was a form of "mental disease" from the *Textbook of Psychiatry* by Professor Emil Kraepelin (1899), a man who would lay the foundations of modern scientific psychiatry (Eysenck, Arnold, & Meili, 1975). His textbooks seem to have had a significant impact on psychiatric classification, extending even beyond the twentieth century (Ebert & Bär, 2010). The remark above about the psychological aspect of the early configuration of schizophrenia concerns not only his scientific approach, but also his personal history and interests.

Kraepelin was born in the same year as Freud, 1856, in the city of Neustrelitz. Having shown an interest in medicine in childhood, he once visited a hospital encouraged by a friend of his father's. There, he found a book that would form his aspirations and influence the approach he would take in his psychiatric endeavours (Briole, 2012): Wilhelm Wundt's lectures on the psyche (1896). Wundt was, of course, as every first year psychology student is told, the founder of the first laboratory of experimental psychology in 1879, and the first scientist to call himself a psychologist.

Yet simply reading the book by the future founder of experimental psychology did not suffice for young Emil. He went on to study with Wundt at the University of Leipzig, where Wundt would later turn a former canteen to his laboratory. Kraepelin soon moved from psychology to the study of psychiatry. Nevertheless, he continued to see himself as a "psychologically inclined psychiatrist" (Gallagher, 2011, p. 26). Indeed, in his renowned *Textbook of Psychiatry*, one can see the influence of Wundt's scientific principles, which aimed at establishing the structure of consciousness through empirical observation.

The first edition of Kraepelin's textbook was published in 1883. Although, as above, this eventually would turn into his magnum opus, its writer was in a professional impasse when he composed it. Kraepelin had just been dismissed from the ward he was working at as a young psychiatrist. Paul Flechsig, also a professor at Leipzig and in charge of the ward, had found him incompetent (Briole, 2012). Ironically, the endeavour that this impasse produced would influence the psychiatry of the following 130 years like no other. As for Professor Flechsig, his name would be forever linked in psychoanalytic literature to one of his future patients presented below, President Daniel Paul Schreber.

Dementia praecox did not constitute a group in Kraepelin's initial categorisation of mental diseases. It originally belonged to other psychotic superordinates. It appeared as a separate and coherent category in the sixth edition of 1899. Yet it is not solely thanks to this innovation that Kraepelin's classification is believed to have considerably affected modern psychiatry: it is also due to the distinction between the so-called affective (i.e., manic-depressive) and non-affective psychoses, where dementia praecox belonged (Decker, 2007). Although Kraepelin did not remain confident about this differentiation, it has lingered in contemporary psychiatry (Leader, 2015). In addition, it has not left the field of psychoanalysis untouched either. Let us now come to dementia praecox.

The term was originally invented not by Kraepelin, as he writes himself (1899), but by the Czech psychiatrist Arnold Pick (Hoenig, 1995). Kraepelin was, however, the one who configured it as a broader diagnostic category and introduced it in his comprehensive system of psychotic forms. Kraepelin did not hide either the fact that most of the forms he would use had already been referred to by previous scholars, such as his own professor, Karl Ludwig Kahlbaum. Yet it was him who went on to unify them and to differentiate them from other forms of psychosis.

The common and necessary characteristic of cases that fell within this new diagnostic category were a) mental and emotional deterioration (*dementia*) and b) their appearance at a relatively young age (*praecox*) (Kraepelin, 1899; 1904). The "great classifier" (Alanen, 2009a, p. 4) also configured categories within dementia praecox. He suggested three groups: "hebephrenia", "catatonia", and "paranoid forms" (Kraepelin, 1899).

Kraepelin (1899) believed that dementia praecox characterised an extended group of cases, examples of which he took great care to give. His intention to apply the principles of psychology to his study of the mentally ill generated graphic portrayals that paint a vivid picture of what a mental asylum looked like near the turn of the twentieth century.

Yet, by focusing on patients' mental processes like apprehension, memory, judgment, consciousness, emotion, and others, Kraepelin failed to attribute a certain status to patients' recurrent complaints about their bodies and organs, like the ones I heard in my first contact with schizophrenic patients described in the *Preface*. On the one hand, Kraepelin is describing quite aptly patients who believe that their throats are occluded or that their bowels are bound together (1899, p, 168), patients whose feet have been transformed to mules' hoofs (p. 175), and patients whose intestines have been removed or replaced (pp. 189, 193). On the other, he does not cease treating such phenomena as nothing more than hallucinations or delusions. This may be indeed the proper psychiatric designations for those complains. Yet, as will be clarified further below, in Freud and in Lacan phenomena like these are not simply treated as secondary manifestations but occupy a central, one might say radical, status for schizophrenia. As for Kraepelin's description of schizophrenics' physical symptoms, they mainly concern the status of nutrition and sleep and in the catatonic type catatonic symptoms (1899).

On the contrary, Kraepelin's textbook is full of examples from patients' discourse with an emphasis on their psychological disturbances. Consonant with his allegiance to Wundt, Kraepelin highlights the particular status of schizophrenics' behaviour, demonstrating his findings with meticulous observation and documentation; so meticulous that in the short *Lectures on Clinical Psychiatry* he refers at least three times to the way patients with dementia praecox shake hands (Kraepelin, 1904)! Yet a comprehensive presentation of a patient in the form of a case history is missing from his magnum opus and from his other descriptions of this disease.

Moreover, in spite of its success, the new concept lacks a comprehensive theory of how this form of psychosis comes about. Kraepelin (1899) acknowledges the specialists' poor knowledge of the cause of that behaviour and presumes that the course of dementia praecox passes exclusively from the cerebral cortex. He even advises psychiatrists not to focus on aetiologies in order to form a diagnosis. In his opinion, they should emphasise the course of the illness rather than any of its other aspects (Decker, 2007).

In effect, Kraepelin (1899; 1904) is rather pessimistic concerning recovery from dementia praecox. His suggestions for therapy regard the treatment of symptoms and not the disease itself, evidencing the time's meagre knowledge of the causes of the disease. This is, of course, consonant with mental deterioration being considered as not only unavoidable but necessary for diagnosis.

So, for example, concerning a patient who would, in the course of their illness, exhibit disturbances like the ones cited above, Kraepelin (1899) suggests that treatment can consist of, among other things and always taking into account the patient's state, a quiet environment, friendly and skilled staff, warm baths, good nutrition, and bed treatment. Nevertheless, the inventor of dementia praecox remains quite pessimistic, implying that the only thing psychiatry can for the moment do with patients presenting symptoms like delusions, looseness of thought, and confusion of ideas is to study them in trying to identify the course of the disease.

It seems, however, that this was not an approach confined to psychiatry. The first psychoanalyst who produced a study of this diagnostic category, which Bleuler would transform into schizophrenia some years later, would adopt a similar perspective. He was Carl Gustav Jung, the man whom Freud would—for some time—consider his "Crown Prince" (McGuire, 1994).

In moving to the examination of another psychiatrist's—and early psychoanalyst's—approach to schizophrenia, one should not rush to abandon the focus on psychology. It seems that Jung's approach is nothing but an attempt to study and portray the discourse of patients suffering from dementia praecox by use of psychological experimentation stemming from psychoanalytic inventions.

Jung

When the sixth edition of Kraepelin's textbooks came out, the Viennese neurologist Sigmund Freud had already published a few papers on the neuroses and defence, as he had encountered them through the talking therapy he had developed in trying to cure hysteric patients alongside Josef Breuer (Breuer & Freud, 1893–1895). In the following decade, a number of influential publications on psychoanalysis attracted the attention of a Swiss trainee psychiatrist at the Burghölzli psychiatric hospital of the University of Zurich: Carl Gustav Jung.

An admirer of Freud's ideas, Jung started corresponding with the founder of psychoanalysis in 1906. A strong relationship developed between them. Before even meeting Freud in person, Jung promised him a study of the clinical condition known as dementia praecox, which he had been investigating at the Burghölzli, from Freud's standpoint (McGuire, 1994).

Freud's influential publications prior to 1906 had been *The Interpretation of Dreams* (1900a), *The Psychopathology of Everyday Life* (1901b), *Jokes and their Relation to the Unconscious* (1905c), and *Three Essays on the Theory of Sexuality* (1905d). The first three have been, quite aptly, called the "birth certificate of psychoanalysis" (Aflalo, 2015, p. 29). Freud's "standpoint" in those publications, "canonical with regard to the unconscious" (Lacan, 1957a, p. 434), concerned his first topographical theory—the division of mental life into conscious, preconscious, and unconscious—and the mechanisms of condensation and displacement occurring in the latter.

Concerning the form of mental illness that we call psychosis today, Freud had not differentiated it radically from neurosis (Freud 1894a; 1896b). His 1890s concept of the "neuro-psychoses of defence" included both clinical categories. He had been focusing upon the common formation of symptoms—which, truth be told, were not irrelevant to the function of the body and its organs—through defence mechanisms in the two categories (Freud, 1896b). Therefore, his "standpoint" on psychosis in the first decade of the twentieth century concerned the formation of symptoms through repression of sexual material in the unconscious.

Jung indeed followed the aforementioned approach in his study, although he attempted to establish it based on psychological research rather than the psychoanalytic technique. His monograph, published in 1906, was titled *The Psychology of Dementia Praecox*. His approach has been described as the first official introduction of Freud's theses into Kraepelinian psychiatry (Dalle & Weill, 1999). I would not hesitate characterising it, alternatively, from a reverse perspective—as the introduction of Kraepelinian "psychologically inclined" psychiatry into Freud's theses—since it is, indeed, psychology and psychiatry rather than psychoanalysis that benefit from his reading.

Jung's main argument is that, as with hysteria, symptoms in dementia praecox are directly related to one or more fixed complexes, which are impossible to be addressed or altered (1906). The function of the complex symptoms, which are observable at the level of affection, is defensive, similar to Freud's neuro-psychoses of defence (1894a; 1896b). Yet the patient's destiny is "psychic mutilation" (Jung, 1906, p. 98).

To show the distorted status of associations in patients suffering from dementia praecox, Jung would conduct a psychological experiment of his own invention, based on the psychoanalytic method of free association. The reader might be familiar with this thanks to the recent film *A Dangerous Method*, featuring the peculiar relations between Freud, Jung, and the future psychoanalyst Sabina Spielrein.

Jung would give a patient a word and ask for an association, which he would time and document. The test was repeated and its findings yielded the main argument: associations in patients suffering from dementia praecox are very shallow; they are not "of the normal state" and can be compared to a dream state (Jung, 1906, p. 12). This, Jung argues, shows that Freud's theory can be generalised to the mental disease in question.

Jung even presents a case example to support this argument, that of a seamstress admitted to the psychiatric hospital in her early forties. She presented an impressive number of active delusions, such as that "she has fortunes of millions" and that "in the night her bed is full of needles" (Jung, 1906, p. 100). This woman also complained of phenomena related to her body, saying that her spinal cord had been torn out and that she would experience back pains caused by magnetism. However, like Kraepelin, Jung would not study them emphatically but continue treating such complaints at the level of the disturbances in mental processes. Year by year, the seamstress' delusions were indeed proliferating and her speech was becoming more absurd. Jung even gives the reader excerpts from her discourse:

> I am Germania and Helvetia of exclusively sweet butter, but now I have no more any supply of butter not even as much as a fly would leave behind—hm—hm—hm –hm—that is starvation—hm—hm.
> I am Noah's ark, the life boat and the esteem, Maria Stuart, Empress Alexander. (Jung, C. G., [1906] 1909, p. 100)

Another aspect of the particular status of this patient's discourse, leaving aside her delusions, are neologisms—which Kraepelin (1899) had also noted in his patients—like "power-word" and "word-salad" (Jung, 1906, p. 112). Jung uses those words to demonstrate the patient's constellation of complexes. He believes that her mental life is occupied totally by the complexes of personal grandeur and persecution, alongside indications of an erotic complex. Like Kraepelin—and soon Bleuler—her complaints about her body and organs are viewed as an effect of distorted association.

Jung (1906) classified the delusional seamstress to the paranoid form of dementia praecox from Kraepelin's three forms. His concern, however, was not to perform treatment of any kind informed by psychoanalytic practice. It was to show that Freud's theory could explain the status of complexes evident in her discourse, which showed nothing but the morbid condition that patients like her are found in.

Regarding the origin of dementia praecox, Jung suggests a theory of "intoxication". He identifies a variable characterised as "toxin (?)" and sometimes "X", which emerges from a somatic disturbance and brings about the fixation of complexes (Jung, 1906). Overall, he had reservations about his theory's capacity to identify the cause and course of dementia praecox. He writes that safe conclusions cannot be easily reached in this field (Jung, 1906).

At the end of the day, it seems that Jung's approach sided with Kraepelin and, as is shown below, with Bleuler, his hospital chief, rather than with Freud. In effect, the founder of psychoanalysis did not see eye to eye about this mental illness with Jung.

In their correspondence one is offered the chance to identify Freud's early reservations, which concerned even the necessity for a separate category of dementia praecox.

His letter replying to the receipt of Jung's book—including his criticism—is missing from their published correspondence (McGuire, 1994). Yet it is obvious in Jung's response that Freud raised objections, which probably regarded the aforementioned intoxication theory and the neglect of sexuality (Miller, 1983). Freud would also remark so in the future (1914d). Unlike with Jung's psychological approach, which was based on the status of associations, Freud wanted to establish a libidinal theory of schizophrenia, still called dementia praecox. A year after Jung's monograph, he wrote about what Jung had described as an "unfortunate" term:

> I write paranoia and not Dem. pr. because I regard the former as a good clinical type and the latter as a poor nosographical term. (Freud, S., [1908] 1994, p. 98)

Freud is certainly justified in denouncing the nosographical origin of dementia praecox, although one is not sure that Kraepelin would necessarily take this as an accusation. That concept had been indeed developed by Kraepelin following extensive clinical observations in a number of psychiatric institutions (Briole, 2012).

Although it is not evident from the specific excerpt whether Freud considers paranoia and dementia praecox synonymous, it is obvious that his viewpoint on its nature concerns its mediation by a libidinal factor, homosexuality. He writes:

> [It] is probably conditioned by restriction to the homosexual component. (Freud, S., [1908] 1994, p. 98)

Freud remarks that the paranoiac (precocious dementia) and the hysteric seek different types of solutions (McGuire, 1994). It is thus their common reference, sexuality—and later on a common recourse to the body—that interests him, rather than their segregation. It would take him some time to distinguish psychosis from neurosis on the vicissitudes of the libido with regard to the self, the ego, and the object.

However, whereas cases of neurosis, like hysteria, had been extensively studied by Freud in the past (Breuer & Freud, 1895d; Freud, 1905c), the same had not happened with regard to psychosis until the second decade of the twentieth century. This would change in 1911. Five years after Jung's (1906) publication, Freud, in a study of a case of psychosis, would refer more explicitly to its conceptualisation and an orientation for its treatment. But let us return, for a moment, to Jung.

It seems that his attempt to combine psychiatry and psychoanalysis to study a psychotic type had produced a psychological approach to dementia praecox that Freud was not enthusiastic about. One more problem seemed to be Jung's propensity to reduce the particular status of patients' discourse to organicity. An advantage to the Lacanian approach to schizophrenia concerns the identification of libido not with the organicity of "toxins" but with that of jouissance, an approach that seems consonant with Freud's, who frequently noted the distance separating the biological from the psychic mechanisms he was putting forward (1915e).

In spite of Freud's criticism, however, Jung's perspective would not disappear soon from the psychiatric study of this psychotic type. In fact, Eugen Bleuler would use Jung's conclusions regarding patients' associations to formulate his understanding of a biologically determined mental disorder too.

As for Jung, within less than seven years after the publication of *The Psychology of Dementia Praecox*, the ultimate break with Freud would occur. The Swiss psychiatrist and psychoanalyst would remain skeptical about the possibility of treating schizophrenia therapeutically and would instead stress psychoanalysis' contribution to the psychology of the disease (Hoffmann, 2009).

Bleuler

As discussed above, Bleuler introduced the term schizophrenia in a speech in 1908, whereas his comprehensive theory of the condition was introduced three years later, in his monograph *On Dementia Praecox or the Group of Schizophrenias* (1911).

Before reconfiguring dementia praecox, Bleuler had been the first professor of psychiatry to embrace Freud's ideas and promote the study of psychosis with the help of the method of free association developed by Jung and other psychoanalysts—Abraham Brill, Max Eitingon, Alphonse Maeder, and Ludwig Binswager (Hoffmann, 2009). He also incorporated the findings from Jung's study in his own configuration of schizophrenia (Ellenberger, 1970). Yet this aspect of psychoanalytic research only proved useful to him with regards to describing the psychological aspects of the condition that were not what interested its psychoanalytic approach.

The new name Bleuler was suggesting came from two Greek words that mean "to split" (or "to cleave") and "mind" respectively (Laplanche & Pontalis, 1973, p. 408). Their combination describes the most important quality in how Bleuler (1911) conceives of schizophrenia: the splitting of the diverse psychic functions, a condition primary to the manifestation of the complexes of the disease.

Although this concept had been suggested by Bleuler only three years earlier, it was not the first time that the idea of splitting was used in a psychiatric attempt to define a psychotic condition (Miller, 1983). Nineteenth-century psychiatric scholars such as Jean-Étienne Dominique Esquirol in France and Wilhelm Griesinger in Germany had also used this notion in the terms "split of psychic functions" and "splitting from the field of consciousness" respectively (Burns, 2007). Therefore, Bleuler did not invent the idea of splitting. He simply used it to describe a new concept by linking that tradition to the idea of psychical impairment, itself suggested in the past by the French psychiatrist Pierre Janet and used in Kraepelin's early classifications (Scharfetter, 2001).

Psychotic symptomatology, which constituted at the same time Kraepelin's success and failure—the second in terms of his admitted inability to locate a single symptom characterising the disorder—was a field where Bleuler proved a master. He suggested differentiating between fundamental and accompanying symptoms in schizophrenia (Bleuler, 1911). The first, where the splitting is found, are considered as typical of the condition. They define its core. It is suggested that they have an organic cause, in contrast to the accompanying symptoms. Those symptoms contribute to the formulation of the phenomenology of schizophrenia and help thus in the formulation of diagnosis (Bleuler, 1911).

The fundamental symptoms suggested by Bleuler concern the patient's simple and complex functions. Simple functions fall into two categories: those affected from the disease (association, affectivity, and ambivalence) and those remaining intact (sensation and perception, orientation, memory, consciousness, and motion). Complex functions relate to the sense of reality—autism, attention, willingness, personality, schizophrenic dementia, activity, and behaviour. The occasional morbid picture of the complex functions is caused by the disturbances in the simple functions (1911). The term "autism", which will be used in the future to describe a distinct clinical entity, points to the schizophrenic's propensity to turn to the self. This does not identify with, but does paint a picture of what Freud and Lacan will describe as a core element of this condition.

The same will happen with a number of Bleuler's accompanying symptoms, which comprise what we are more accustomed to define as psychotic manifestations. They are sensory errors, delusional ideas, accompanying disorders of memory, symptomatic personality, language and writing, body symptoms, catatonic symptoms, and acute symptoms (Bleuler, 1911). Although, unlike Kraepelin, Bleuler describes body symptoms as separate to delusions and hallucinations, he still emphasises the disturbances in mental processes rather than introducing a distinctive status for those phenomena.

Yet Bleuler did not stop his reconfiguration of dementia praecox there. He did not simply stick to the definition of core and accompanying symptoms. He also reshaped the schizophrenic types. He created "schizophrenia simplex" and added "special groups" to Kraepelin's three pre-existing types (1911).

The significance of the introduction of simple schizophrenia should not go by unnoticed, because this innovation indicates a latent type of schizophrenia. Bleuler (1911) specifies that the latent type is the commonest form. This concept means that no specific sign can exclude its diagnosis (Leader, 2011). Therefore, the splitting might be there without the individual presenting manifest signs of psychosis.

It seems that this supplementation deals a great blow to Kraepelin's construction. Thanks to Bleuler, schizophrenia—formerly dementia praecox—no longer leans solely on phenomenology. It involves a core that is independent of secondary phenomena, despite being defined as biological and being linked to mental processes.

It might be not unimportant to note that one would hardly be able to support that someone was suffering from schizophrenia without presenting manifest symptoms before Bleuler's differentiation between fundamental and accompanying symptoms and introduction of schizophrenia simplex. Kraepelin had made it clear: first the course, then the diagnosis (1899; 1904). Yet this is not the only area where the two psychiatrists disagree. Bleuler (1911) argues that patients suffering from dementia praecox do not necessarily present mental deterioration (dementia) and that such deterioration does not necessarily occur early in one's life (praecox). He also suggests that schizophrenia refers to a group and not a single disease, characterising it from the beginning as a syndrome, that is, a cluster of different manifestations (symptoms) of the same diagnosable condition (Miller, 1983).

Bleuler produces a theory of schizophrenia that is coherent and even ontological (Baud, 2003). After this monograph, things were never the same again in the psychiatric perception of schizophrenia, formerly dementia praecox (Miller, 1983).

Yet it seems that Bleuler's conceptualisation still remains influenced by psychology, following Jung's psychological experiments and Kraepelin's empirical observations. Moreover, like his German predecessor and colleague, the Swiss psychiatrist did not stop considering schizophrenia an incurable mental disease (Bleuler, 1911). It seems therefore that his monograph's homage to psychoanalytic theories—especially as passed on by Jung—concerned the phenomenology of schizophrenia rather than its generation; the ability to demonstrate the splitting in association rather than a libidinal causation (Zenoni, 2012). Bleuler seems to owe more to Janet, who had also influenced Jung extensively, than to Freud (Moscowitz & Heim, 2011).

On the other hand, Bleuler's approach to the treatment of schizophrenia seems much more liberal than Kraepelin's. Of course, he believed that patients could not be cured of schizophrenia. Some of his indications for pharmaceutical treatment concern symptoms such as nervous excitability (Bleuler, 1911) but he also contended that no treatment of the condition per se was possible, let alone one advocated by psychoanalysis.

However, a recovery at the social level or enhanced by beneficial conditions was not completely overruled. Bleuler recommended that patients be given tasks like cutting wood, or even simpler activities for younger individuals (1911; 1934). He also encouraged entertainment on less busy days and preached against the disadvantages of idleness. Like Kraepelin, Bleuler favoured the provision of a caring environment and emphasised the importance of informing the patient's family about the nature of the disease (Bleuler, 1934). In addition, in contrast to his German colleague, Bleuler first and foremost argued against hospitalisation, judging that admission should be avoided if at all possible and that any hospital stay should be as short as possible. There might, however, be a historical and socioeconomic explanation for this disagreement between the two scholars. Bleuler's approach might have been easier to apply at a progressive hospital in Switzerland, a country with low unemployment and poverty compared to the countries where Kraepelin worked (Warner, 1994).

With respect to the schizophrenic body, it is important to summarise at this point that the frequent and recurrent phenomena concerning the schizophrenic's body and organs are very loosely associated to the core of the condition, which, for Jung and Bleuler, is the splitting of the mind. Since they are, moreover, linked to organicity, not much can be done about it.

This approach would change radically thanks to Freud. The founding father of psychoanalysis, who would publish a paper on paranoia that contained several pages on schizophrenia the same year, would show that what psychoanalysis really had to say about this condition differed greatly from what Kraepelin, Jung, and Bleuler were suggesting.

Freud

Freud's comprehensive theory of psychosis is situated mainly in two papers of the years immediately preceding the First World War: the study on President Schreber of 1911 and the paper introducing the theory of narcissism of 1914 (De Waelhens, 2001a). Studying them in combination sheds light upon Freud's original ideas and differences between the psychotic types of paranoia and its "poor relation", schizophrenia, based on the vicissitudes of the libido and defence mechanisms at play.

However, to grasp the totality of Freud's approach on schizophrenia that will be later linked to Lacan's approach to the schizophrenic subject and its body, one also needs to look before and after those years.

1895–1910

As was noted above, before the turn of the twentieth century Freud treated cases that fell "under the heading of paranoia"—adding in a footnote of 1924 "no doubt, dementia paranoides" (1896b, p. 174)—as "neuro-psychoses of defence". Neurotic symptoms were formed as defence against material repressed in the unconscious, which were linked to sexuality (Freud, 1895f; 1896a). This viewpoint would not be maintained in its entirety in the future, when dementia praecox would be turned into schizophrenia.

However, for the moment the mental disorder to become dementia praecox and then schizophrenia belongs to a category that is being contrasted to "neurasthenic neuroses" (Freud, 1896a): "neurasthenias" and "anxiety neuroses" (Freud, 1895b). These are disorders in which one finds symptoms of anxiety or bodily implication somehow related to the patients' sexual life, but whose role is not defensive; they are linked to the "somatic" rather than the "psychical" field (Freud, 1895b, p. 107).

Although Freud (1895b; 1895f; 1896a) does not deny the role played by heredity in both types, he argues that the neuro-psychoses cannot be produced without the factor of sexuality. He therefore suggests that apart from its defensive character against sexual material, the outbreak of a neuro-psychosis like dementia praecox is caused by a psychical rather than organic factor.

It was under this approach, further developed in Freud's publications of the first years of the 1900s, that clinicians interested in psychoanalysis, like Jung, Binswager, and Abraham, had studied psychotic patients and/or tried to treat dementia praecox. Thus, during the first decade of the twentieth century psychoanalytic papers appeared on the psychology of dementia praecox—and then schizophrenia—like Jung's aforementioned study and Sabina Spielrein's doctoral dissertation on a case of dementia praecox. Psychoanalysis was advocated as clinical therapy for psychosis at the Burghölzli—not by Bleuler, who only encouraged its psychological application—and the Bellevue Sanatorium, which Binswager took up as a director in 1910 (Hoffmann, 2009).

However, within less than five years this optimistic approach would fade away. The same year to Spielrein's dissertation and Bleuler's monograph, Freud published his study on paranoia and three years later he wrote his paper on narcissism. Both papers put schizophrenia in a different context to that of the old "neuro-psychosis of defence." Although in the previous years the psychotic subject was not clearly excluded from the "other scene" (Freud, 1900a) of the unconscious accessed through the dream process, a demarcation line would be gradually drawn.

Consequently, a few years later, many psychoanalysts stopped addressing clinically the psychoses and, following Freud, returned to their theoretical study (Alanen, 2009b).

1911–1914

The two papers forming Freud's comprehensive viewpoint of paranoia and schizophrenia are "Psycho-Analytic Notes on an Autobiographical Account of a Case of Paranoia (Dementia Paranoides)" (1911c) and "On Narcissism: An Introduction" (1914c). The first was dedicated to the study of the case of a psychotic German judge, President Schreber, who had suffered a number of breakdowns and was hospitalised three times. The second, which expanded the theory presented there furthermore, was a rather theoretical paper.

The surname Schreber was a familiar one in the German-speaking world at that time. President Schreber's father, Daniel Gottlob Moritz Schreber had been a renowned German physician and aspiring social reformer. He was also a professor at the University of Leipzig, the same university where, seventeen years after his death, Kraepelin would attend Wundt's psychology lectures. His son, Daniel Paul, was born in 1842. He went to law school and became a judge and rose relatively quickly to the position of court president. President Schreber had gotten married at the age of thirty-six but did not have any children. The Schrebers would only adopt a girl relatively late in life (Dalzell, 2011; Maleval, 2000).

At the age of forty-two Schreber suffered a defeat in an electoral bid for a seat in the German parliament, the Reichstag. He then presented a moderate psychotic episode. It led to his hospitalisation. He was transferred to the psychiatric hospital of the University of Leipzig in Sonnenstein and was there treated by the renowned psychiatric professor Paul Flechsig, who had dismissed thirty-year-old Emil Kraepelin for being unfit for psychiatric work (Briole, 2012). After his treatment, Schreber returned home and was believed to have made a full recovery (Dalzell, 2011).

A second crisis occurred nine years later. It followed his appointment as president of a five-judge panel at the Supreme Court of Appeals in Dresden—hence, the title "President" by which he is known in psychoanalytic literature, his full title being "President of the Senate" (*Senatpräsident*). This hospitalisation would last for almost ten years. During that period he wrote his autobiography, *Memoirs of my Nervous Illness* (Schreber, 1903), which had attracted the attention of Jung, Bleuler, and, subsequently, Freud.

Schreber suffered a third, and final, breakdown in 1907. It followed his mother's death, his wife's stroke, and his having been asked by an association to grant them exclusive rights of his father's intellectual heritage; in fact, it seems that this last relapse was characterised by auditory hallucinations and physical deterioration (Maleval, 2000). He was once again admitted to the asylum, where he died after four years (Dalzell, 2011).

Schreber's diagnosis was "severe hypochondria" in his first two hospitalisations, which is indicative of phenomena related to his body. Yet during his second hospitalisation Guido Weber, his doctor at Sonnestein, diagnosed him with "paranoia" (Dalzell, 2011)—after all dementia praecox, let alone schizophrenia, had not been configured yet as a separate clinical entity. The second hospitalisation was longer and apparently more of a torment for him than the first. His relapse had started with the idea that occurred to him one night in June 1893—that it would be a fine thing to be a woman engaging in copulation (Schreber, 1903). His memoirs would be constructed around this idea and used in support of an appeal for his release.

Schreber believed he was a victim to God's wish to turn him into a woman. He had to become God's wife and restore mankind, which had in the meantime vanished, by producing a new race of humanity (Schreber, 1903). He had developed a comprehensive system in order to substantiate this idea. Different roles were assigned to himself—eventually, as redeemer—and to figures like Professor Flechsig and God—gradually, as persecutors. His system involved ideas such as: "God nerves", an "anterior" and "posterior God Realm", an "upper" and "lower God", and even a new language, the "fundamental language" (*Grundsprache*), a form of antiquated German full of euphemisms and neologisms. All these ideas were linked to a new form for the German judge's body too, a feminised body that connected to God through divine rays. Schreber's idea about emasculation, which had generated the delusion, would act as the starting point for Freud's discussion of Schreber's case.

Freud's hypothesis was that Schreber's delusion had not been the primary manifestation of his disease. It was a secondary process, the symptom addressing the disease. The delusion was an attempt at self-healing responding to the condition's causal factor, which Freud believed to be repressed homosexual "impulses" (Freud, 1911c). In Schreber's delusional ideas of becoming God's wife there was manifested a repressed desire for men like Professor Flechsig, a desire that had started with his homosexual feelings for his then dead brother and father (Freud, 1911c).

Freud is therefore interested in explaining Schreber's breakdown and delusion on the basis of his theories on defence and sexuality, which were the pillars of his approach to the neuro-psychoses of defence (1894a; 1896b). He argues that what appear as morbid phenomena were produced from the patient's resistance against the attack of homosexual libido, which Freud had also suggested for dementia praecox in 1908. The defensive struggle against the phantasy—whose object was Flechsig—took the form of the delusion (Freud, 1911c). To explain how this happened, Freud introduced the theory of *narcissism*.

He suggested that the libido, the psychical force of the drive, normally passes from auto-eroticism to object-love through the stage of narcissism (Freud, 1911c). Psychoses like Schreber's are linked to fixations of the libido throughout that course. This happens in the following way: The individual is required to select an object for their libido, a love-object that unifies their sexual instincts. That object is initially the self. This is the stage of narcissism. It takes its name from Narcissus, the young man in Greek mythology who admired his own reflection on the surface of a lake and drowned thus. The stage following narcissism, which leads to heterosexuality, is the choice of an external object, a love-object with different genitalia (Freud, 1911c).

Therefore, the homosexual desire Freud notes in Schreber's case is related to a regression and fixation of the libido to a stage prior to object-love. The paranoid defence, which has generated Schreber's impressive delusion, emerges from it. He uses individuals with the same genitalia as his as love-objects, and this generates the delusional system that revolves around the idea of God turning him to his wife, defending himself from homosexual inclination coming from himself.

This takes place in paranoia. Defence in dementia praecox or paraphrenia, on the other hand, which is separate from it, must be sought for at a stage even earlier than narcissism. Freud writes:

> This attempt at recovery, which the observers mistake for the disease itself, does not, as in paranoia, make use of projection, but employs a hallucinatory (hysteric) mechanism. This is one of the two major respects in which dementia praecox differs from paranoia; and this difference can be explained genetically from another direction. The second difference is shown by the outcome of the disease in those cases where the process has not remained too restricted. The prognosis is on the whole more unfavourable than in paranoia. The victory lies with repression and not, as in the former, with reconstruction. The regression extends not merely to narcissism (manifesting itself in the shape of megalomania) but to a complete abandonment of object-love and a return to infantile auto-eroticism. The dispositional fixation must therefore be situated further back than in paranoia, and must lie somewhere at the beginning of the course of development from auto-eroticism to object-love. Moreover, it is not at all likely that homosexual impulsions, which are so frequently—perhaps invariably—to be found in paranoia, play an equally important part in the aetiology of that far more comprehensive disorder, dementia praecox. (Freud, S., [1911c] 2001, p. 77)

The detachment of dementia praecox from the factor of homosexuality is an aspect of the condition that will mark its psychoanalytic conceptualisation in both Freud and Lacan's perspectives. This is because, for Freud, homosexuality concerns a person's capacity for establishing a relation to otherness, in what he here calls the choice of a different person with the same genitalia to project libido to. Lacan would later reformulate that as the image of the other's body. The schizophrenic will be thus treated as the person in whom this might not play "an equally important part".

On the other hand, Freud will not maintain the idea of victory lying with repression in schizophrenia (dementia praecox). In 1915 he will express doubts on the correct use of this term for this condition (Freud, 1915e). In addition, three years after his study on Schreber, he will change his mind on the differentiation between dementia praecox, which he has suggested calling paraphrenia, and Schreber's original diagnosis, paranoia. This is what he suggests in 1911:

> Our hypotheses as to the dispositional fixations in paranoia and paraphrenia make it easy to see that a case may begin with paranoid symptoms and may yet develop into a dementia praecox, and that paranoid and schizophrenic phenomena may be combined in any proportion. And we can understand how a clinical picture such as Schreber's can come about, and merit the name of a paranoid dementia, from the fact that in its production of a wishful fantasy and of hallucinations it shows paraphrenic traits, while in its exciting cause, in its use of the mechanism of projection, and in its outcome it exhibits a paranoid character. (Freud, S., [1911c] 2001, pp. 77–78)

For Freud (1911c), Kraepelin was justified in merging what was hitherto called paranoia with catatonia and other forms of the disease to create dementia praecox. His reservation, shared in the past by Bleuler (1911) and Jung (1906), concerns the name used for the disorder. He finds it unhappy (Freud, 1911c). Yet, he thinks the same of Bleuler's schizophrenia too. He does not disagree with the creation of this concept, but he objects to its name's connotations and suggests labelling it, instead, paraphrenia. The two conditions, paraphrenia and paranoia, share a similar nature and they are differentiated with regard to the stage of libidinal fixation. Freud writes that even the suggestion of the new term for dementia praecox, paraphrenia, was there in order to signify the common ground with paranoia (1911c).

Yet three years after this study, in his paper dedicated entirely to the study of narcissism, Freud would deviate to some extent from this approach. In "On Narcissism: An Introduction" (1914c), he developed further the concept of narcissism and wrote about paraphrenia as a term that signified a different concept to that of 1911.

On the first page of the paper, Freud (1914c) remarked that the attempt to substantiate the knowledge of dementia praecox or schizophrenia under the libido theory had given rise to the theory of narcissism. He also refers to Schreber once more. In discussing the therapy brought about by the German judge's delusion, Freud suggests a new conceptualisation of paraphrenia and the clinical entities it consists of (1914c):

> Our chief means of access to it [narcissism] will probably remain the analysis of the paraphrenias. Just as the transference neuroses have enabled us to trace the libidinal instinctual impulses, so dementia praecox and paranoia will give us an insight into the psychology of the ego. (Freud, S., [1914c] 2001, p. 82)

Freud no longer suggests using paraphrenia as a term separate from paranoia. In 1911, "paraphrenia" was a new term for dementia praecox or schizophrenia as linked to, but also distinct from, paranoia. In contrast, its use here signifies an umbrella term that includes both paranoia and dementia praecox (Freud, 1916–1917), corresponding, in fact, to the second pole of the Kraepelinian dichotomy, which Freud had praised in 1911. This does not seem to clash with Bleuler's (1911) view of a group of schizophrenias either.

Yet it is important to note that Freud (1914c) is now separating those disorders from the "transference neuroses": hysteria, anxiety neurosis, and obsessional neurosis. This introduces a split in the old "neuro-psychoses of defence", which will create the group that we now call psychoses. In fact, thanks to the introduction of narcissism, paraphrenias will be contrasted, as "narcissistic neuroses", with the other neuroses, as an effect of the patient's inability to develop transference, a fundamental for psychoanalysis. This will, in fact, be the gravestone for the treatment of paraphrenics (paranoiacs and schizophrenics) through psychoanalysis, since they will be considered unfit for it, due to their narcissistic propensity (Freud, 1916–1917).

Nevertheless, it seems that Freud does not close all doors concerning treatment that can come about for these subjects. In 1911 and 1914 he explained why he considered the paranoiac's megalomaniac delirium, which others took for a morbid expression, to be self-healing. For dementia praecox he had suggested hallucination, but in the following year he would suggest something different.

Although Freud's theoretical approach to schizophrenia and paranoia was presented in 1911 and 1914, it seems that his 1915 paper "The Unconscious" should stand out regarding the treatment for schizophrenia that Lacanian psychoanalysis can take interest in, due to a "linguistic" explanation it offers to phenomena related to schizophrenics' bodies and their organs. In the first half of the 1910s, Freud analysed in detail his approach to schizophrenia based on the libido and defence mechanisms. What is different in the paper in question is that he is now, for the first time, linking the libido to the status of language—and, as an effect, of the body—in schizophrenia.

Freud's (1915e) aim in "The Unconscious" is basically to summarise the layout of his so-called first topographical theory: to expose the division of the mental life into conscious, preconscious, and unconscious and outline the dynamics between them and mechanisms at play, such as repression (Freud, 1915e). Freud says he has gathered the findings to substantiate his theory from dream life and transference neuroses. He argues that a study of the mechanisms at play in schizophrenia can contribute to the understanding of the enigmatic "Ucs." system, which he does not stop characterising as an "assumption". This is a fundamental principle in psychoanalysis and not irrelevant to the Lacanian approach to psychosis: the unconscious is a supposition, not a fact; "it is ethical and not ontic" (Aflalo, 2015, p. 32). This is, in fact, one more reason for which I find the current popular attempts to trace the foundations of the unconscious in the structure of the brain, which take place under signifiers like "neuro-psychoanalysis", to be far from Freud's standpoint.

In "The Unconscious", Freud (1915e) returns to the particular status of the language of schizophrenics highlighted as early as in the formulation of this category by Kraepelin (1899) and Bleuler (1911). He attempts to explain it by use of the mechanisms he used to analyse the paranoid phenomena in Schreber's case.

Schreber's paranoid delusion had emerged from an attempt to make up for the loss of object-cathexis by libido having been cathected to the self. In schizophrenia, in the place of "self", we need to read "words" and not overlook that the body and its organs are words too. Freud (1915e) writes about dreaming and schizophrenia: the same processes that are at play in the dream—that is, condensation and displacement (Freud, 1910)—happen in the schizophrenic's words, followed by the respective cathexis of the libido. This may go on until it reaches a single word, which "if it is especially suitable on account of its numerous connections, it takes over the representation of a whole train of thought" (Freud, 1915e, p. 199). He adds that:

> If in schizophrenia object-cathexes are given up [...] the cathexis of the word-presentations of objects is retained. (Freud, S., [1915e] 2001, p. 201)

As a result of the aforementioned dream-like processes, Freud writes, the schizophrenic is characterised by a "predominance of words over what has to do with things" (1915e, p. 200). Therefore, if paranoiacs channel libido to themselves and similar others (narcissism), in schizophrenics this happens with word-presentations, which in Lacan's teaching will be read as signifiers. Borrowing Hegel's terminology, Lacan will say that for the schizophrenic, for the psychotic, moreover, the Word is the Thing, instead of its murder. Yet this is not the only part of Freud's rethinking of schizophrenia that will mark Lacan's approach to the psychoses.

Another of Freud's suggestions will help Lacan formulate the boundary between psychosis and neurosis, a major element in the first period of his teaching. Freud (1915e) writes that it might be worth rethinking and modifying the formula of repression, the term he had used for the transference neuroses and which he had suggested were at play in the neuro-psychotic form of schizophrenia (Freud, 1911c). Lacan would pick up on this many years later and suggest a different type of negation—instead of repression—that takes place in psychosis, in contrast to neurosis (and perversion).

How about treatment, however? If schizophrenics treat things like words and cannot perform a recovery in the fashion of Schreber, what can they do? According to Freud, the cathexis to the word instead of the self or the object is, by itself, a first step in the reparation that schizophrenia involves. He writes:

> It turns out that the cathexis of the word-presentation is not part of the act of repression, but represents the first of the attempts at recovery or cure which so conspicuously dominate the clinical picture of schizophrenia. These endeavours are directed towards regaining

the lost object [...] but then find themselves obliged to be content
with words instead of things. (Freud, S., [1915e] 2001, p. 203)

Therefore, instead of hallucination being the mechanism at use in a
schizophrenic's attempt at therapy (Freud, 1911c)—in contrast to the
paranoiac's projection that establishes narcissism—Freud (1915e)
now highlights the significance of the cathexis of the libido to word-
presentations, which lies in the field that extends from "auto-eroticism"
to "object-love".

Of course, this treatment comes about in a similar way to Schreber's
self-healing, that is, as a singular attempt initiated by the patient.
Although this viewpoint opens a window for a treatment within the
clinic of schizophrenia, which will be discussed further below in the
light of Lacan's teaching, it closed the door in the face of the clinician
who aspired to treat this former neuro-psychosis of defence through
psychoanalysis.

Indeed, the psychoanalytic treatment of schizophrenia of the first
two decades of the twentieth century, which had begun enthusiastically
at the Burghölzli, Bellevue, and elsewhere, came to a halt. Discouraged
by Freud's pessimism about the treatment of psychoses, his followers
withdrew for some time from the idea of being able to treat schizophrenia
through psychoanalysis (Alanen, 2009a). If a cure can be brought about
in schizophrenia, this will be built upon the way the person himself or
herself treats word-presentations. The psychoanalyst cannot do much
about this, since he or she cannot occupy the position of the target of
object-love.

Nevertheless, whereas Freud's publications of the 1910s (1914c;
1915e; 1916–1917) were indicating that a psychoanalytic treatment was
impossible with a schizophrenic, some psychoanalysts of the second
generation had undertaken seeing schizophrenics based on psychoanalytic theory. One of the first to do this was Victor Tausk, a Viennese
journalist, lawyer, and neurologist who had a peculiar relationship
with the founder of psychoanalysis. One of the clinical examples Freud
had used in "The Unconscious" had come from the former's clinical
practice (1915e).

In an example Freud had borrowed from Tausk, the latter was referring to a patient complaining of her eyes having become "twisted"
after quarrelling with her husband, whom she reproached as an

"eye-twister". In another case, the same patient had felt a jerk while standing in church, pushing her to change her position. That feeling was related to another reproach to her lover: he had misled her concerning his position and urged her to change, metaphorically, her position instead (Freud, 1915e). Freud agreed with Tausk's remarks that those physical changes had corresponded to the metaphorical meaning of "eye-twister" and "changing positions". A schizophrenic property that Freud (1915e) does not forget to note—neither had Bleuler (1911c)—and which will return in its psychoanalytic conceptualisation and more specifically in the way it is viewed in the later Lacan, could not escape our attention: that the eyes are body organs. They can thus speak their own language (Morel, 2011). Freud remarks that:

> Some reference to bodily organs or innervations is often given prominence in the content of those remarks. (Freud, S., [1915e] 2001, p. 197)

The challenge for the schizophrenic in Lacan will be to "acquire" those organs and the whole body with the help of language: to obtain a feeling of them as proper body organs instead of words, as Freud suggests happening. It seems that this is what Freud was describing already when in 1911 and 1914 he compared dementia praecox to hysteria, where symptoms related to the body are predominant.

Tausk, on the other hand, did not point to the same direction. He seems to have contributed to contemporary psychoanalytic approaches to schizophrenia thanks to his idea of a weak ego with difficulties maintaining boundaries, which was taken up by Paul Federn (Sledge, 1992). Yet Tausk himself did not claim to have cured schizophrenia with psychoanalysis. He only argued that, through his examination, he was able to prove that the organisation of libido that has been termed narcissistic takes place in the developmental stage preceding object-finding. In fact, he remarked that one of the symptoms he was able to isolate in schizophrenia was the "loss of ego boundaries" (Tausk, 1919, p. 194).

Other students of Freud's who contributed to the formulation of a psychoanalytic theory of schizophrenia up until the 1920s were Ferenczi, Abraham, and Federn (Dalle & Weill, 1999). Federn particularly spoke of an ego that becomes poor of libido, which contrasts greatly Freud's idea of the return of the libido to the ego (Miller, 1983). Yet, as is obvious, the work of the second wave of psychoanalysts to treat schizophrenic patients was no longer based on the first topography, which compared schizophrenia to a dream, but on the second, which was gradually developing. Freud would formulate it in the first half of the 1920s. The way those psychoanalysts tried to implement that theory for their treatment of schizophrenia is discussed in the following chapter, since Lacan opposed their approach in defence of his own view of psychosis and its treatment.

1923–1924

That influential theory, summarised in *The Ego and the Id*, was introduced by Freud in 1923, although it had already been sketched for some time, in his papers of the previous decades. In it, Freud (1923b) presented an "amplification" to the theory of narcissism.

It is important to highlight—and Freud does so himself in the first lines of this paper—that his second topographical theory does not in any way cancel out the first: the division of the mental life into conscious, preconscious, and unconscious (Freud, 1923b). The ego, which had been referred to numerous times in the theory of the libido, is where consciousness is attached. It is, according to Freud (1923b, p. 25), what can be called "reason and common sense", whereas the id, which is for the most part unconscious, is where "passions" are contained; libido rests there. Repression derives from the ego trying to defend itself against the requests of the id. Thus, psychoanalysis is considered as an instrument that helps the ego achieve a progressive "control over the id" (Freud, 1923b, p. 30).

Yet the ego does not only have the id to fight, but two more factors: the ego ideal or superego and the external world. The first is an outcome of the well-known Oedipus complex. In effect, it is the agent that the ego has created so that its oedipal wishes can be repressed. It is the mental life's censor, a moral and ethical preacher which has, as a prototype, the prohibiting character of the father. On the other hand, the external world or reality is mainly what the ego must adhere to. The ego is therefore caught between three factors, not two:

> We see the ego as a poor creature owing service to three masters and consequently menaced by three dangers: from the external world, from the libido of the id and from the severity of the superego. (Freud, S., [1923b] 2001, p. 56)

In Part II the reader is given the chance to observe the route of an ego struggling to serve three similar masters and the way invented by a subject to address those challenges to its precarious constitution.

The "amplification" to the theory of narcissism suggested in this paper concerns the formation of the ego, in relation to the use of this term in Freud's earlier theories of the vicissitudes of the libido. Here is what Freud writes about this:

> At the very beginning, all the libido is accumulated in the id, while the ego is still in the process of formation or is still feeble. The id sends part of his libido out into erotic object-cathexes, whereupon the ego, now grown stronger, tries to get hold of this object-libido and to force itself on the id as a love object. The narcissism of the ego is thus a secondary one, which has been withdrawn from objects. (Freud, S., [1923b] 2001, p. 46)

The idea of the weak ego, which, as was seen above, tries to serve three masters, will have two significant impacts on the psychoanalytic treatment of schizophrenia: a theoretical and a clinical.

Concerning its clinical implication, some of Freud's influential followers, such as Melanie Klein, would suggest a psychoanalytic treatment of schizophrenia based on the idea of strengthening that weak ego (Leader, 2011). This is what Tausk and Federn had also been implying.

Its theoretical effect is found in two papers that Freud wrote the following year, "Neurosis and Psychosis" (Freud, 1924b) and "The Loss of Reality in Neurosis and Psychosis" (Freud, 1924e). In those papers the "genetic" difference between neurosis and psychosis is that neurosis comes from a conflict between the ego and the id, whereas psychosis is generated from the conflict between the ego and the external world (Freud, 1924b). The phenomena that result from these conflicts are that neurosis ignores reality, whereas psychosis disavows it, trying to replace it with something else (Freud, 1924e).

It is clearly observed that not only the psychoses (paranoia and schizophrenia) are differentiated from the neuroses, but that they are also excluded radically from the field of the unconscious, since their cause is their conflict with the external world and not with the id, which is partly situated in there. They thus seem now closer to the neurasthenias than to the neuro-psychoses of defence (Freud, 1894a; 1895b; 1896b).

Those developments, however, concerning how the psychoses are treated do not seem to have met with unquestioned approval from Freud's direct and influential followers, like Melanie Klein. Klein did not adhere to a radical differentiation between the psychoses and the neuroses. Lacan, on the other hand, will would start formulating his own theories on psychosis after a few years, will make this distinction structural, even though his own teaching will implicate an open dialogue with Klein as well.

In effect, one day in the year that she published her *Psycho-Analysis of Children* (Klein, 1932), which supports this direction, and while Freud was preparing his *New Introductory Lectures on Psycho-Analysis* (1933a), the founding father of psychoanalysis received in the post a French psychiatrist's thesis on paranoia. He sent a postcard thanking the author but wrote nothing about the thesis on it (Roudinesco, 1997).

The sender was the thirty-one-year-old Frenchman Jacques Lacan, who was finishing his psychiatric formation in Paris and would soon enter an analysis with Rudolph Lowenstein (Roudinesco, 1997). In his extended theoretical and clinical work on psychoanalysis and psychosis, we find indications for a treatment of schizophrenia that extends beyond the Tauskian and Kleinian suggestions about the ego, one that Lacan contends that he has found in Freud: the status of the subject and the signifier. What the first psychologically inclined psychiatrists and psychoanalysts had noted in passing about schizophrenics—a particular relation to language and their bodies—will prove to be the compass for a treatment potential distinct from the post-Freudians' stress on the ego, an idea about which Freud himself had already expressed his doubts in 1911.

CHAPTER TWO

From the ego to the subject

L acan's conceptualisation of psychosis was a dynamic process lasting for almost fifty years (Miller, 1987; Vanheule, 2011a). It should not thus come as a surprise that what he was suggesting in the thesis he sent to Freud changed very soon, generating a theoretical framework that would not be maintained for long either. Lacan never stopped questioning his own understanding of psychosis (Miller, 1987). There is at least one impressive shift in the way he views psychosis almost every ten years (Ribolspi, Feyaerts, & Vanheule, 2015; Vanheule, 2011a).

In changing his viewpoint Lacan cannot but remind one of Freud, whose endeavour also included theoretical impasses and reformulations during an intellectual and writing activity lasting for more than forty years. Discontinuity seems to mark both psychoanalysts' theoretical formulation (Miller, 2003a).

The imaginary: the predominance of the image

Paranoia and personality

Lacan's first theoretical formulation of psychosis dates before his direct involvement with psychoanalysis. His first relevant monograph, the thesis he sent to Freud, was produced when he was a trainee psychiatrist at the Hospital of Saint Anne in Paris. It was influenced by his psychiatric masters, mainly Gäetan Gatian de Clérambault, whereas there were also direct references to Freud.

Lacan's dissertation was based on the case of a woman named Marguerite Anzieu, whom he nicknamed "Aimée". She was a psychotic patient hospitalised at Saint Anne's and the mother of the future psychoanalyst Didier Anzieu.

Lacan saw "Aimée" almost every day for an entire year (Roudinesco, 1997). He used the content of interviews with her and her case history in support of a new diagnostic category: "self-punitive paranoia". He argued that Anzieu's homicidal attempt against a French actress, Huguette Duflos, was directly related to her personality (Lacan, 1932). That attempt, which was linked to the patient's paranoid delusion, was seen as a breakthrough in her psychosis, leading to her eventual treatment.

This approach of Lacan's is consonant with Freud's theory of psychosis presented earlier. In paranoia, in contrast to schizophrenia, the subject can "cure" himself or herself through a secondary projection of the libido onto the other as object, as happened in Schreber's case. Libido in "Aimée's" case was projected onto the French actress, having been cathected to herself and initially projected to her sister. Young Lacan thus makes her a female version of Schreber. In the place of the sequence *Schreber—brother—father—Flechsig—God*, we find *Marguerite—sister—Huguette Duflos*.

Despite the absence of focus on schizophrenia, the reader is advised to keep in mind its title: *On Paranoid Psychosis and Its Relations to Personality* (Lacan, 1932). Forty years later, Lacan would admit regretting having picked it, for a reason that will contrast paranoia further to schizophrenia and is discussed at the end of the following chapter.

Four years after completing his thesis and having in between entered his own analysis, Lacan presented a new psychoanalytic theory at the congress of the International Psychoanalytical Association (IPA) of 1936, held in Marienbad. The concept he introduced would permeate his work: it was the so-called theory of the "mirror stage" (Roudinesco, 1997). Inspired by the work of French developmental psychologist Henri Wallon (Feyaerts & Vanheule, 2015), the mirror stage describes a phase during which the ego is formed through the process of identification. It shows how the imaginary constitution of the "me" is formed (Nobus, 1999).

The mirror stage

The theory of the mirror stage was introduced as part of the individual's "normal" development. However, it bore a significant effect for the structure of paranoia and for schizophrenia too. This is because it re-reads Freud's ideas of 1911 (Morel, 2011). Its effects might be better understood in connection with Lacan's following publication, presented further below: *Family Complexes* (1938).

The mirror stage constitutes the model for what Lacan calls the imaginary. This is one of three registers that he will later suggest as making up human subjectivity, next to the symbolic and the real (Lacan, 1953a).

When this theory was being developed, the ego, which holds a significant part in it, was dominating psychoanalytic theory. It had played an important role in the fierce debate between psychoanalysts Anna Freud and Melanie Klein concerning the psychoanalysis of children. The abandonment of the importance of the ego would be the step that differentiated Lacan's approach to psychosis from that of post-Freudian psychoanalysts.

In his speech at Marienbad, Lacan placed emphasis on the fact that the human infant, in contrast to animals, is born prematurely. It presents deficits, such as inability for motor coordination. Yet there comes a point, at the age of six months at a minimum, when this changes. The baby becomes capable of recognising, in front of the mirror, its image as a totality, a *Gestalt*. Eventually it exhibits a series of gestures that produce a "playful experience" between the movements reflected in the image and itself standing in front of the mirror—which needn't be an actual mirror, but a place where its image is reflected, actually or metaphorically. This image of totality contrasts with the feeling of the fragmented body preceding this stage. The recognition of the infant's body as a complete image gives birth to a jubilant sentiment and produces the Freudian Ideal-I. This form will give rise to the agency of the ego as well as secondary identifications (Lacan, 1949).

The impact of the mirror stage is not simply limited to the human being's first experiences. According to Lacan (1949), the outcome of identification with an image of totality determines the subject's destiny:

> The mirror stage is a drama whose internal pressure pushes precipitously from insufficiency to anticipation—and, for the subject caught up in the lure of spatial identification, turns out fantasies

that proceed from a fragmented image of the body to what I will call "orthopaedic" form of its totality—and to the finally donned armour of an alienating identity that will mark his entire mental development with its rigid structure. (Lacan, J., [1949] 2006, p. 78)

The alienating identity at stake, which the mirror stage gives birth to with its "orthopaedic totality", will be of immense importance for the destiny of the psychotic subject, as is described in Lacan's following publication, three years later. This happens because, as is obvious, the mirror stage corresponds to the generation of narcissism, which is vital for Freud's differentiation between paranoia and schizophrenia, as well as between neurosis and psychosis. The fragmented body that precedes the emergence of the ego is the destiny of the schizophrenic subject, an aspect of which is seen in patients' complaints about their bodies and organs, such as Tausk's patient with the "twisted-eyes" (Freud, 1915e), Jung's seamstress who complained about her spinal cord having been removed (1906), and the patient I met during my undergraduate psychology placement, who identified his mother's genitalia in his throat. To cut a long story short, one's failure to establish the outcomes of the mirror stage leaves the person lacking this "orthopaedic" perception of their body. Instead of their body parts being concentrated in a Gestalt, they are scattered. The body parts, the organs, and the body itself can be found anywhere "above the ground and beneath the clouds", to use the words of a wanderer whose identity will be revealed in a subsequent chapter. The idea of a problematic relation to the imaginary will pervade Lacan's teaching about and dominate the contemporary Lacanian conceptualisation of schizophrenia.

Nevertheless, back in the 1930s, the presentation of the theory of the mirror stage, from which this thesis stems, did not receive an enthusiastic response. Ernest Jones, who was chairing the panel, stopped Lacan after ten minutes (Lacan, 1946). Overall, the immediate reaction of the community of the IPA to his announcement was rather disappointing (Roudinesco, 1997). Nevertheless, the mirror stage still appeared in Jean Laplanche and Bertrand Pontali's (1973) "orthodox" psychoanalytic dictionary *The Language of Psycho-Analysis*—which Lacan (1976a) later claimed to have almost ruined psychoanalysis in its entirety—next to the relative concept of the imaginary and two concepts from his following period of teaching: the symbolic and foreclosure.

But Lacan did not give up. Two years after Marienbad, he attempted to explain further the status of schizophrenia and paranoia in relation to the mirror stage on the occasion of a paper requested from him on the effect of family on human cognitive development by the editors of the *French Encyclopaedia* (Roudinesco, 1997). He composed the article *Family Complexes: The Role of Family in the Formation of the Individual* (Lacan, 1938). In it, Lacan (1938) configured a sequence of complexes appearing during child development and their possible morbid outcomes. He thus attempted to combine contemporary psychoanalytic knowledge consonant with Freud's ideas—but basically dominated by the perspective of Melanie Klein—with his own innovations earlier in that decade. But what exactly was Klein's ground-breaking approach that Lacan would later oppose in his teaching (Guéguen, 1992)?

Klein

Born in Austria, Melanie Klein had emigrated to the United Kingdom in the 1930s, invited by Ernest Jones. Her "Merovingian" (Lacan, 1953b, p. 67) rivalries with Freud's daughter regarding the psychoanalysis of children came to mark the history of the psychoanalytic movement even before Freud's death.

Klein had undertaken her formation with Ferenczi and with Abraham, who had contributed to the concept of the object and its significance for the psychoanalytic view of schizophrenia through his correspondence with Freud (Dalle & Weill, 1999; Miller, 1983). Based on her extended and innovative work with children, Klein had developed a theory of early human development that utilised the stages of the formation of the ego and its relation to objects, originally an idea of Freud's. For her elaboration of the "positions", which mark human development, she would use terms that characterise psychotic states, as in the "schizoid-paranoid" position.

Klein considered one of the aims of psychoanalytic work to be to relieve anxiety, which is present from the beginning of one's life. She would thus try to alleviate it drastically by interpreting the content of her young analysands' discomfort (Klein, 1932; 1961). This had been one of the major points of disagreement with Anna Freud (Laurent, 2003). Freud's daughter had been arguing that what needed interpretation was not the content of one's anxiety, but the defence to which the individual has recourse. Therefore, her approach was to divide the child's ego and cause anxiety in him or her by obtaining the position of the superego (A. Freud, 1936). For Klein, on the other hand, in the early stages of development there are no ego or superego formations.

Klein held that, during its first year, the infant passes from two positions, which lead to Oedipus: the schizoid-paranoid and the depressive (Klein, 1932; 1946). These are not called stages or phases—as in Freud, who was speaking about the oral, anal, and phallic phases of the development of the libido—for a reason that is not irrelevant to her original view of psychosis: they are indeed periods where fixation points for the psychotic sub-types are to be found, but they are also loci to which the individual can return at any point in life (Klein, 1946). Therefore, individuals are not done with it as soon as a following stage has been reached. They run the risk of regressing there.

The first position initially took its name from paranoia and was only later supplemented with the prefix "schizoid". According to Klein, when the infant is first found in this position it experiences great states of persecutory anxiety (Klein, 1932). Those are projected onto the first object, the mother's breast, which is split. Hence, the characterisation "schizoid" (remember the meaning of schizo in Greek from Bleuler's definition of *schizo*phrenia: "to split" or "cleave"). The object is seen as both good, when it is remedying the infant's need, and bad, when it does not. The paranoid aspect of this position corresponds to the sadistic and persecutory anxieties projected onto the object, which corresponds to the organisation of the ego. The splitting of the object reflects the infant's own splitting. The development of the ego is based on the internalisation of the object from the beginning of post-natal life (Klein, 1960).

The second position, which follows the schizoid-paranoid, is the depressive position. It arises from feelings of guilt about the destructive and sadistic fantasies and feelings towards the primary object (Klein, 1932). This is a second important step in the organisation of the ego, after the processing of the schizoid-paranoid position. Whereas the previous position offers the prototype for schizophrenic psychoses, the depressive position acts in the same way for the manic-depressive disorder (Klein, 1960). When that position has been processed too, the infant arrives at the stage of the Oedipus complex. This is set rather early, at least compared to Freud.

The Oedipus complex is the well-known story about the child feeling love for the parent of the opposite sex and rivalry for the one of the same sex (Freud, 1900a). For the boy, it is resolved by the fear of castration by the bearer of the phallus, the father, through identification with him and the formation of the superego or ego-ideal. Klein (1932) locates its first phases much earlier in human development than Freud, even as early as the first half of the infant's first year. Moreover, she argues that the phallus is not initially considered as being part of the father, but fantasised by the baby as belonging to the mother's body—in fact, to an amalgam of father and mother—among other contents, like babies. Therefore, the infant's sadistic impulses are projected, following the mother's breast, onto the mother's whole body (Klein, 1928; 1932). Klein (1932; 1946; 1960) argued that although the first two positions, when worked through, are part of normal human development, they also form the basis of any psychosis that might appear in the person's life; the first concerning schizophrenia and paranoia, the second concerning manic depression.

Therefore, by speaking of "positions" instead of stages, Klein seems to deviate from what was earlier described as Freud's radical differentiation between the neuroses and psychoses, as well as from his indication about psychotic patients being unfit for psychoanalysis. This approach is observed in a remark of hers from the early 1930s:

> I have come to the conclusion that the concept of schizophrenia in particular and of psychosis in general as occurring in childhood must be extended, and I think that one of the chief tasks of the children's analysis is to discover and cure psychoses in children. (Klein, M., 1930, p. 244)

Klein's innovations therefore included the abandonment of a radical differentiation between psychosis and neurosis and a suggestion for its psychoanalytic treatment. This view seems to derive from the significance of the ego that needs strengthening, which Tausk had suggested already in the late 1910s. For the moment Lacan would not deviate significantly from an approach like this, but that would change within the next decade.

Family complexes

In his *Family Complexes*, published a few years after Klein's influential publications of the early 1930s, Lacan formed his own theory of the stages of human development as if he were in a dialogue with her. A few years later, he would pave the way for a psychoanalytic praxis that depends not on the significance of the ego, but on that of the subject.

In his article for the *French Encyclopaedia*, Lacan defines a complex as "being understood with reference to the object" (Lacan, 1938, p. 12). According to Lacan, the sequence of stages in human development depends on the subject's response to an object, which is consonant to Freud's idea of the progress of the cathexis of the libido. For Lacan, the fundamental element of the complex is an unconscious representation, an *imago* (Lacan, 1938). The way this imaginary concept is treated defines the progress of human development. The individual undergoes three basic complexes: the "weaning complex", the "intrusion complex", and the "Oedipus complex", which appear in this order in normal human development (Lacan, 1938). Paranoia and schizophrenia appear in relation to problems in processing those complexes. This approach resonates with the theoretical formulations on object relation and its role in human development introduced by Klein's analyst, Karl Abraham (Miller, 1987).

The weaning complex is the primary complex, appearing in the child's first year. Lacan argues that the subject's emotional condition at this age is not mature enough to recognise its own body and the external world (1938). Thus, this complex is located before the mirror stage, which, for its part, identifies with the complex that follows it: intrusion complex.

Lacan highlights the absence of a self- or ego-formation in the weaning stage, since the mirror stage has not yet taken place. The infant is left with only the primordial form of the maternal imago (Lacan, 1938). Later on in this article, Lacan affirms that schizophrenia is caused by regression to this stage (Vanheule, 2011a). It is obvious that this complex is deducible from Klein's work (Guéguen, 1992). The infant's only imago is *mother*. Schizophrenia corresponds to regression to this primary stage, in which, Lacan argues, we do not find Freud's auto-eroticism. This stage even precedes that (1938).

The second complex is characterised by intrusion. It occurs when agents of otherness enter the individual's world. They participate in family life in a way similar to the child. Those agents are usually its brother(s) or sister(s). Thus, the prevailing imago in this stage is that of *sibling*. Its image is being perceived as a competitor. Lacan writes about the appearance—the intrusion, in fact—of an "other as object" (Lacan, 1938, p. 25). Libidinal homosexual demands trigger the emotional relationships of love and identification toward this object regardless of the sibling's sex. The other's image is thus perceived by the subject as a figure prone to identification through which the subject forms its own image of the self, the ego formation, which takes place through the mirror stage (Lacan, 1949). The product of this process is thus, apart from a primordial ego, a "narcissistic world" (Lacan, 1938, p. 31). A secondary function related to identification is aggressiveness. This occurs because, consonant with the theory of the mirror stage, the recognition of the individual's complete image on the mirror precedes his or her comparison to the fragmented body (Lacan, 1938; 1949). Lacan writes clearly about schizophrenia for the first time when outlining the implications of the intrusion complex and the traumatic character of the sibling's invasion:

> If he is surprised by the intruder while still disorganised by weaning, this experience will be reactivated every time he sets eyes upon him. He then regresses in a way that will reveal itself according to the fate of the ego as a schizophrenic psychosis or as a hypochondriacal neurosis. (Lacan, J., [1938] 2003, p. 35)

This differentiation between the psychotic sub-types, which is clearly rooted in Freud, can explain a number of phenomena in the clinic of schizophrenia, where the precarious status of the other's image with which the subject identifies is observed. It is not infrequent to come across schizophrenic subjects where a vacillation of that imaginary agent can have detrimental effects for them, indicating the unstable nature of imaginary identification alone. This figure is often a close friend or a relative and, as was explained above, their unstable nature is linked to the status of the body.

Take, for example Amelia, a young schizophrenic woman hospitalised in her early twenties. Amelia's hospitalisation, following her first psychotic breakdown, came when her father was diagnosed with cancer and started visiting hospitals for chemotherapy. Very soon the girl started saying she was ill, believing she was suffering from AIDS or some other incurable disease, and she stopped taking care of her physical appearance and, gradually, of her body as a whole. As her father's image gradually faded due to his illness, her ego lost that point of specular dependence too. It thus started echoing the fragmented body that precedes the mirror stage, when the body is not yet jubilantly perceived as a totality. She believed her body to be rotting, an idea seen as early in schizophrenic symptomatology as in Kraepelin's textbook entry on dementia praecox (1899).

For Lacan of this period, schizophrenic psychosis is thus viewed as an outcome of an inability to process an invasion of otherness (in the form of sibling). This seems totally in accordance with Freud's (1911c; 1914c) theory about the "therapeutic" outcome of narcissism in paranoia, from which the schizophrenic is excluded.

In effect, the successful undergoing of the intrusion complex will establish the system of the paranoid ego, if the individual processes the intrusive imago. This attributes to the imago the property of persecutor. Lacan argues that this has happened in President Schreber and his first two studies of paranoid cases, "Aimée" (1932) and the Papin Sisters (1933), whereas other deviant identifications of the ego occurring at this stage produce the typical demands of homosexuality or sexual fetishism (Lacan, 1938).

The third stage in Lacan's early theory of human development does not have to do with psychosis, since it is linked to the already configured Oedipus complex. The imago at stake is that of the parent, more specifically the *father*. Lacan (1938) discusses the typical Oedipus complex in combination with the castration complex and Freud's myth of the primordial horde of *Totem and Taboo* (1912–1913) and identifies the emergence of neurosis at this stage (Lacan, 1938).

This is where one of Lacan's disagreements with Klein can be identified (Guéguen, 1992). For Lacan, the imago of the Oedipus complex is not the mother and father, as an amalgamated formation where the phallus is to be found, among others. The father is strictly the bearer of the phallus for both boys and girls. Moreover, there is no feminine position in both sexes owed to that early parent formation; the father is the single locus of the phallus the individual must process.

In the last part of this article Lacan discusses extensively the impact of family complexes upon psychopathology. His analysis concerns two distinct groups: psychoses and neuroses. A further development of his early conceptualisation of schizophrenia is found in this part, when he presents the three complexes and a relatively more elaborate reference to paranoia and its self-punitive type.

Lacan suggests two options for the delirium related each time to a different complex: a) the "normal genesis" of the object in a specular relation to the other and b) subjective participation in the fragmented body (Lacan, 1938, p. 47). Those conditions point towards paranoia and schizophrenia respectively, in the way Freud had discussed them in his papers of the 1910s and Klein had described them in her positions of human development of the 1930s. In addition, in the closing paragraph of *Family Complexes*, Lacan (1938, p. 65) says he agrees with the contemporary psychiatric belief in the possibility of the aggravation of paranoia "towards paraphrenia", which Freud (1911c) had also noted in his study on Schreber.

It seems, therefore, that Lacan's first theoretical approach to schizophrenia and his establishment of the register of the imaginary are in accordance with Freud and—partly—with Klein. Despite his occasional disagreements with both psychoanalysts, he will agree that a schizophrenic is lacking the ego formation that exists in paranoia and—let us not forget this—in neurosis. However, when he turns his focus from the role of images to that of signifiers, Lacan will shift the question of the treatment in psychosis from the importance of the ego to that of the subject. This is presented below.

The symbolic: the predominance of the signifier

The subject and the Other

Family Complexes (Lacan, 1938) was published just one year before the outbreak of WWII and Freud's death in London, which both happened in September 1939. Lacan published nothing during the war. His teaching commenced after more than ten years of silence, in the early 1950s, and lasted for almost thirty years. Its first decade took place in the Hospital of Saint Anne.

However, what is considered as the inaugural paper of his teaching was not read at Saint Anne's, but at a conference in Rome. Thus, it is known as the "Discourse of Rome", its original title being "The Function and Field of Speech and Language in Psychoanalysis" (Lacan, 1953a). There we find the cornerstone of this period of Lacan's teaching: his contention that the unconscious is structured like a language.

Near the end of the 1940s, Lacan interacted with disciplines other than psychiatry and psychoanalysis, such as Ferdinand de Saussure's structuralism, Roman Jakobson's linguistics, and Claude Lévi-Strauss' social anthropology. Lacan's reading of Freud's writings on psychoanalysis and the psychic life was affected by them (Ribolspi, Feyaerts, & Vanheule, 2015). The teaching this interaction generated suggested a "return to Freud".

As was seen above, Lacan's fruitful period of publications of the 1930s had been dedicated to a study of the importance of images for the creation of the ego (1949) and human development (1938). This is when the register of the imaginary was configured. These were the years of Lacan the phenomenologist (Miller, 1987). In a meticulous re-reading of Freud during the 1940s and 1950s with the help of the aforementioned disciplines, Lacan found the elements he would use to explain the constitution of a second register, the only one he calls an *order*, the symbolic.

In a few words, the symbolic order is the field of language "plus law" (Leader, 2011, p. 49). It is speech deprived of its imaginary connotations. This is the only "ordered" register of human life. Every aspect of the symbolic fits in a category and obeys rules, laws, and orders. Unlike the imaginary, which is established in the mirror stage, it has nothing to do with the image. Think about how the imaginary resists obeying rules— although not like the real, the third register to be emphasised later in Lacan's teaching: as schizophrenic patients frequently show us, it is not easy to insert a pause in the mirror, to state that this is you and this is your image, end of the story. Without the symbolic's intervention, one's constitution popping from one side to the other can be eternal.

The symbolic is a component of human subjectivity that is conditioned by the function of the signifier, which is governed by specific rules that were suggested but not clearly formulated by Freud (Lacan, 1958a). Lacan reads Freud in pursuit of the coordinates of the symbolic and, prominently, the *signifier* and the *subject*. The next few paragraphs are dedicated to their analysis, since their status in psychosis will help us discuss their conceptualisation and treatment in Lacan.

In his seminar of the same year as the "Discourse of Rome", Lacan said that nothing else is at stake in psychoanalysis but "recognising what function the subject takes on in the order of the symbolic relations which covers the entire field of human relations" (1953b, p. 67). To specify the nature of the symbolic in psychosis, we must turn to the basic differentiation Lacan suggests in his "Discourse of Rome" between speech and language.

Lacan suggests that whereas the psychotic subject uses speech, it is not therefore outside language, it is "out of discourse". Instead of speaking, it is being spoken. The subject in madness is "in a language devoid of dialectic" (Lacan, 1953a, p. 231). What does this phrase, as well as the term "subject", stand for?

Let us, first, take language. In language per se, there is no subject. For example, the language that we will speak exists before our birth and our constitution as subjects (Lacan, 1957a). It is ignorant of our existence (Miller, 2009b). Our coming to this world will probably have no effect at all on its corpus.

This is the starting point for all of us. Our subjective constitution takes shape after we gradually grasp language through symbolisation, which generates the function of the signifier and its passive effect, the subject (Evans, 1996). Let us turn to an example from human development, in fact to an example from Freud, which Lacan uses in the "Discourse of Rome". It is taken from Freud's influential text *Beyond the Pleasure Principle* (1920g) and concerns a game invented by his one-and-a-half-year-old grandson.

In a few words, that boy would throw away a reel attached to a string and pull it back, re-enacting, by means of this primordial symbolisation, his mother's absence for a few hours. The two acts of the game were accompanied by the phonemes "ooo" and "da" respectively, which for Freud—and the boy's mother—corresponded to the words *Fort* and *Da*, German for "there" or "gone" and "here" respectively. The second act was less frequent than the first, which sometimes consisted of the boy simply throwing his toys out of sight and saying "ooo". Freud (1920g) suggested that by means of this game the boy was trying to assume an active role with regard to the unpleasant condition of his mother's absence; in contrast with being its passive observer, he was trying to become "master" (Freud, 1920g, p. 17).

What Lacan saw in the boy's game was a gradual acquisition of the signifier and the abandonment of language in the status described earlier, when it ignores the person's existence. By using "fort" and "da", the young boy was inserting a lack in the field of language, signifiers were used and their effect, the subject, could gradually emerge. In effect, he was being represented by the signifier "fort". Freud's testimony (1920g) can be of help in confirming this suggestion, when he writes that the boy once presented himself to his mother using the sound "ooo!" This will become Lacan's definition of the signifier: far from being simply a word, it is what represents the subject for another signifier (Lacan, 1960a). Using Freud's remark about the boy trying to become a "master", we might call "fort" a master signifier in this case. That simple game is an example of the gradual mastery of subjectivity through the use of the signifier (Lacan, 1962), the entrance to speech and the abandonment of language as an exterior and pre-existing closed circuit addressed to no one.

The subject emerges therefore when a person starts using the signifier by inserting a lack in language. The new field of language created is what Lacan will call the symbolic Other or big Other, for which he will give a number of definitions, such as the "battery of signifiers" and the "treasure trove of signifiers" (1960a, pp. 682, 694). Yet the big Other is more than that. It is a dimension (Zenoni, 2012). It is the Other of language, the Other of universal discourse, the Other of truth, the third party in every dialogue, a point of reference for agreement and disagreement, the Other of good faith and the Other of speech, fundamental interlocutor, a field to which discourse without its interpersonal direction is addressed (Miller, 1979, p. 19).

The big Other is therefore the locus of language following symbolisation inserted thanks to the signifier. The subject, in fact, is defined as such by being *subjected* to this Other, the field of signifiers. For it to emerge it must succumb to the big Other and the person must lose that original condition where "pure" language instead of the signifier prevailed.

This conceptualisation of language regulated by law as the big Other will mark Lacan's theory and practice of psychoanalysis for a long time. He will (Lacan, 1953a; 1957a; 1958a; 1960a) refer to the unconscious as the Other's discourse, a reflection of Freud's "other scene" (1900a). Similar to what Freud's grandson did to mark his mother's absence, the subject borrows everything from the Other—not simply its language, but also his desire. Lacan will note that desire is the Other's desire (Lacan, 1958b). Everything for the subject comes from the Other in this period of Lacan's teaching.

The status of the subject, the signifier, and the Other also guides Lacan's new approach to psychosis, which stems from his re-reading of Freud and is contrasted to his theories of the 1930s (Lacan, 1956a). He is now arguing against focusing on the imaginary relation, which Klein, Anna Freud, and others had stressed (Lacan, 1953b), in favour of the symbolic register. The concepts that make that up present a particular status in psychosis, observed in the discourse and conduct of psychotic patients. Of course, this status, especially as far as schizophrenia is concerned, had been already described in the past by its pioneers, Kraepelin (1899) and Bleuler (1911), as well as Freud (1915e). Yet Lacan now turns this from a phenomenological problem, which was his earlier approach (Miller, 1987), into a radical status for the psychotic subject.

Two years after the "Discourse of Rome", Lacan introduces into his seminar a shape that illustrates the interrelation—and clash—between the imaginary and the symbolic registers, whose status must be amended for psychosis. This is the so-called "schema L".

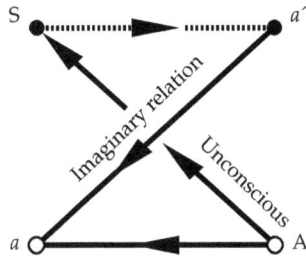

Figure 1. The "schema L".

The first part of this schema, the imaginary relation, is what psychoanalysis has mainly dealt with ever since Melanie Klein and Anna Freud took over the psychoanalytic community. In the figure above, *a* stands for the ego and *a'* for the specular other. Both come from the first letter of the French word for "other", *autre*. Between them lies the imaginary relation, which is inaugurated in the mirror stage (Lacan, 1949). This is the already known matrix of the imaginary.

The second axis is the one Lacan added in the 1950s. It consists of the new terms "subject" (S) and "big Other" (A). As was previously noted, the unconscious unfolds between these entities.

However, as was also explained earlier, the symbolic is the field of law; it is governed by specific rules, being in this respect different from the imaginary. It is not simply a game of signifiers, which flow incessantly. This is one of the effects of the unconscious being structured like a language: one cannot use language as he or she wishes; specific rules, as in grammar and syntax, must be followed. The signifier, whose structure is "that it is articulated" (Lacan, 1957a, p. 418) fulfils its role—of representing the subject—by being articulated with other signifiers and forming a signifying chain, like "Fort! Da!"

Two laws of closed order (Lacan, 1957a) condition the articulation of the signifying chain: metaphor and metonymy. The first stands for the replacement of one signifier with another; the second stands for the "word-to-word" (Lacan, 1957a, p. 421) combination of signifiers, that is, the way those are articulated within a signifying chain. Lacan calls them the "synchronic and diachronic dimensions" of the signifying chain respectively (1953a; 1960a). They are the equivalents to Freud's (1900a) condensation and displacement (Lacan, 1957a).

Yet although the signifier is articulated according to those two unbreakable rules, the same does not happen in its outcome: signification.

Signification, which leads to the production of meaning, is an effect of the signifier's function but not its primary aim. For example, Freud's grandson used the signifiers "Fort" and "Da" to create the signification that Mummy is gone and she will come back. Yet this is not what those two signifiers alone signify. Somebody else might use the same signifiers to throw a stick to their dog and mean "fetch, Spot!" Signification is therefore more personal—unlike the signifier, it can be filled with anything. The arbitrary outcomes of the signifier—signification and meaning—belong to the register that does not obey predefined rules: the imaginary (Lacan, 1956a). Hence, in schema L the imaginary and symbolic axes are clashing: the propensity for meaning does not identify with the use of the signifier, although—as must be noted—they are somehow articulated.

By use of this symbolic "toolbox", we are now ready to examine Lacan's re-thinking of psychosis, where those instruments appear in a distorted form.

The destiny of the paternal signifier in psychosis

In this, second, approach to psychosis, following his phenomenological period, Lacan will emphasise the dysfunction in the symbolic next to that in the imaginary. He will indicate that the study of linguistic phenomena is the most fruitful lesson for the psychoanalytic conceptualisation of psychosis (Lacan, 1955a).

This innovation will eventually have an impact upon the Lacanian approach to psychosis and schizophrenia, since the problematic status of the imaginary of the body will be linked to the unstable status of the symbolic. As was noted in the preceding chapter, psychoanalysts before Lacan would attempt to explain and treat psychosis on the grounds of Freud's cathexis of the libido to the ego and the object. They viewed schizophrenia as an effect of the loss of the cathexis of the libido to the ego due to its weakness and thus attempted to strengthen it through identification (Tausk, 1919; Klein, 1932; 1942; Deutsch, 1942). Based on Freud, Lacan will explain schizophrenia not simply on the basis of a problematic relation to the ego, but to the Other too. This theory was presented in the third year of his seminar (1955–1956), dedicated to a re-reading of Freud's analysis of Schreber.

In *Seminar III* Lacan suggests a rule of thumb for the safe diagnosis of psychosis: the presence of disturbances of language (1955a).

These disturbances stem from the psychotic subject being barred from the use of speech in terms of the regulated big Other of the symbolic (1953a). Psychosis is a field where the big Other, as, for example, in the form of the unconscious, is excluded. Lacan goes on to say that without language being addressed to someone, there would be no problem with psychotics, who would simply speak like talking machines—which is not infrequently encountered in the clinic of schizophrenia either. Therefore, the matter does not seem to be the use of language per se, but of signifiers stemming from the field of the Other.

The core of psychosis should therefore be sought at the level of the signifier, which is linked to the subject's subsistence (Lacan, 1956a). Lacan's example to demonstrate this, as well as the treatment that can occur to counter it, is Schreber. Yet he no longer investigates the German judge's case on the basis of the imaginary, as Freud did, but on that of the symbolic—without ignoring the former, of course. Lacan argues that the cause and treatment orientation of Schreber's delusion does not lie in homosexuality, which is found on the axis of the imaginary, but in paternity (1955a). He demonstrates this for Schreber by returning to the circumstantial incidents preceding his breakdowns.

What were the events that triggered Schreber's hospitalisations? As was noted earlier, the first two had been his failure to be elected to the Reichstag and his success in being appointed president at a relatively young age; the third had been an appeal to Schreber by an association to grant them the exclusive use of his father's heritage on social reform, next to his mother's death and wife's stroke. It seems, indeed, enigmatic that both a failure at rising to a position of authority and a success can trigger a breakdown, let alone the fact of being asked for permission to use one's father's name, which Lacan does not discuss. Those ambiguous phenomena cannot be explained by a mere focus on homosexuality.

In contrast, according to Lacan (1955a), the answer only comes by highlighting the common theme at stake: *paternity*. It is less important whether the circumstance regarded success or not. What mattered was that paternity came into question from the side of the Other. Schreber's inability to subjectively undertake this position was caused by the lack of a particular signifier related to paternity and its respective imaginary lack.

In effect, during this period in Lacan's teaching not all signifiers are of equal status. There is one signifier that is considered responsible for the "normative" articulation of signifiers that the subject depends on. This signifier is called the "Name-of-the-Father" (Lacan, 1953a; 1956a). Whether the subject becomes psychotic or not will depend on its function or dysfunction (Ver Eecke, 2009).

This happens in the following way: during its first experiences, the human being depends on others to answer its needs and provide it with the essentials to survive. The infant, having no capacity for signification, cannot make meaning of the desire of this entity upon which its life usually depends: its mother. Therefore, it stands frustrated before the omnipotence of that agency that can provide or withdraw care at will (Cordié, 1993). This figure is the first Other, the *mOther* (Fink, 1995; 1997), which is not regulated in the sense of the symbolic Other. Imagine Freud's grandson before he invents his little game, watching Mummy come and go at her own will. Isn't this a confusing experience, before becoming simply unpleasant?

The only way such states come to an end, according to Lacan (1956a), is through the intervention of the paternal function. The agent of this function is not one's father in flesh and blood, but the signifier Name-of-the-Father. The paternal signifier bears the symbolic function of an element that adjusts the mother's enigmatic desire by naming it. When this happens, desire and law are linked (Solano Suarez, 2006). Since, as has been remarked already, law and desire come from the Other, the Name-of-the-Father is the Other's regulatory agent: the "Other of the Other". The prototype for this operation is the well-known Freudian Oedipus complex.

Lacan (1938) had disagreed on this occasion with Klein's interpretation of it, highlighting that its agent is specifically the father as the bearer of the phallus. However, at this point he modifies his approach further. The father is not simply a figure, an image to which the phallus is attributed, like the maternal imago, but a symbolic function. Anything can occupy this position. It is not exclusively—and certainly not necessarily—one's father. It does not matter who performs this role, as long as it protects the infant from the arbitrary behaviour of the primary Other the infant is attached to. In Freud's grandson's case, the function of the paternal signifier could be attributed to the elementary game with the piece of string attached to a reel.

Indeed, one of the effects of the successful function of the Name-of-the-Father is the regulation of the signifying chain. The subject can make a signifying use of the signifier, as was shown on the occasion of the "Fort! Da!" game. This happens thanks to the establishment of the so-called *points-de-capiton* or "quilting points" (Lacan, 1955a). This is where the signifier is quilted on the signified (the meaning unit it produces) through the course of the signifying chain. Operating on the enigma of the maternal desire (Laurent, 2012), the Name-of-the-Father establishes the first quilting point that quilts the signifier to the signified (Lacan, 1955a). The quilting point is thus an outcome of the successful paternal metaphor (Grigg, 2001).

Therefore, the signifier's intervention makes language less threatening, since meaning is conditioned by signifying rules. It does not flow. It cannot appear anywhere. The imaginary axis is thus regulated by the symbolic. Freud's grandson's mummy cannot come and go at her own will any more. She can, of course, do this in actuality, but her presence and absence can now be regulated by two phonemes coming from the Other: the signifiers "gone" and "here!"

Yet, as was noted above, there exists the possibility for this particular signifier to be absent, as in Schreber's case. There then appear phenomena explicable on the basis of the non-regulation of the Other and a use of the signifiers for reasons that are not semantic. Lacan understands at this point psychosis in relation to the Name-of-the-Father not having acted as the operator of this regulation (Laurent, 2012). It has been, in contrast, rejected by the subject. This happens through the mechanism Lacan will call "foreclosure".

This term, *Verwerfung* in German, is borrowed from Freud. Foreclosure is used for a fundamental rejection of an element from the subject's system and not simply its repression (Lacan, 1956a). As was highlighted in the preceding chapter, Freud had as early as 1915 expressed the idea that repression might not be suitable for characterising the negation that takes place in schizophrenia. By borrowing this term from another reference of Freud's, Lacan establishes at this point the radical difference between psychosis and neurosis Freud had been implying since the 1910s.

When the Name-of-the-Father therefore is foreclosed, psychotic phenomena can appear. According to Lacan (1954; 1955a), what was not introduced in the symbolic reappears in the real, the register that cannot be accessed like the symbolic or the imaginary. This is the logic behind phenomena such as the delusion of the cut-off finger of the Wolfman, one of Freud's five famous case studies (Freud, 1918b; Lacan, 1954). Lacan returns to his case in the first lecture of *Seminar III* as an example of the foreclosure of castration (1955a).

Lacan therefore founds his theory of psychotic structure and phenomena, along which we will review the schizophrenic's relation to language, its body, and its organs, upon the ground of a symbolic dys-function. He thus shows that psychosis—and therefore its potential treatment—is not a matter of simply curing the ego, which falls within the category of the imaginary, but the symbolic, whose importance has in the meantime been introduced even in his theory of the mirror stage, in the form of the affirmation of the baby's image from the side of the Other. The discussion, which had dominated the psychoana-lytic approach to psychosis via the work of Klein, has moved from the importance of the ego to the primacy of the signifier.

A return to Schreber

In effect, Lacan's audience is encouraged to revisit Schreber's case thus concerning both the cause and treatment achieved. Schreber's dysfunc-tion did not concern exclusively the level of the imaginary—that is, homo-sexuality, which stems from narcissism—but the symbolic. The paternal signifier in his case did not help him give an answer to the question of paternity arising from the field of the Other (1958a). He thus lacked the symbolic factor to regulate the primordial Other and generate the subjec-tive use of the signifier. Schreber could not say "Fort! Da!" Well, he may have been able to mouth the very words, since German was his mother tongue, but for him there was no regulating agent upon the field of signi-fiers that come from the Other; there was no Other of the Other.

On the other hand, Schreber—and the psychotic in general—is not incapable of using signifiers (De Waelhens, 2001b). In fact, Schreber's self-healing system did not only involve the imaginary register, but also a partial—and particular—use of the symbolic. For Lacan (1955a), Schreber builds his solution starting from the mirror stage and the relations that derive from it, and reaches the construction of a new pseudo-symbolic system written in a neo-code, the *Grundsprache* (1958a). What appears as a psychotic phenomenon therefore is in fact a treatment attempt related to structure, which cannot but remind one of Freud's remark of 1911.

Yet Schreber's construction also reminds one of Freud's indication about the cathexis of libido to words in schizophrenia of 1915. In fact, Lacan does not forget to note the part played by the "fundamental language" in the German judge's delirium. In 1911, Freud had not neglected it, but he had not yet articulated his suggestion on schizo-phrenics' discourse. At the end of the day, like Lacan, he is not using Schreber to talk about schizophrenics' language or body phenomena, but about paranoid constructions. Yet Lacan does not pass by the fact that in terms like "soul-murdering" or "nerve-voluptuousness", one can see that the signifier is utilised for the construction of Schreber's delusion (Lacan, 1955a). The German judge might not be able to use "Fort" and "Da" while adhering fully to the Other's discourse—a simple task, one might think—but he uses some of them and thus a subject, a subject distorted and precarious nevertheless, emerges. A negativity is inserted into the body of language—not into the German language, but into Schreber's personal language, the *Grundsprache*. Thus the floating imaginary, the body, and its organs that can lie anywhere above the ground and beneath the clouds, are anchored thanks to a "delusional" use of the signifier.

However, at this point Lacan will differentiate the creation of Schreber's "delusional symbolic order" (Miller, 2009a) from what schizophrenics, for which "all of the symbolic is real" (Lacan, 1954, p. 327), do. Unlike the paranoiac, the schizophrenic cannot historicise his experience (Lacan, 1954). In other words, the schizophrenic cannot create a distorted but relatively coherent big Other in the paranoiac's style, to bring one's specular dependence to a halt.

In fact, in *Seminar III* Lacan (1956a) argues that there are two types of compensatory mechanisms for the lack of the paternal signifier: a) the delusional metaphor and b) conformist imaginary identifications. The first concerns cases like Schreber and the structure of his paranoid delusion. The second is related to one among very few references in this seminar to schizophrenia per se: the "as-if mechanism" that Helene Deutsch (1942) had highlighted on the occasion of "a significant dimension of the symptomatology of the schizophrenias" (Lacan, 1956a, pp. 192–193).

Helene Deutsch was another influential Austrian psychoanalyst and Freud's analysand, interested in the study of schizophrenia, as that had been inaugurated by Tausk and perpetuated by object-relations theorists like Melanie Klein. In fact, she had been Tausk's psychoanalyst on Freud's suggestion.

Based on the idea of the weakness of the ego which her now deceased analysand had highlighted, and after working with schizophrenics, Deutsch constructed a theory of a mechanism at work in schizophrenic subjects: the "as-if" personality. This phenomenon characterises individuals whose life might appear to be complete and normal and yet, in the way they live it, lacks genuineness (Deutsch, 1942). Freud had apparently suggested to Deutsch that she pick another term for this category of hers, since "as-if" had been coined in a translation from the German by a neo-Kantian philosopher named Hans Vaihinger, but she retained it (Galiana-Mingot, 2010).

In her relevant paper, Deutsch was highlighting the absent or impoverished egos that psychoanalysts prior to her, like Tausk and Federn, had also described. She argued that schizophrenic individuals who created such artificial personalities did so as a counter-effect of the failure to develop an object-cathexis, an idea consonant therefore with Freud and Klein's earlier theories. Deutsch's (1942) argument derives from her having observed that when a schizophrenic develops a delusional form, this always happens through an "as-if" phase. She would also suggest that although a standard psychoanalysis cannot take place with such patients, the clinician can help, through a strong identification with them, to achieve far-reaching results. She specifies, finally, that psychoanalysis with "as-if" individuals seldom succeeds (Deutsch, 1942).

Now although we see Lacan differentiating between the delusional metaphor and conformist imaginary identifications, he does not seem to exclude the schizophrenic from treatment attempts resembling Schreber's construction. In fact, Schreber's diagnosis itself might not be as clear as it seems.

In effect, Freud himself (1911c) had argued that elements from both schizophrenia and paranoia are present in the case of the German judge and he chose to focus on the paranoid aspects evident in the delusion. Lacan highlights the fact that Freud treated Schreber's case as a paraphrenic, i.e., schizophrenic, rather than paranoid (1955a). Moreover, it seems that the existence of a discontinuity in Schreber's case points in that direction too, rather than to mere paranoia (Laurent, 2007a).

One might be able to suggest therefore that a "so-called" schizophrenic Schreber (Miller, 1983) treated—temporarily, in fact—the disturbed field of the signifier through his delusional attempt as illustrated in his memoirs (De Waelhens, 2001a; 2001b). Let us not overlook that a few years after having finished the memoirs and being released from the asylum, Schreber suffered his third relapse (Dalzell, 2011), which was not devoid of auditory hallucinations and bodily deterioration (Maleval, 2000). Having abandoned the pseudo-symbolic system built during his second hospitalisation, his relation to God was not enough to hold his body and organs anchored and to keep him away from the asylum.

To sum up, it seems that if Schreber is viewed from the schizophrenic aspect of his case history, a didactic endeavour encouraged by

Jacques-Alain Miller (1983), including the years after his second hospital-isation and the writing of his memoirs, it can be assumed that what gave his system its relatively therapeutic quality was the creation of a personal discourse that substantiated the identity "God's wife", which was not itself irrelevant to a metamorphosis of the body. Wasn't Freud suggesting something similar in "The Unconscious" (1915e) when he highlighted the therapeutic effects of at a cathexis of libido in word-presentations?

If, in the end, Schreber's relation to God did not generate a solid construction through the projection of libido to the other's image, this might have been due to the fact that, as schizophrenic, he presented a fundamental dysfunction in processing otherness as an object (Lacan, 1938). Libido was, then, projected to the units of the *Grundsprache*, ele-ments of which, like "nerve-voluptuousness" referred directly to his body; thus, his organs were temporarily anchored to his feminised body in a "delusional" Gestalt.

Lacan's theory of psychosis of the 1950s did not stop in *Seminar III*. It was developed further in a paper, published two years later, entitled "On a Question Prior to Any Possible Treatment of Psychosis". That paper was included in his famous *Écrits* (Lacan, 1958a). According to Ver Eecke (2009), this is where Lacan's first theory of psychosis is actu-ally formulated.

The first metaphor

In the very first line of this paper, Lacan (1958a) argues that psychosis had yet to be reconceptualised by psychoanalysis in spite of fifty years of Freudianism having been applied to it. He claims that the privilege of his own contribution to the psychoanalytic approach to psychosis, following Freud, was that he had come up with a "structural analysis" (Lacan, 1958a, p. 449).

Two years after *Seminar III*, Lacan's teaching is still under the pre-dominance of the symbolic. In this paper therefore he is highlight-ing the effect that the subject's relation to the signifier had upon both the understanding of human subjectivity and the status of psychosis (Lacan, 1958a). Based on his hitherto limited references to the Name-of-the-Father and the idea of foreclosure, Lacan formulates the theory of the paternal metaphor. This theory shows the comprehensive way in which he conceives of the causation of subjectivity. The effects of its failure for the subject are elaborated upon further than in *Seminar III*.

In the theory of the paternal metaphor, the Name-of-the-Father is given the role of the regulator of the primary Other's enigmatic desire. An example of such an operation was presented earlier, in the game "Fort! Da!" What is explained further than *Seminar III* is that *phallic* signification emerges by the replacement of the desire of the mother by a signifier.

Phallic signification means that the Other, represented in this primary form by mother, can become desirable (Vanheule, 2011a). The Phallus is introduced in the second phase of the operation. Having held an imaginary role in the past ($-\varphi$), it turns into a positive factor (Φ). It will act for significations in the same way that the Name-of-the-Father does for signifiers (Menard, 2009). It organises signification and thus meaning; phallic meaning is one of the effects of the paternal metaphor (Grigg, 1999).

It needs to be clarified without further ado that when Lacan says "phallus", he is not referring to the actual phallic organ, the penis, in the way this term is seemingly used by Freud or Klein. He initially speaks of an image ($-\varphi$) and then a signifier (Φ).

Therefore, to the Kleinian theory that the child initially attributes the phallus to the mother's body—a point of disagreement with her already from the 1930s—Lacan suggests that the child wants to be what the mother desires, to become the phallus itself in order to satisfy her desire (Lacan, 1958a). He claims to have taken this idea from Freud when the latter suggested that the castration complex was the pivotal point for a symbolic process in both sexes (Lacan, 1958a). In the successful processing of the paternal metaphor the phallus is not imaginary; it does not simply relate to an imaginary agent that supplements mother, but to what regulates significations, the field of language—in other words, a signifier (Φ). As far as psychosis is concerned, since the symbolic axis is fundamentally problematic, the person subsists primarily in the place of $-\varphi$.

In *Seminar II*, Lacan had written that the madman is someone who, purely and simply, adheres to the imaginary (1955b), whereas a few years earlier he had suggested that "madness is experienced entirely within the register of meaning" (Lacan, 1946, p. 135). Is, however, the imaginary enough to keep the psychotic subject going? It seems that it is not. At this point, the side of the symbolic is deemed so significant that Lacan writes:

> If the Other is removed from its place, man can no longer even sustain himself in the position of Narcissus. (Lacan, J., [1958a] 2006, p. 460)

There might be no clearer summary of what Schreber achieved thanks to the writing of his memoirs. Applying this remark to his case as it was analysed by Lacan in *Seminar III*, we can suggest that the imaginary axis itself is not enough to safeguard the ego's strength, and certainly not the subject's subsistence. Even in a problematic form, an Other is vital for one to be able to sustain subjectivity. This is what, in the end, the paranoiac—and whoever undergoes successfully the mirror stage—succeeds in.

This seems to be the orientation to answer the "question prior to any possible treatment of psychosis": it is the existence of an Other, a field towards which the psychotic subject can develop "delusional transference", as President Schreber did (Lacan, 1958a, p. 456). When the Other towards whom transference is developed is abandoned, people like Schreber cannot even sustain themselves in the position of the specular other, since that position is, as was remarked above, fundamentally precarious. In the field of the regulated Other there is an emergence of a subject according to signifying laws that brings about a pause in the mirror and offers it a sense of an acquisition of their body and organs.

Aren't the effects of its absence evident in the case of the tormented German judge? His semi-therapeutic paranoid construction constituted a discourse that sustained his existence as subject, built on a language characterised by a personal use of the signifier that covered the void created from the lack of the Name-of-the-Father. When that stopped, after his release from the asylum, his imaginary relations to God and Professor Flechsig did not suffice for him to get by. Unable to sustain himself in the position of Narcissus, he was taken to the asylum experiencing physical phenomena and he died there after four years.

This, however, presents something that might look like an impasse for the clinician. As was noted above, Lacan's suggestion for the treatment that can take place in psychosis concerns the question of the handling of transference (1958a). Yet, as was remarked as early as in Freud's time, this is not the kind of transference developed in a proper psychoanalysis, where, as Klein and Deutsch were implying, the analyst can represent a kind of otherness.

What is therefore the clinician's task when it is not to become an "other" for the psychotic subject? This is found in the sixteenth lecture of *Seminar III*. Lacan writes that we must become "secretaries to the insane" (1956a, p. 206).

The importance of secretarial support

Becoming secretaries to the psychotic. Is that all, one would naturally ask. We are encouraged to drop the suggestion of offering our brilliant egos as points of identification for becoming … secretaries? This might sound like an inferior task, but it is not.

First of all, being a competent secretary to the insane concerns handling skilfully the major role played by transference in psychosis. As above, Freud (1916–1917) noted the incapacity for transference in psychotics as a factor depriving such subjects of the ability to undergo a proper psychoanalysis. However, this does not mean that psychotic subjects do not develop transference.

In contrast, transference to the clinician can be developed, yet this runs the risk of becoming erotomaniac or persecutory (Allouch, 2015; Grigg, 2015; Maleval, 2015; Voruz & Wolf, 2007). The clinician's task therefore is to avoid encouraging the development of transference in the style of a proper psychoanalysis. This might prove a challenging task itself.

In effect, what the psychotic, as well as the analysand, need is not something that will offer them one more imaginary point to identify with, especially when the former's problematic relation to this has been extensively discussed. In fact, the guidance to avoid implicating the imaginary is seen in another frequent remark of Lacan's: to evade aiming at the effect of signification—meaning.

From the early stages of his teaching until the last period of his seminar in the 1970s, Lacan warned his audience against comprehension: do not try to understand! If one goes through Lacan's entire oeuvre they will find this piece of advice appearing again and again.

Why is that? In a few words, because understanding belongs to the field of meaning, signification, and thus the imaginary. It stops nowhere: it goes on and on, it continues eternally, which is something that can also happen with psychotic transference. The psychotic is in need of a pause in his or her continuous wandering and not its perpetuation (Klotz, 2009).

This pause can come about by means of the introduction of a negativity, which will bring about the subject. In neurosis, this negativity is offered by the Phallus (Φ), which puts a stop to the subject's incarnating what fulfils the desire of the mother ($-\varphi$). In psychosis, this signifier is absent.

Consequently, at this stage in Lacan's thinking, clinicians are encouraged to support the psychotic subject in inventing his or her own point of reference: try to maintain a cut, in other words a negativity, in the person who is tormented by a continuous wandering, in the absence of the break offered by the phallus. His or her task as secretary is to introduce a negativity in what appears to the psychotic as an excessive experience (Malengreau, 2003). If the "madman is a theoretician of his own experience of madness" (Allouch, 2015, p. 119), the secretary's task is structuring, symbolising, and supporting the subject to construct their theory. How? The elements to do this can be found by listening to the subject's discourse. Lacan suggests:

> Like Freud, I hold that we must listen to the speaker, when what is at stake is a message that does not come from a subject beyond language, but from speech beyond the subject. For it is then that we will hear this speech, which Schreber picked up in the Other [...].
> (Lacan, J., [1958a] 2006, pp. 478–479)

The psychoanalyst therefore is not discouraged from seeing psychotics—not, however, with any unwarranted ambition to cure them, but with the humble ambition of offering them his or her secretarial skills, trying to benefit from their abilities in inventions (Maleval, 2015). At the end of the day, when Freud discussed Schreber he spoke of "self-healing" and not a treatment brought forward by a clinician through transference—which he also noted for recovery in schizophrenia (1915e). But how can this be attempted in actual terms?

Let us take the example of a nineteen-year-old psychotic man, Paul, who had to see a psychotherapist due to his behaviour troubling his divorced mother and her new family. A tall and overweight young man, Paul believed that his tiny four-year-old half-brother, who supposedly swore at him and called him names, wanted to throw him off the balcony. He sometimes saw himself crawling on the ceiling and heard his step-father asking him to do naughty stuff. In addition, his expressed wish to have sex was puzzling the family who did not know how to address it. Should they look for a sex worker experienced with the mentally ill or not?

Whenever he was encouraged to speak in session, Paul would respond with an unstructured delusion. This included everyone and everything he knew—people, animals, inanimate objects, and body parts—procreating. For example, "the duck fucks the ear and they give birth to the door", or "the priest fucks the pen and they give birth to chicken" he would say. It took me some time to realise that some of the elements of those couples were present during the session, like the office door, the pen resting on a desk or even my ear! Signification was unstoppable. The only way to stop Paul from being delusional was to stop encouraging him to speak, which I did for some time with no outcome. So, encouraged by supervision, I tried becoming his secretary.

I was advised to support a structurisation of that chaotic system, which included me, and tried to do so for some time. The attempt to transmit to a piece of paper that procreating phantasmagoria once gave out an impressive illustration of the need to insert a pause into the body's precarious imaginary constitution: having finished writing, Paul touched his tongue with the tip of his pen and said: "now I put a full stop!"

Yet after numerous desperate attempts, something caught my attention: that there was someone escaping being "fucked" in Paul's system: Satan. "Satan fucks everyone but no one fucks him", Paul said. So, although this might sound an unorthodox thing to do—quite ironic come to think that I was raised a Christian Orthodox—I "allied" with Satan, trying to use him as a regulating agency in the attempted structure in the absence of the phallus. My objective was not the creation of an "other scene", but "taming" what filled those signifiers, which is not simply meaning, and is further explained below. I aimed for such an orientation to help Paul fasten to the parts of his floating body.

In the next period in Lacan's teaching, which developed in the 1960s, the area where the clinician-secretary to the insane will be called to act upon will not simply be unstoppable signification, as one might think on the occasion of Paul's case. Lacan will argue that the use of the imaginary and the symbolic do not suffice to maintain such a discourse. At the end of this period, it will be suggested that if a subject within the clinic of schizophrenia must create a personal discourse to fight the effects of the paternal foreclosure, this must also involve the third component of subjectivity: the real, a relation to which could have been implied in Paul's comments about Satan.

CHAPTER THREE

From the subject to the speaking being

S̲ix years after "On a Question Prior to Any Possible Treatment of Psychosis", Lacan (1964a) taught his eleventh seminar, *The Four Fundamental Concepts of Psychoanalysis*, which constituted a second stage in his teaching (Miller, 2003a). The step towards it was accompanied by an institutional change: Lacan was, in his words, "excommunicated" (1964a; 1969) from the French Psychoanalytic Society, on the grounds of his controversial teaching and what was being considered as an unorthodox practice of psychoanalysis (Nobus, 1999; Roudinesco, 1997). He thus left Saint Anne's for the prestigious École Normale Supérieure, a Parisian *grande école*.

The four fundamental concepts that gave that year's seminar its title were the unconscious, the drive, repetition, and transference (Lacan, 1964a). All of them are related to a focal shift in Lacan's teaching: from the prevalence of the symbolic to that of the real (Verhaeghe, 1999). This fundamental shift shed new light on the understanding of the subject (Vanheule & Geldhof, 2012) and psychosis.

After a few years, when the last period of Lacan's teaching, the so-called "later Lacan", unfolded, the promotion of one register after the other would be abandoned (Voruz & Wolf, 2007). Miller (2003a) identifies a cut between Lacan's teaching of this period compared to the preceding ones and an attempt to detach himself from Freud. Lacan's later theory overshadowed many of his earlier but even more recent theoretical formulations. Even the unconscious was replaced with the "speaking being" (*parlêtre* in French), whereas language lost its predominance to *lalangue*. This paved the way for an understanding of psychosis relatively different to what had been hitherto developing in psychoanalysis. These developments are discussed below.

The real: the predominance of jouissance

Jouissance

During Lacan's teaching on the symbolic, which had dominated the 1950s, Freud's concepts like the libido and the drive were understood on the ground of desire, demand, and the big Other (Lacan, 1958c). Thus, Freud's (1915e) remark about schizophrenics' language and their relation to body organs were to be understood in a similar way. Yet in the 1960s the libido was rethought of in a different context, which emerged from an effort to conceive of the aspects of subjectivity beyond the symbolic and the imaginary.

One might wonder what the need for this change was, especially since Lacan had spent an entire decade encouraging psychoanalysts to reject the prevalence of the imaginary—which he had emphasised in the 1930s—for that of the symbolic. The truth is that the need to examine subjectivity from a perspective other than that of the symbolic and the imaginary arose from clinical observations.

Freud had been the first to highlight the power of repetition—one of the four fundamental concepts—in the form of "negative therapeutic reaction" (Freud, 1920g). This concept describes the clinical phenomenon of patients who would get worse after a temporary suspension of symptoms (Freud, 1924c).

I have already referred to Freud's first relevant example of repetition: "Fort! Da!" Unlike the first Lacan, Freud's (1920g) attention had not been attracted to his grandson's game by the articulation of the signifiers, but by the boy's intentional revival of a distressing experience. That observation along others had led him to form the hypothesis of an instinctual urge, independent of the pleasure principle—hence, the paper's title—which leads to a return to a primordial, inanimate condition of things (Freud, 1920g). He was led to support the existence of a death drive running counter to the sexual drives and drives of life (Freud, 1920g).

This is the economy of the libido that Lacan, who, on the other hand, did not adhere to Freud's approach of the duality in the drives, would reformulate (Aflalo, 2015). For Lacan there is only one drive, the death drive (1964a). In contrast to Freud, who wondered why somebody would revive an unpleasant experience, Lacan would bestow upon such experiences a character of painful pleasure, which he called *jouissance* (Evans, 1996). French for "enjoyment", jouissance is a term that corresponds to Freud's concept of libido concerning its dimension of the real. Whereas Freudian libido, which is not absent from *Seminar XI*, signifies sexual pleasure, jouissance is a type of satisfaction or drive gratification that goes beyond pleasure (Aflalo, 2015; Vanheule, 2011a). It becomes the—unpleasant—satisfaction of the drive (Lacan, 1960b).

The fundamental shift in Lacan's understanding of the real must be noted at this point. In the previous period of his teaching, the real was what resisted signification (Lacan, 1955a–56a), what simply "ex-sisted" (Lacan, 1954, p. 327). It was therefore what could not be grasped by the symbolic—yet there was no link between it and the jouissance of the living being. The first Lacan placed jouissance on the side of the imaginary (Miller, 2011).

At this stage, however, jouissance is subtracted from the imaginary and is linked to the real of the body. Lacan suggests an aspect of the body that has nothing to do with the image, the form or vision: jouissance as such is reduced to an event of the body (Miller, 2011). Jouissance thus turns into a concept of physical, material nature, less related to the body of the imaginary and desire and demand of the symbolic. It is an aspect of the real, which concerns the body's libidinal life (Leader, 2011) yet still resists signification and symbolisation (Vanheule & Geldhof, 2012).

Lacan's emphatic introduction of jouissance as linked to the real against the imaginary generated a new approach to the causation of subjectivity and the subject's libidinal route. This change introduced an alternative aspect for the big Other and the subject and generated a new significant concept, the object *a*.

The big Other as field of the signifier is not absent from *Seminar XI*. Lacan argues that the subject arises from this field. The emergence of the subject through the articulation of signifiers had already been described in the 1950s, as the effect of the minimal signifying chain S_1–S_2, of which Freud's grandson gave us a simple but graphic example.

Yet what is different to the past is that now the subject is represented by a barred S ($). This was a development of the late 1950s in Lacan's teaching, to show that the subject is divided by language (Evans, 1996). It was his way to join Freud's two convictions about the subject: that it is being manifested in the language of the formations of the unconscious and that it is marked by division (Aflalo, 2015).

One more of this period's innovations concerns the texture of the Other as "field of [that] living being in which the subject has to appear", besides its symbolic nature (Lacan, 1964a, p. 203). Lacan argues that the Other is the field from which the drive emanates (1964a). Yet the drive is now linked to the corporeal texture of the act (Soler, 2014).

Let us return for a moment to the causation of subjectivity suggested in the paternal metaphor. The entity that required regulation through the intervention of a special signifier was mOther, the subject's first Other. In the paternal metaphor, the desire of the mother was named and it became possible for the person to make use of the signifier for means of signification, thanks to the positivisation of the phallus. Consequently, subject and regulated Other of the signifier, the two sides of the axis of the unconscious in the schema L, were established. A new alienation was opened for the subject, following its form as the unregulated Other's phallus ($-\varphi$).

In this new theoretical perspective of the emergence of subjectivity, things change, since the field that requires regulation is not considered any more as primarily imaginary or symbolic. It is rather occupied by jouissance, which is now closer to the real rather than the imaginary. Lacan (1964a, p. 205) writes that the real lack "situated at the advent of the living being" precedes the lack born from the advent of the subject in relation to the signifier. It is there from the start for the speaking being (Morel, 2011). Therefore, the necessary regulation in the field of the Other through a symbolic intervention does not concern originally the signifier, not separated yet from the signified, but jouissance. The Other of the signifier succeeds this. According to Miller (2009b) the subject is an effect of inserting the symbolic into the real; in "the jouissance of the body undifferentiated from the surrounding world" (Grasser, 1998, p. 2).

The way in which the subject emerges from the field of jouissance is analysed in *Seminar XI* in two operations Lacan defines as "alienation" and "separation" (Lacan, 1964a; 1964c). Necessary for the constitution of the subject (Glowinski, 2001), they are characterised by a temporal ordering (Miller, 2007).

Alienation and separation

Unlike the paternal metaphor, this theory of the causation of subjectivity has everything to do with the drive (Verhaeghe, 1999). The operation of alienation produces a subjective formation within the Other of the drive that the child is entirely attached to, whereas separation generates an agent that makes the subject believe it can recuperate a part of it. How does it work?

Alienation establishes the subject divided by the signifier (Miller, 2007). In Lacan's words, it realises the subject in its signifying dependence in the field of the Other (1964a). Remember Freud's grandson's game. The introduction of a minimal signifying chain like "Fort! Da!" starts evacuating the locus of the drive from jouissance and producing the Other of S_1–S_2 and the subject (Lacan, 1964c). Thus, the child assumes an identity of some kind thanks to the intervention of the signifiers of the Other (Verhaeghe, 2008). It is alienated by the signifier, having chosen to make sense or meaning instead of being (Glowinski, 2001). Meaning is, indeed, promoted in this operation. Freud's grandson attempts to turn from being what his mother is lacking to creating meaning about her desire through his alienation by the minimal signifying chain. This is achieved by images linking to words (Verhaeghe, 2008).

After alienation comes separation. This operation concerns the subject's actual parting from the otherness they are attached to in this primary stage. As was described in the process of alienation, this otherness has been marked by the intervention of the signifying chain in the field of jouissance. Yet signifier, image, and jouissance are still undifferentiated to an extent. In other words, we are still talking about psychosis. In separation, the subject parts from the minimally regulated Other it is attached to and incarnates its lack. The lack that the separation of the subject from the Other constitutes generates desire in that field; thus, the subject leaves jouissance for desire. The neurotic subject is established. The construction it will make use of to access that lack is the object *a* (1962–1963). This is the cause of desire that will condition its libidinal life (Lacan, 1964a; 1964c). The subject will assert itself as that object (Miller, 2007).

Have we seen such an entity in Freud's grandson's game? It seems we did. Apart from the phonemes "ooo" and "da", there is an actual object in the operation, the reel attached to the string, which represents a primary object. In the 1960s Lacan suggests that, at the end of the day, it was not a pure activity of mastery that was taking place in that game, but an alienation, which is practiced with the help of the reel, that is, the object *a* (1964a). This is not the mother's body itself reduced to an object—as Klein was suggesting—but a part of the subject (Lacan, 1964c). Next to the signifying opposition of "Fort!" and "Da!", the presence of the object shows what is at stake at the level of jouissance (Morel, 2011).

Thus, in contrast to the previous period in Lacan's teaching, the emergence of subjectivity from *Seminar XI* onwards is not without a secondary product. After all, if it were repetition would make no sense, since signification would have been able to fully absorb jouissance. What remains, according to Lacan, from the completed intervention of the signifier onto the human being is the object *a*. The object *a* represents a minimum quantity of jouissance that cannot enter to the symbolic (Vanheule & Geldhof, 2012). It is a small entity signifying the subject's relation to the real. It lingers and motivates the subject's desire. Lacan will use it in his quest for the ways through which a circumscription of the real can occur (Voruz & Wolf, 2007).

Lacan (1964a; 1964c) will even create a myth to describe the emergence of the object *a*, which is linked to the partial drives: the "lamella"; the primordial form of the libido as "pure real" (p. 717). The lamella, which he also calls *h*omelet (h stands for *homme*, French for "man") is an imagined thin-layered organ condensing the organism's primordial status of jouissance. An effect of separation is for the subject to aim at restoring this lost status of the organism "further than the body's limit" (Lacan, 1964c, p. 719) that can be only partially pursued through the object *a*.

We observe therefore that jouissance and the new approach to the real bring a significant alteration to Lacan's conceptualisation of subjectivity. In the past, the subject had been thought of as a mere effect of signification; the small other was considered a specular image and the Other was thought of as the field of the signifier, which regulates the former. Now, the divided subject is an effect of jouissance; the object small *a* is its agent and the unregulated Other is primarily a field of jouissance. However, this new theoretical formulation does not cancel out its preceding theory. It acts as something supplementary to it. The subject is not divided by either the signifier or jouissance but by both.

Specular others maintain their status. Finally, the Other can be both the field of the signifier and the field of jouissance. Lacan (1964a) speaks of a conjunction of the subject as it appears in the field of the drive, and as it does in the field of the Other.

As above, the supplementation of Lacan's theory of the causation of subjectivity will lead to a different approach to psychosis too. From that theory it derives that separation does not take place in psychosis. The subject remains un-separated from the signifying chain (Rodriguez, 2001); thus meaning is promoted. Yet the same happens with jouissance, since the object *a* is not extracted. Hence, Lacan will argue that the madman has the object *a* in his pocket (1967a).

It might seem that these effects have been partly referred to in Lacan's previous teaching. The regulation of the signifying chain and the signifying use of the signifier were what the psychotic subject was deprived of as a result of the paternal foreclosure in Lacan's thinking. Yet thanks to this new focus on jouissance the problem is not any more seen in psychosis as the result of the non-regulation of the imaginary by the symbolic but the non-regulation of jouissance too. Incomplete separation leaves the subject attached to the amalgamated real, symbolic, and imaginary that alienation has partly established. Therefore, the "mad Other" (Vanheule, 2011) schizophrenic subjects confront is not only the inconsistent Other of the symbolic, but also the real, jouissance that is linked to the body. Thus, the schizophrenic is treating actual body organs (eyes, spinal cord etc.) like words—remember Paul, who attempted to put a full stop on his tongue, as if it were a word—not only as an effect of the signifier not having parted from the signified, but also as an effect of it being still attached to its aspect that is closer to the real; jouissance. Freud's word-presentations and Lacan's signifiers are bearers of jouissance when separation has not taken place.

In fact, at the beginning of the next decade, Lacan would help us clarify this in stating that the schizophrenic is found without a ready-made way to relate to his or her body and organs, from which subjects who are not called schizophrenic benefit: the four discourses.

In and out of established discourses

The theory of discourses was introduced five years after the configuration of alienation and separation of *Seminar XI*. It was presented in Lacan's *Seminar XVII, The Other Side of Psychoanalysis* (1969–1970).

In it, Lacan was still trying to answer the question of the subject's articulation to the signifier and its jouissance.

In *Seminar XVII*, Lacan (1969) introduced four exclusive types of discourse: the discourse of the master, the hysteric, the psychoanalyst, and the university (or academic discourse). They are a psychoanalytic writing of the four basic types of social bond that exist in Western civilisation (Gallagher, 2002; Laurent, 2012). Each of them delineates a fundamental type of relationship (Verhaeghe, 1994). Lacan (1972–1973, p. 17) says "discourse should be taken as a social link, founded on language."

Discourses are not produced randomly. This is because the formulae of discourse are not mere depictions of operations. They are governed by specific rules. Thus they are configured as algorithms. The positions occupied by the four different terms in the algorithms are in the upper left side that of "agent", in the lower left that of "truth", in the upper right that of the "other", and in the lower right that of the "product" (Lacan, 1969). Moreover, the form of the composites of those positions—S_1, S_2, $, and a—changes whenever they occupy a different location in the four discourses. Here they are:

$$\text{M} \qquad \text{H} \qquad \text{A} \qquad \text{U}$$

$$\frac{S_1}{\$} \rightarrow \frac{S_2}{a} \qquad \frac{\$}{a} \rightarrow \frac{S_1}{S_2} \qquad \frac{a}{S_2} \rightarrow \frac{\$}{S_1} \qquad \frac{S_2}{S_1} \rightarrow \frac{a}{\$}$$

Figure 2. The four discourses.

The master's discourse (M), depicted first in the figure above, is the prominent discourse. It acts as matrix for the remaining three (Lacan, 1969). In it, the master signifier (S_1) acts as the *agent* whose *truth* is the divided subject ($), it addresses the *other* of knowledge (S_2), and the object a is *produced* (Lacan, 1969).

An example seems appropriate at this point. Paul Verhaeghe (1994) gives one I find simple and understandable: A father tells his son to work hard at school; the son, instead, brings home nothing but failures. In this example the agent is the father, the other is the son and the product is failure. The most important part of every discourse, however, its moving force, is what lies on the lower left side: truth, which, according to Lacan, is always half-said (1969). What triggers the father to ask for such a performance from his son? It is not merely him as a master, but a truth unknown even to him—unconscious—that motivates the discourse. In this case, himself he is divided: the divided subject is in the place of the truth.

Another enlightening example is Éric Laurent's (2007b) reference to the compilation and writing of the Homeric epics in sixth-century-B.C. Athens, commissioned by him whom Laurent calls the first tyrant. The master who commissioned such a task, which would praise the heroic deeds of the Athenians' ancestors, was motivated by nothing other but his own truth. That was the fact that heroic eras, where he could himself emerge as hero, had been long gone (Laurent, 2007b). Another example for the master's discourse from ancient Greek history is Lycurgus, the harsh Spartan lawmaker (Soler, 2014).

As observed in the figure above, the remaining three aforementioned discourses are generated by a quarter turn of the coordinates of the master's discourse on the right or the left. As above, the composites always maintain their position with regards to each other. Other historical examples for the established discourses suggested by Colette Soler (2014) are Charlemagne for the discourse of the university, Socrates for that of the hysteric, and, of course, Freud for the analytic discourse.

Of course, one could claim that the social bond presents many more modalities than the four discourses described above. However, for Lacan, no other turns of the master's discourse can take place and no arbitrary positioning of the four components or their function is allowed—despite the fact that Lacan (1972) himself added a fifth type, the capitalist's discourse, a few years later. Nevertheless, these are the only four established ways that a subject as speaking being can use in the social bond. In fact, discourse defines the position of the subject even before the subject utters any statement (Rodriguez, 2001). They are already there, like empty bags with a predefined structure, waiting for the subject to fill them (Verhaeghe, 1994).

This, however, presents a challenge for psychotic subjects, where the composites of the four discourses do not appear in forms that can fit those algorithms. Since separation has not taken place, there is no object a, divided subject $ or segregated S_1 and S_2 to fill those empty bags. How do they relate to the signifier and to their jouissance therefore?

With regards to the subject's use of established discourse, Lacan will link the schizophrenic subject to the real of the body in a reference that will surprisingly bring it closer than before to the other subjective modalities. This reference is found in a text of 1973 entitled "L'Étourdit" (1973a).

"L'Étourdit", included in his *Autres Écrits*, is a paper in which Lacan discusses the impasses of the signifier and suggests a treatment of the real beyond meaning (Fierens, 2002). It establishes a "second return to Freud" (Soler, 2003). His reference to schizophrenia can act as a return to Freud's indication of not only what is at stake in this psychotic sub-type, but also the treatment that can take place with such subjects. It is found in the part where Lacan discusses an aspect of the real and its effects on the subject's body: the inexistent sexual relationship.

That there is no relation between the sexes is one of those famous aphorisms of Lacan's that may have generated the greatest controversy of them all (1972–1973, p. 17). Yet there is much more to it than simply an acknowledgment of the impossibility of a man relating sexually to a woman. By calling this an "aspect of the real", Lacan (1973a) shows that it cannot enter the symbolic, a predefined, ordered position, yet has a direct effect on the subject's singular relation to the libidinal body. Indeed, nothing about the relation between the two sexes can be found in the unconscious. The only relation possible is to the object a—the structure of the fantasy—which is a proper part of the subject subtracted in the operation of separation and which the schizophrenic is missing.

Yet the challenge stemming from the hole that the real of the inexis-tent sexual relationship creates in the symbolic concerns every speaking being's attempt to "inhabit" language. Inhabiting language will help any subject obtain the use of their body, its organs, and their functions. Language is, in fact, the first of those organs whose use must be obtained by the subject and this takes place with the help of the established dis-courses. As for "so-called schizophrenics", who, just like any other sub-ject, must inhabit language to acquire their bodies, their organs, and their functions too, they are called to do so without the help from the established discourses (1973a).

Marie-Hélène Brousse notes that the Name-of-the-Father returns in established discourses (2009). Therefore, the schizophrenic subject's lack of help from the established discourses could be parallelised to the lack of belief in the Father and the processing of the paternal metaphor. Indeed, the effects of the lack of help from the established discourses are similar to those of the lack of help from the paternal signifier: the unregulated big Other. Yet things have changed drastically since the 1950s, since, as was remarked above, in the 1960s the signifier fell from its pedestal in Lacan's teaching and lost its predominance to jouissance, which is linked to the living body.

In effect, the four discourses, which offer a divided subject an estab-lished way to articulate with their jouissance, are not idealised as was the Name-of-the-Father. On the contrary; the four discourses are bound to portray an impossibility due the aforementioned absence of the sexual relationship, which is their real (Miller, 2015). Discourses are thus built around holes; Verhaeghe (2008) adds the father—who also loses his predominance in Lacan's teaching—and the sexual difference to the hole of the sexual relationship (p. 117).

In order to describe the artificial constructions that attempt to cover the holes that the real creates in the symbolic, Lacan will suggest the term *semblant*, French for "make-believe". In his seminar of the following year he will re-define the position in the upper left side of discourses: from "agent" to "make-believe" (Lacan, 1971). This will indicate that discourse, which is always a discourse of make-believe (Soler, 2014), only exists in the context of the discourse that produces it, which appears as true, whereas it is not (Braunstein, 2015).

This development is leading us to change the way we view the schizophrenic subject in comparison to Lacan's theories of the 1940s and 1950s. This should not be viewed anymore as a subject who presents a deficit in front of reality, but as a subject showing disbelief in artificial constructions, such as the established discourses (Zenoni, 2012). The schizophrenic is not fooled, like everybody else, by the make-believe, the moving force of established discourse. This stance against the make-believe, which has abiding consequences for the schizophrenic's relation to their body and organs has, in fact, generated this book's title, as will be explained further below.

So what happens to the body when the composites of established discourse are missing? As was observed in the theory of alienation and separation, the introduction of the signifying chain results in the emergence of the subject divided by the signifier and jouissance and the production of the object *a*. Yet when separation is unsuccessful jouissance does not leave the subject's body. As a result, signifier and jouissance, or words and things (Freud, 1915e), are not segregated. Thus, the subject is not represented by one, master signifier, a unary trait, but, instead, by a swarm of signifiers (Miller, 2001; Sauvagnat, 2000; Soler, 1999; Zenoni, 2012). Moreover, the object *a* as regulator of jouissance is not ballasted. It can appear anywhere. According to Miller, the lack of help from the established discourses signifies the lack of a position for the object *a* (2001) for the schizophrenic.

As above, a subject who is not schizophrenic—which makes one think of not only the neurotic, but the paranoiac too—can make use of the established discourses to assume its body, its organs, and their function. Those four discourses offer a ready-made access for subjects divided by the signifier and jouissance to undergo that process. Discourse "gives us our bodies", notes Soler (2014, p. 178). Thus, when we are not given our bodies through the help of established discourse and the make-believe, jouissance can overwhelm them; it can turn them to its prey at any point, generating the phenomena of detached spinal cords, twisting eyes, procreating ears, and female genitalia inhabiting one's throat. The examples from literature and the clinic used in the preceding chapters (Jung's delusional seamstress, Schreber, Peter, Amelia, and Paul) show exactly this effect of the schizophrenic being deprived of the treatment of jouissance that established discourses offer. However, in contrast to the past, this theoretical formulation seems to leave a possibility for treatment open.

A discourse that is not established

As was remarked above, the schizophrenic is not described in "L'Étourdit" as deprived of the help from any discourse but from the established ones. He or she must find a way to assume the function of his or her body, its organs, and their function without the help from the established discourses. We read nowhere that there is not a way other than the established for someone to assume their body organs and those organs' functions.

The schizophrenic is thus not by definition excluded from inhabiting language and acquiring thanks to this their body and its organs. Their difference to other subjects concerns the way this is achieved. The schizophrenic is taken beyond the help of established discourses, which are the modalities used by other—divided—subjects to articulate with their jouissance (Laurent, 2012).

Therefore, the objective for the "so-called schizophrenic" that can be drawn from this extract is to invent a singular, out-of-ordinary way to exist as a subject who has a body. The fact that the schizophrenic cannot be helped by the established discourses shows therefore that there is no standard means for them to become divided by the Other and articulate with their jouissance so that this does not become directly attached to the body and its organs.

The subjects that are deemed schizophrenic are not therefore necessarily doomed. If they can invent a way to acquire or inhabit language before this "acquires" or "inhabits" them, and through this their body and its function, they can somehow deal with the jouissance deriving from the hole that the real creates in the symbolic. What is at stake therefore is to preserve the body against the onslaught of language that is inhabited by jouissance, something that does not seem to be the primary challenge for other psychotic subjects, like paranoiacs, since in the aforementioned excerpt Lacan is not talking about the psychotic in general, but about the schizophrenic. It seems that the paranoiac makes use of a discourse linked to otherness, although he or she creates this alone, in the style of Schreber's delusional metaphor. Like the neurotic, they may not be in need of an original modality aimed at assuming the organ of language and their body, since they seem to adhere to some form of otherness stemming from the mirror stage.

Not far from the end of his teaching—and his life—Lacan will use a case example of a man who, despite his inability to make use of the established discourses, proceeded to an instrumentalisation of the organ of language that allowed him to acquire his body and its organs. It seems that in this case, where the Other did not hold a central role, the subject's body was won over from jouissance inhabiting language. Moreover, this kind of language was treated in a way that probably kept our well-known psychotic phenomena in a latent state. That was the case of the Irish writer James Joyce.

Joyce's invention is studied below in relation to the articulation of four elements, but this time they are not the composites of established discourse that link the subject to the Other. Instead of S_1, S_2, $, and a, what attracted Lacan's interest was how the real, the symbolic, and the imaginary were linked thanks to a fourth element that allowed the subject's subsistence: the *sinthome*. This offered Joyce the capacity for an acquisition of the body of a different kind to the established. A development in Lacan's teaching beyond the theory of the established discourses is that although there might not be such thing as a sexual relationship, there "is something of the One" (Lacan, 1972–1973).

The sinthome

Borromean knotting

For a long time Lacan had been supporting the idea of the supremacy of one register—imaginary, symbolic or real—over the other along his structural differentiation between neurosis and psychosis (Voruz & Wolf, 2007). Yet with time his interest shifted to the connection of the three registers that subjects achieve regardless of their structure. In an introduction to a German edition of his *Écrits* appearing the same year as "L'Étourdit", he wrote that there is not a unique meaning deriving from a given structure (Lacan, 1973b).

This new approach brings a radical change to the way psychosis is approached, since the cornerstone of the psychoanalytic view of one's life is now considered a subject's singular symptom. Its significance for the treatment of psychosis relates to a formation like this helping the subject to keep hold of its body and the body's organs against language outside reference to established otherness, a fundamental deficit for the schizophrenic since Freud (1911c; 1914c).

The concept of the sinthome was introduced in Lacan's *Seminar XXIII*, taught in 1975–1976, based on references to topology and knotting. Using mathematical theory and knots, Lacan presented an approach to the equal relation between the real, the symbolic, and the imaginary (Vanheule & Geldhof, 2012).

Lacan suggested the idea of a symptom that represents subjectivity itself (Cordié, 1994). This symptom bore no reference to an Other (Skriabine, 2009). Unlike therefore the good old neurotic's symptom, which is linked to the Other's discourse in terms of the "other scene" of the unconscious, the sinthome speaks of the subject itself as One.

To illustrate the effects of this new concept, Lacan used a design borrowed from the coat of arms of the Borromei, an Italian aristocratic family (Lacan, 1975–1976). Both topology and the coat of arms of the Borromei had been introduced in *Seminar XIX, Ou pire …* (Lacan, 1971–1972), and Lacan (1972–1973) had been developing their study ever since. The Borromean knot, shown below, illustrates the coordinates of this new concept. For Lacan (1972–1973), it is a metaphorical use of the fact that we only move forward "on the basis of the One" (p. 128):

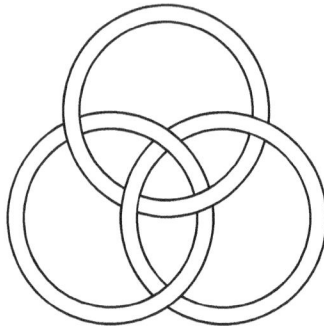

Figure 3. The Borromean knot.

Lacan's attention was drawn to the Borromean knot by the way the three rings are held together in this shape. Its particular quality is that if one of them is removed the remaining two are also disconnected from each other. This, fourth, knot created from the interrelation of the three corresponds to the new conceptualisation of the symptom he had in mind.

In contrast to the past, its theoretical foundation requires treating the real, the symbolic, and the imaginary as equal and interconnected registers. In fact, their properties for Lacan in *Seminar XXIII* are respectively what ex-sists (real), hole (symbolic), and consistency (imaginary). If those are disconnected from each other—not therefore knotted in a Borromean style—then a fourth knot is needed to connect them, the sinthome (Lacan, 1975–1976).

Of course, the symptom was not a new concept in psychoanalytic theory. Freud treated it as an unconscious formation with metaphorical meaning (1926d). That was also Lacan's view before this groundbreaking suggestion of the mid-1970s (Morel, 2003). The symptom is, moreover, still used widely in the mental health domain, treated as a disorder's morbid expression that calls for eradication.

This is exactly what Lacan tried to orient his audience against by his new view of the symptom: the sinthome is not something clinicians should try to remove or cure (Voruz & Wolf, 2007). Lacan (1976b) writes that "their symptom is the most real thing many people have" (p. 7). It represents the One's most intimate mark, what organises subjectivity (Vanheule, 2011a; 2011b) in terms of a compromise between the subject and the jouissance inhabiting it (Aflalo, 2015). The subject is therefore no longer viewed it terms of division, but unification: it is not simply subjected to the Other of the signifier or divided by the Other of jouissance. Subjectivity is achieved by the symptom knotting the enigmatic link of three registers—imaginary, symbolic, and real—and keeping them together in a way comparable to the three rings in the coat of arms of the Borromei (Lacan, 1975–1976).

Therefore, the symptom requires delicate care instead of eradication for the following reason: disconnecting the three registers that make up subjectivity by lifting a single ring leads to detrimental effects for the subject. In Lacan's new formulation of the sinthome, the subject *is* the symptom. Hence, the title of two lectures on Joyce he gave during and after this seminar: "Joyce the Symptom" (Lacan, 1975–1976; 1975a). When the symptom is removed therefore the same happens for the subject.

Thanks to this new approach to subjectivity, the phenomena encountered in psychosis—like the body phenomena in schizophrenics we have examined so far—are viewed as outcomes of the disconnection of the three registers (Vanheule, 2011a). Thus, psychosis is not viewed any more in terms of foreclosure of the paternal signifier in Lacan, but as related to un-knotting (Thurston, 1999). It is the effect on subjectivity of the disconnection of the three registers. As is shown below, the sinthome in Joyce was constructed to tackle that fundamental deficit and avoid the further manifestation of psychotic phenomena, such as the detachment of the body image. Yet this does not cancel out Lacan's previous theory; the theory of knotting seems to substitute for the function of metaphor (Soler, 2014). Consequently, the old forms of the symptom have not been eradicated.

Ordinary and extraordinary symptoms

Indeed, the singularity of the sinthome is not significant only for the psychotic subject, who is faced with the absence of a standard connection of the real, the symbolic, and the imaginary. In the first pages of *Seminar XXIII*, Lacan argues that the Oedipus complex, as such, is a symptom (1975–1976). Yet this is not the first time this idea appears in Lacan's teaching.

In the early 1960s, Lacan had started teaching a seminar entitled *The Names of the Father* (in the plural) (1963). He intended to develop the idea that paternity, connected to castration and the Oedipus complex, is not a unique solution, the sole factor of metaphor (Thurston, 1999). He had hinted at this idea already in *Seminar VI, Desire and its Interpretation*, when he said that the big secret of psychoanalysis is that there is no Other of the Other (1958c). Yet after his "excommunication" he had decided to never return to that idea again.

Nevertheless, in the 1970s he articulates something from that old story. He argues that the belief in the Father, the common denominator of Oedipus complex and paternal metaphor, is a commonplace symptom. It is a ready-made solution that common mortals use to make sense of the world and subsist as subjects (1975–1976).

Therefore, *a* Name-of-the-Father—against *the* Name-of-the-Father—is a symptom. It can be an intimate way to resolve jouissance with meaning (Lacan, 1975–1976). Therefore, the established discourses, where the Name-of-the-Father returns (Brousse, 2009) and from which the schizophrenic is excluded are offered for the use of ready-made symptoms.

As was noted above, Lacan suggests a new way to write this new concept of the symptom: sinthome, an older version of the same French word, which has been maintained in English (Lacan, 1975–1976). Apart from being a medieval synonym of "symptom", "sinthome" also plays with the similar-sounding *saint-homme* ("saint man") (1975a) and Saint-Thomas. The reference to the Catholic saint is used in relation to Joyce, who was interested in Saint Thomas Aquinas's theory of clarity.

Lacan's study of Joyce in *Seminar XXIII* is a profound investigation of an extraordinary way of knotting the real, the symbolic, and the imaginary, producing a new consistency at the level of jouissance (Dravers, 2005). Joyce needed to establish such a consistency in the absence of the object *a*, the regulating factor of jouissance produced by separation for subjects who evade psychosis and inhabit language via the help from the established discourses.

For Lacan (1975–1976), Joyce starts the writing endeavour that will produce the sinthome in order to address the consequences of his father not having been a father for him. Indeed, the radical lack of Joyce's father was a recurrent theme in the Irish writer's case.

If Joyce had been a subject for whom the symbolic father existed, a Name-of-the-Father would have worked. Thus, he would not have needed to invent a fourth element to knot the imaginary of the body to the real and the symbolic. A ready-made type of symptom would have been generated by his insertion into one of the established discourses. In contrast, Joyce had to come up himself with an invention that tackled the lack of an established unifying element of the three registers. He was excluded from the commonplace belief in the Father and its privileges, such as the entry to the established discourses and the consequent acquisition of one's body. So, how were the effects of the absence of a Borromean knot avoided through artifice in his case?

Lalangue

A recurrent reference in Lacan's approach to psychosis had been that symptoms like elementary phenomena are a manifestation of a reappearance of the non-symbolised in the real (Lacan, 1954; 1955a). Thanks to the emphasis placed upon the concept of jouissance in the 1960s, that reappearance can be viewed as one of unregulated jouissance. As was seen in the preceding chapter, what exists before the advent of the subject is no longer simply an unregulated array of signifiers, a mixture of the symbolic and the imaginary, but the field of jouissance. This field, which the subject encounters during its alienation, is a language that traumatises, ravages (Miller, 2006). It is a language rooted in the real (Soler, 2003).

Lacan (1973a) will suggest a new name for it, *lalangue*, and will argue that it is not built for communication, highlighting its distance from language. He will even go as far as to say that language does not exist and that it is rather an attempt to know something about the function of lalangue (Lacan, 1972–1973).

Lalangue refers to the singular way through which a subject incorporates common language (Biagi-Chai, 2014). It appears at the beginning of one's life, before one starts becoming gradually constituted as a subject (Fink, 1995). Thus, lalangue traumatises the subject's body before it meets the regulated Other's discourse. It is the subject's first partner (Gault, 2007). It is a symbolic without metaphor (Soler, 2014). Lacan (1954) has described this occasion in the past as the "first moment of symbolisation" (p. 320), as an intersection of the symbolic and the real unmediated by the imaginary. Yet at that period the real was not conceived of in relation to corporeal jouissance, but as what resists signification.

During the period when he introduces lalangue, Lacan (1972–1973; 1975–1976; 1976a) will speak of a "motierialism", making a pun on *mot* ("word") and materialism, hinting at the material impact of lalangue striking the person's body, its material constitution. Lalangue troubles one's body and soul (Briole, 2003). Doesn't this pun remind one of Freud's (1915e) reference to words having a material quality in schizophrenia? Soler (2014) writes that the schizophrenic may dispense with the symbolic, "but not with lalangue" (p. 28).

On the other hand, lalangue establishes the person's singularity, so to speak—the subject's relation to its mode of jouissance (Biagi-Chai, 2014). This relation to jouissance is primary in relation to that to the object *a*, since it is not established through separation but during alienation, the subject's first encounter with the language or the Other's signifiers: it is relative to the mark of the One, which Freud had called the *einziger Zug*, "unary trait". In the past Lacan (1960a) was discussing this as the Other's insignia, but later described it as a commemoration of an eruption of jouissance (1970, p. 77): "The body in the signifier leaves a trait", he said (Lacan, 1976a, p. 23), "and a trait that is a One." This might be a body beyond the mirror stage, in its Aristotelian definition of "what maintains itself as one", that Lacan encourages us to return to

(1972–1973, p. 142) and from which the schizophrenic is not excluded this time. The unary trait in the sense of a symbolic identification, a S_1, may be absent or have disappeared in schizophrenia, hence, the subject's representation by a swarm of signifiers, but his relation to lalangue is there; it still suffers reality's trauma of language (Zenoni, 2012).

If therefore there is no sexual relationship, which causes specific problems for the schizophrenic in relation to their body, there is the One, which is a mark left by the person's first contact with language, and from which they cannot be excluded. Yet whereas, thanks to repression, neurotic subjects are not conscious of it, for psychotics this does not necessarily happen. In fact, by their having "unsubscribed" from the unconscious, it seems that lalangue returns continuously in language.

In fact, even if schizophrenic subjects are excluded from the unconscious, as they are also excluded from the established discourses, there is no similar indication about the new term Lacan invented to replace the Freudian unconscious: *parlêtre*, a suggested translation for which is "speaking being". Alfredo Zenoni (2012) suggests that schizophrenia testifies about the real the speaking being confronts.

The speaking being thus concerns the real aspect of the unconscious (Miller, 2015; Soler, 2014). It is not any more an idea made from the imaginary and the symbolic, but a convergence between the unconscious and the id (Miller, 2015). As far as what is at stake for the schizophrenic is concerned, the body in the speaking being changes register (Miller, 2015). There is a different relation to the body in it to the one built thanks to the mirror stage. The speaking being has his body, rather than being it (Miller, 2015), thanks to a jouissance grasped through speech. It is not an articulation of signifiers according to specific rules, like the unconscious, but it is contaminated with the jouissance of lalangue.

Joyce is an exquisite paradigm of how a speaking being managed to acquire his body leaning on a sinthomatic operation upon lalangue (Miller, 2015). Something of a similar nature is suggested in *Part II* about another writer.

In *Seminar XXIII*, Lacan (1975–1976) refers to an incident from Joyce's childhood that might remind one of the danger that the schizophrenic is running in relation to the body (Lacan, 1973a). This incident is included in Joyce's semi-autobiographical *Portrait of the Artist as a Young Man* (Joyce, 1916). Psychotic structure, shown in the disconnection of the imaginary from the real and the symbolic, is implied there.

In *A Portrait of the Artist as a Young Man*, we read of the writer's school-mates tying him to a fence and beating him up. The author says about the incident that he had no bad feelings against his torturers. He had only felt that "some power was divesting him of that suddenwoven as easily as a fruit is divested of its soft ripe peel" (Joyce, 1916, p. 87). This description illustrates graphically the un-knotting of the imaginary (in the form of the body image) from the two other registers, the real and the symbolic. If Joyce cannot be helped from the established discourses to hold onto his body, his body runs the danger of slipping away. Like Paul, it can be seen crawling on the ceiling. It can thus be found anywhere "above the ground and beneath the clouds" as another subject later put it.

Joyce's way of addressing the disconnection of the imaginary from the other two registers was the construction of a fourth ring. That ring gave him a body by knotting the real, the symbolic, and the imaginary. Joyce achieved this in creating the sinthome (Leader, 2011) depicted in the figure below. It is observed that the otherwise disconnected rings are held together by the imaginary knotted to the real and symbolic thanks to the black ring, which represents his ego.

A new ego

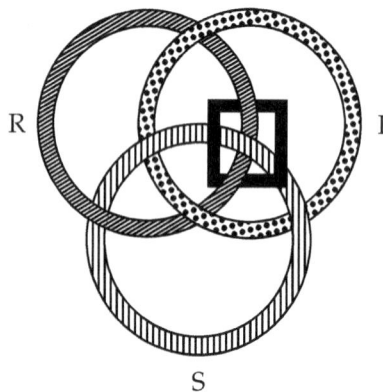

Figure 4. Joyce's ego.

According to Lacan (1975–1976), the outcome of Joyce's artistic creation was the construction of an ego, which lies in him being "The artist". His aspiration is explicit in Joyce's quote that he wanted academics to study him for at least a few hundred years (Ellmann, 1983; Lacan, 1975–1976; Leader, 2011; Miller, 2012). The identity of artist is linked to this symptomatic function. Joyce subsisted as subject by identifying with this sinthome, his ego. Hence, "Joyce the Symptom" (Lacan, 1975–1976; 1975a).

Yet this construction did not merely comprise Joyce having a megalomaniac or narcissistic belief that stemmed from specular otherness. It does not find support in the image (Morel, 2003). That would probably mean he was a paranoid—or even a neurotic—subject. The success in his artistic activity concerns first and foremost an instrumentalisation of language through writing. His sinthome was a formation produced during a work in progress comprising an elaboration upon lalangue, which gave it a literary value (Gault, 2007). Joyce's symptom compensates for his relation to lalangue (Soler, 2014). In effect, language and literary style in Joyce's work change continuously. The creation therefore of the sinthome started with it and was based on his processing an elaboration of lalangue as traumatic.

Lacan writes that it is difficult not to see that a certain relationship to the word is increasingly imposed on Joyce (1975–1976). The elaboration of language in the sense of lalangue is fundamental for the creation of the sinthome. Elements of this are already evident in *Ulysses* (Joyce, 1922). Yet it is in his final piece, *Finnegans Wake* (Joyce, 1939), that language is literally decomposed, it becomes a "litter". It is a "language of a new world, a 'newspeak' whose role is not to be spoken; it does not say anything" (Gault, 2007, p. 76). Joyce's writing transformed language in an enjoyment lying outside meaning (Grigg, 1999). Soler (2003) highlights that this is where Lacan finally found the supreme display of what Freud had perceived about schizophrenics' discourse: their propensity to treat things as words, outside meaning. In fact, in *Seminar XXIII* Lacan is discussing words imposed on Joyce just after referring to Joyce's daughter, Lucia, another "what is called" schizophrenic whose father believed her to be telepathic (1975–1976).

The importance of Joyce's ego might rightfully beg the question as to what makes it so unique. This is not the first time we encounter ideas of grandeur in psychotics, as for example in the case of Schreber claiming he is God's wife.

Lacan's equation of the ego with psychosis was an old story. It had concerned paranoia. In his doctoral thesis, he had argued that his paranoid patient's solution lay in her personality (1932). In addition, in

Seminar II (1955b, p. 247), Lacan had said that paranoia "as compared with schizophrenia" always has a relation to the alienation that the ego creates. Why wasn't thus Joyce simply a paranoid subject whose writing endeavour was used in order to substantiate his grandiose belief of being "The artist", as supposedly happened in the case of Schreber as "God's wife"? Because, as above, "The artist" primarily involves the subject believing in himself without reference to the other's image—note that to become "God's wife", Schreber needs a God.

In fact, Lacan differentiates between the coordinates of the sinthome and paranoia in terms of knotting by equating paranoid psychosis to personality. In *Seminar XXIII* he admits regretting having linked the two terms in the past in the title of his thesis (Lacan, 1932) but not because he considers them irrelevant. On the contrary; he finds them identical: a personality is the same as paranoia (Lacan, 1975–1976).

However, albeit that paranoia and sinthome produce a similar outcome (i.e., the real, the symbolic, and the imaginary do not stand disconnected), this does not happen in the same way. Paranoid psychosis consists in I., S., and R. being one and the same consistency (Lacan, 1975–1976, p. 53).

The effect that the fourth knot brought in Joyce's case therefore is supported in paranoia by the continuity of the three registers. Consequently, in paranoia the subject is not in need of a fourth ring, as Joyce was. The three registers have merged together to form one thing: personality. The challenge may be the same, the successful outcome may seem similar but it is not; neither is it achieved in the same way. Joyce's ego is not the outcome of this solidification of the three registers, but an "open ego" that can allow "experience and enjoyment" to flow through it (MacCannell, 2015, p. 216).

In fact, to further portray the difference between Joyce and a paranoid construction dependent to the mirror stage, it seems that this ego is related to a narcissism of a different kind.

In his first lecture on "Joyce the Symptom" Lacan (1975–1976) used another term to describe the impact of Joyce's writing upon acquiring his body, which he called *escabeau*. In the future, he would write this in various ways, such as *est-ce cas beau*? ["is this case beautiful?"], *est-ce cabot*? ["is it a mutt?"], or even *SK … beau* (Soler, 2014, p. 63). This concept is the stepladder, a small pedestal on which the speaking being ascends to make itself *beau*, beautiful. It is a mixture of Freudian sublimation with narcissism (Miller, 2015). Mostly, it has to do with the body, which is raised to the dignity of the Thing through a process that lacks the specular character of the mirror stage. Laurent speaks, on this occasion, of a "modified narcissism" (2015a, p. 6).

Miller (2015) suggests that Lacan was attracted to Joyce by his capacity to conjoin the sinthome—which does not lean on meaning, whose matrix is the mirror stage too—with the beautification of the stepladder; a narcissistic construction therefore that attributed his body to him by raising it upon a small pedestal.

Thus, if a psychotic subject is, indeed, condemned to either be megalomaniac or not be anything (Biagi-Chai, 2014), it seems that the coordinates of the paranoiac's narcissism are, following schizophrenia, much different to those of the sinthome too. The *escabeau's* beautifying role will very soon prove helpful to our reading, when in the following part we will examine the case of an ugly man who died in a psychiatric hospital and whose writing endeavour bore such an effect.

Paranoia and schizophrenia

It seems, in fact, that based on those remarks from the later Lacan, we are led to further disengage schizophrenia from paranoia, a story as old in psychiatry and psychoanalysis as Kraepelin's textbook (1899) and Freud's study of President Schreber (1911c). It seems that we must take a similar path for sinthome and paranoia.

Paranoia consists of the three rings (R, S, and I) having formed a rigid construction, one ring that supports the subject's personality, founded upon narcissism depending on otherness. In schizophrenia, on the other hand, the subject is lacking a fourth ring to knot the real, the symbolic, and the imaginary. The necessary narcissistic position could thus pass through the construction of a small pedestal. We return therefore to both Freud (1911c) and Lacan's (1938) remarks about the schizophrenic's incapacity to lean on narcissism founded upon established otherness.

Another radical difference between the two—mentioned earlier—which, in my opinion, also makes Joyce's case resemble the schizophrenic rather than the paranoid constitution concerns the role played by the Other in the subject's invention. In a publication of Schreber's *Memoirs* in English contemporary with *Seminar XXIII*, Lacan links paranoia to the act of identifying jouissance in the place of the Other as such (1975b).

From this point onwards, Lacan will emphasise paranoia as the identification of jouissance in the Other in the form of a fundamental evil: κακόν (kakon)—Greek for "evil" (Miller, 2001). This is realised in persecutory figures in paranoia, like Flechsig or God in Schreber's delusion: a figure that incarnates the enjoying Other. Paranoia makes an evil Other exist (Miller, 2010). A quilting point is established between the Other and jouissance. In fact, if the persecutor is not defined or limited, then one cannot speak of paranoia (Deffieux, 2014).

This is not, however, the form in which the Other appears in Joyce. If we understand Joyce's only Other as the amalgamated formation of real and symbolic, the effect of his sinthome is not to make an evil Other exist.

In fact, it seems that this did not happen in Schreber either. In *Seminar III*, Lacan (1955–1956) had emphasised that the quintessence of Schreber's writing was the invention of his God. Yet, as was discussed earlier, that formation where jouissance was identified did not prove helpful in the end. At some point, Schreber suffered the third relapse, which being God's wife did not deter. On the other hand, in *Seminar III*, Lacan (1955–56) had also shown how Schreber's discourse comprised a treatment of his body by means of language—by inventing his "fundamental language". Couldn't this invention be viewed as an elaboration of lalangue? The element in his invention that favoured treatment might have to be rethought, especially when viewed in relation to Freud's reference to recovery in "The Unconscious" (1915e). The channelling of the libido to words may have been more therapeutic toward the acquisition of one's body and organs than the one to images of specular others.

It seems that the aforementioned radical differentiation between the paranoid and sinthomatic solutions constitutes the coordinates of the schizophrenic's discourse more relative to the sinthome. The treatment by means of lalangue that subjects like Joyce achieve does not take place through the real, the symbolic, and the imaginary merging into one ring. It takes place in another direction that knots the speaking being to the body without depending on the narcissism of the mirror stage.

Therefore, if the schizophrenic subject is deprived of the help from the established discourses as an effect, among others, of the absence of the object *a*—condenser of jouissance, the utilisation of the jouissance of lalangue might create an alternative discourse than can help them address the same challenges described in "L'Étourdit" (1973a): to inhabit language and, through this, their bodies and organs.

Alongside the maintenance of a setting where the subject is welcome to speak—not in any way in the sense of neurotic transference—the potential "secretary to the insane" might benefit from inventions that utilise this aspect of schizophrenia.

In the following part I present and discuss the case of another subject who achieved such a construction but did not avoid, in the end, being admitted to a lunatic asylum. Next to reading about a fascinating life and impressively varied literary work, studying his case could enrich the clinician's knowledge of how this can be applied and answer the question as to whether a schizophrenic's acquisition of their body, their organs, and their functions can come from a sinthomatic construction.

Summary to Part I

For a considerable part in the more than hundred-year-long history of schizophrenia, psychiatry and psychoanalysis treated this concept as paranoia's "poor relation". Although the psychoses are not disposed to psychoanalytic treatment for Freud or Lacan, the capacity for the projection of the libido or channelling of jouissance to a formation of otherness was considered as a breakthrough in paranoia. The schizophrenic's incapacity to achieve such a process was, equally, viewed as excluding such subjects from a chance to address the challenge to acquire their body, their organs, and their functions against language, which generates the well-known body phenomena of schizophrenics.

However, in the later Lacan we find a new conceptualisation of subjectivity and the subject's relation to the body, which does not depend on established otherness but on the One. There are limited references to the schizophrenic subject during that period. Yet we are led to conclude that a psychotic subject's capacity to acquire its body is not limited to the paranoiac's dependence on the other's image. This new form of the subject, along with the *speaking being*, *lalangue*, the *sinthome,* and the *stepladder,* have not been excluded from the clinic of schizophrenia.

Thus, in the following chapters they are implicated in the study of a case of a subject who acquired his body against the amalgam of language and jouissance in a way different to that of neurotics and paranoiacs.

PART II

THE BEAUTIFYING RISE AND THE DISASTROUS FALL OF THE CHILD'S BODY IN GEORGIOS VIZYENOS

Introduction to Part II

In the evening of April 15th, 1896, citizens of Athens and international guests attended the closing ceremony of the first modern Olympic Games. In the following day's newspapers, next to euphoric articles on the revival of an ancient Greek tradition, there was a distressing announcement: the poet and professor Georgios Vizyenos, admitted to a psychiatric hospital four years earlier, had passed away the same night.

Not many were surprised by the writer's death. For the past four years, newspapers had been reporting on his deteriorating condition following a dramatic admission accompanied by psychotic symptomatology: megalomaniac and erotomaniac delusions, intense physical excitation channelled to incomprehensible speech and writing, and two suicide attempts. Those symptoms had appeared in the writer's early forties, following a dramatic vacillation of the consistency of the body image.

His life and work are studied in the following chapters as a case whose acquisition of a body and its organs took place without reference to established otherness, from which clinicians can draw lessons for the treatment of patients in need of such an invention. The study of his case in the light of Freud and Lacan's conceptualisation of schizophrenia presented in *Part I* can thus act to the "secretary to the insane" as an example of an orientation in treatment that can be supported or encouraged in theory and in the clinic.

The paradigm employed here is the psychoanalytic case history. For Lacan, the privilege of the case history is that it is identical to the progress of the subject, that is, "to the reality of the treatment" (1951, p. 178). My aim is a biography enlightened by psychoanalysis (Biagi-Chai, 2014); a biography that will focus on the relation between the subject and the real, Lacan's two major contributions to the study of human experience and psychosis. I find Francesca Biagi-Chai's reading of the case Landru, who puts forward this approach, as fascinating and truly didactic (2014). I have attempted to draw lessons from it for my own reading of Vizyenos.

The present part consists of four chapters: in the first, I describe the writer's childhood and youth. I examine the particular status of the signifier "child" in the family history with regards to the mad poet and scholar's two dead sisters and to their mother. In the second, I analyse how Vizyenos managed to acquire the child's body despite his manifest unfitness to established discourses. In the third, we read of how his edifice collapsed and the organ of language took over his body leading him to the asylum, whereas the fourth is a summary of his case history quilted with instruments from the later Lacan's theory of knotting: speaking being, lalangue, sinthome, and stepladder, all of which pertain to the One rather than the Other.

CHAPTER FOUR

A body orphan and poor

Vizyenos was not the real surname of the unfortunate writer who died in a lunatic asylum on the last day of the first modern Olympic Games. It was a signifier with which the subject renamed himself in late adolescence.

In the present chapter, I discuss the lineage with which this man proceeded to a rupture by renaming himself thus. His childhood and family background are viewed in the light of the psychoanalytic theories analysed in *Part I*. In researching the writer's recollections from his childhood and youth, one comes across a paternal lack, the prevalence of maternal jouissance, and respective structural problems in signification. The reader is reminded that such are the conditions that deter a schizophrenic from acquiring his body, its organs, and their function (Lacan, 1973a) as happens when one is able to enter the established discourses, in which the Name-of-the-Father returns (Brousse, 2009).

The family constellation

Paternal poverty

George—short for "Georgios"—Vizyenos was born in 1849 (Athanasopoulos, 1992; Koutrianou, 2003; Moulas, 1980). His birthplace was Vizyi, a Greek village in Eastern Thrace, modern-day European Turkey. It is not really clear what his surname was at birth: Syrmas or Michaelides.

According to the first version, Syrmas was his father's surname and Michaelides was an artificial name he adopted or was given in his early school life as more "appropriate" to the school environment. Although in the short story "The Only Journey of His Life" Georgios will write that Syrmas was the surname of his maternal great-grandfather (Vizyenos, 1884a), this was not true; it was probably that of his paternal grandfather (Koutrianou, 2003).

On the other hand, since George never referred to Syrmas as his surname, Michaelides could have been his father, Michael's, actual surname. Its etymology should not escape our attention.

This name includes the patronymic suffix "ides". This is a very old suffix in the Greek language. It is even used in the first verse of Homer's *Iliad*, where Achilles is called Pelides, that is, the son of Peleus (2014). "Ides" stands for "son of". Consequently, "Michaelides" means "Michael's son". This was therefore a name with a rather literal meaning: that the person who bears it is, indeed, Michael's son. This was a name that our man needed to change for reasons analysed below.

Nevertheless, the obscure nature of George's father's surname does not clash with the available information about this man. Not much is known about Michael. We know that he had come to Vizyi from another Thracian village, Kryonero, and ran a grocery shop for some time. After closing it he became a peddler, like his father-in-law, known in the village as Grandfather Georgie. Like his wife, Michael was an Orthodox Christian, spoke Greek and followed the Greek traditions (Vizyenos, 1881a) despite living just a stone's throw from the capital of the Ottoman Empire.

George was the second son and third child born in the family, which had two more boys, Christakis—which means "little Chris"—and Michael, and two girls, both named Annio, a rural version of "Anne" (Athanasopoulos, 1992).

One of the few things we read about the father's relationship with George comes from one of the autobiographical short stories the latter wrote in his early thirties: that due to a girl born directly after him and her having received more care and tenderness, his father frequently called him "his wronged one" (Vizyenos, 1883a, p. 9). We cannot know if this is exactly true, but in George's writings as an adult we find frequent complaints about lacking something on the part of his father.

According to Vizyenos' biographers, Michael died of typhus while returning from a business trip to Bulgaria when George was five (Athanasopoulos, 1992; Moulas, 1980). However, according to an account of his, that happened two years earlier (Vizyenos, 1881a).

His father's death is an event to which the adult George indeed keeps returning. He will write about it in poems, short stories, and even in a document attached to his doctoral dissertation. Yet it seems that his actual complaint—since very little is known about his siblings either—does not primarily concern the symbolic absence of a father, but his imaginary aspect. George writes about the paternal lack in a CV written in Latin at the age of thirty-two, attached to his thesis in philosophy:

> My father, a poor man, passed away during the third year of my age and left me an orphan living in poverty and to my wretched mother. (Vizyenos, G., [1881b] 2009, p. 205)

If one wanted to identify the paternal foreclosure in this excerpt, their attention should not be attracted by the father's real absence—the mere fact that three- or five-year-old George's father died. After all, people who never meet their father do not necessarily become psychotic and vice versa. The real father's absence is not in any way incompatible with the existence of the paternal signifier (Lacan, 1958a). In effect, I do not hold that the foreclosure of the paternal signifier is indicated in Michael's death per se, which could, on the contrary, stand for its presence, since the symbolic father is the dead father for Lacan (1958a). It is in the adjectives "poor" and "orphan" and the noun "poverty" used in this citation, and which reappear frequently in George's writing as an adult, where one must look for the kind of father that exists in his cosmos, and for its corresponding status for the child's body.

In reality, the reference to poverty does not reflect the father's or the family's actual economic and social background. It seems that they were not particularly poor according to the time's standards, since they were able to build a house with two floors, which was infrequent at the time (Koutrianou, 2003; Paschalis, 2009). In addition, George's father's death only left him partly an orphan, since his mother was alive and well. Therefore, as was viewed later on, George's father's poverty did not concern the family's financial status, but the poverty in naming; the name he was given on the side of his father did not suffice to safeguard his subjective constitution and his right to a body of his own. What was actually poor, or powerless, was the paternal signifier.

In fact, if in the description of George's childhood and family background we were looking for a parallelism to the failed paternal metaphor, apart from the frail paternal signifier we would also need to affirm the subject's first Other, mOther, as a source of ineffable desire or jouissance. Indeed, to contrast the "poor" father, young George's mother is described like the figure whose imaginary phallus the child grows up condemned to incarnate. As was explained in Chapter Two, this turns the infant to what can fulfil mother's desire.

Mother's desire

As was noted in Chapter Two, the function of the paternal signifier is to name the desire of the mother, which constitutes an enigma for the child. The positivisation of the phallus that the paternal metaphor brings about puts an end to the subject incarnating it.

Indeed, the status of George's mother, as we read about her both in his short stories and in his biography, does not remind one of a regulated Other stricken by the bar of desire, but an enjoying Other, the mother Lacan (1970) compares to a crocodile with open jaws, ready to devour the child. Whereas that woman complained of having been deprived of the joys of marital life, events from family history do not lead us to suggest that her enjoyment—in the Lacanian sense of jouissance—suffered the bar of privation. In contrast, it seems that no limit was put to it.

Michael's wife was called Despoinio. She was better known as Michaliessa or Michalena, which stand for "Michael's wife" in Greek rural tradition. As "Mother", she will be the leading character in two short stories George will publish in the first half of the 1880s, when he will reside as a poet and scholar in London. In those stories he offers the reader a magnificent portrait of his mother and her psychic life (Moulas, 1980): an unfortunate, hard-working, superstitious, and at the same time deeply religious woman who strives to raise her children alone, which was actually true following her husband's death. It seems, however, that if this woman was good at something besides having children, it was losing them.

As is written in Vizyenos' most famous short story, "My Mother's Sin" (1883a), Michaliessa accidentally killed her first daughter, the forty-day-old baby girl Annio in bed, a true story (Papakostas, 2004). Tired from a wedding feast, she tried to breastfeed the baby in bed and awoke having smothered her. In Georgios' second autobiographical short story, "Who Was My Brother's Killer?" (Vizyenos, 1883b), Mother is associated with the actual death of the narrator's older brother, Christakis. Having initially expressed second thoughts, she consents to his taking a position that she knows to be dangerous while at the same time she nurses—unintentionally once more—her son's future killer (Chrysanthopoulos, 1994). As for George's second sister, also named Annio, who was quite sickly, the former narrates how she died in the presence of him and his brothers. This happened during a magic ritual performed by Mother, following her having prayed to God to take one of the boys to spare the girl's life (Vizyenos, 1883a).

In effect, Michaliessa will outlive all her surviving children too. Michael, her youngest son, died of apoplexy during George's first year at the asylum. Moreover, she will live for eleven more years after the writer's death in 1896. She will stay with her daughter-in-law, her son Michael's widow, who will marry another man. Mother will die with pure clarity of mind and ask to be buried in white, saying that she wishes to do so because she spent most of her life dressed in black, since she was a widow and a mourning mother (Xireas, 1949). However, only young or unmarried people are buried in white in Greece, which makes her wish unusual and peculiar, regardless of her justification.

Thus, in both George's biography and his fiction, in which he is elaborating upon actual events in his family history (Chrysanthopoulos, 1994; Papakostas, 2004), we read of a motherly figure whose desire—which later on in Lacan's theory is attributed the texture of jouissance—is not named by a paternal signifier, leaving children attached to it (Lacan, 1958a).

As was remarked above, the desire of the mother not being named as an effect of a "poor" paternal signifier leaves the phallus $(-\varphi)$ in the negative (Φ_0). It leaves the child, therefore, in the position of an imaginary substitute for it $(-\varphi)$. This is the status of Michaliessa's children: what she is having and, consequently, what she is losing. But as for those children's being, this will not be named for them. At least not from the side of a father, who cannot act as the Other's Other (see Chapters Two & Three).

Indeed, what we see young George narrating about his life before leaving his village at the age of ten, when no one intervenes between him and Mother, is that he is something at her disposal: one of those children that his mother can have or lose, like his two sisters and later on Christakis, Michael, and, finally, himself. As was seen above, in his CV he will write that he was left attached to his "wretched mother". His destiny at that stage therefore could be described in the first Lacan's terminology as what Mother had or not: $-\varphi$. We can also describe the child's destiny with a term from Lacan's following period of teaching, the object a, using a very rare allusion of his to the schizophrenic's mother. Lacan describes her as voicing what her child had been in her belly as a body "conversely convenient or cumbersome, namely, the subjectification of a as sheer real" (1962–1963, p. 119).

It seems that the Other's first signifiers George is given, probably with his father's permission, of which he also writes in his fiction, point with great precision to such a condition. The signifier(s) following him in childhood, George, "Michael's George", "Michaliessa's tiny George" (as he is called after his father's death) and Michaelides, only indicate who belongs to whom.

Let us take his first name first: George, which is short for the Greek Christian name Georgios. Until recently, it was a somewhat unbroken rule in Greece that grandchildren were given their grandparents' first names. Since Georgios was the family's second male child, his brother Christakis had apparently been given the paternal grandfather's name. So what was left for him was the name of the maternal grandfather, Grandfather Georgie, a name stemming from a story about a child being a body acquired by someone else in a rather literal way.

George's mother had not been Grandfather Georgie's biological daughter. Michaliessa had not even been born in Vizyi, but in St. Stephen, another Thracian village, near the modern-day Turkish-Bulgarian border. She probably came from a wealthy family (Koutrianou, 2003) but had lost her parents at a very young age and had ended up at a provost's house in a town called Tzogara (Athanasopoulos, 1992). This was where Grandfather Georgie found her and took her back to his village, adopting her. George took his name therefore from his mother's foster father.

Thus, besides inscribing him on his mother's lineage, the name George comes from the story of someone who obtained a child in a rather pragmatic way. Grandfather Georgie, who has no children, acquires one during his trips as a peddler, as if that child was a piece of merchandise. "Michael's George", as he is called by fellow-villagers till the age of three, is only its metonymy.

The dead girl's body

Then, aged three or five, our writer becomes "Michaliessa's tiny George", a nickname hinting a quality as mother's imaginary phallus or her *a* "as sheer real". Isn't this the child's status preceding the paternal metaphor? The child is what mOther is missing and what can fulfil her enigmatic desire; it belongs to her.

As was discussed in Chapter Two, this was the way Lacan supplemented Klein's theory about the mother as container of the phallus (1958a). If metaphor is linked to the question of being and metonymy to its lack (Lacan, 1957a) we must not be surprised to encounter a metonymy like this (*Georgios*—"*Michael's George*"—"*Michaliessa's tiny George*"—*Michaelides*) that does not give a name to this subject's being beyond what the primary Other can lack and have.

Now, concerning our interest in the schizophrenic's relation to its body, this condition corresponds to a specific status for it too. Let us remind ourselves of how in lack of a symbolic process (metaphor) that introduces phallic signification, the image of the body established through the mirror stage does not enter an established dialectic with the other's image, but remains attached to mOther, in our case to Mother. This is exactly what Lacan was suggesting since the 1930s concerning the schizophrenic: this subject is characterised by a return to the weaning complex, where only the maternal imago lies, due to its inability to process and establish otherness through the imago of the sibling (1938). Thus, metonymy prevails.

This propensity in Georgios' family's constellation is seen in the case of his siblings' naming, which is not mediated by a regulatory factor like the Name-of-the-Father. Chrysanthopoulos (1994) writes that for this family, name-giving goes hand in hand with metonymy. Let us take a quick look at it.

George was preceded by Christakis and then the first Annio. As noted above, she was accidentally killed by Mother as an infant. The daughter born directly after George was also named Annio. Thus, the only sister he knew was not worth a signifier of her own (Chrysanthopoulos, 1994). That girl was named after a dead sister, to replace the void in the desire of the mother.

Yet it is somehow implied that the same could have happened for George too. In "My Mother's Sin" (Vizyenos, 1883a) the author writes that he was expected to be a girl, to replace the first dead daughter called Annio. We read therefore of his coming to this world not in order to be someone, but to replace a daughter had and missed, not entitled to the status of a being but destined to fulfil a pre-existing void. That was the status imposed upon him before he was even born; the status of a missed girl. One might not be necessarily wrong in bringing to mind Otto Fenichel's equation of girl to phallus, which Lacan will pick upon in "On a Question Prior to Any Possible Treatment of Psychosis" (1958a) and suggest that this finds its imaginary roots in the paths by which the child's desire identifies with the mother's want-to-be (p. 471). Yet the problem in George's case lies in the fact that the girls' status as $-\varphi$ or object a in Mother's belly is a dead body, a corpse.

Therefore, if during the period of the mirror stage or the processing of the intrusion complex, George was in need of the body of a sibling as a specular other (as Lacan suggested in 1938), that could have been, instead of his brother's body, the image of a body preceding this stage, a girl's body in decay. He might not have rejoiced in a *Gestalt* that belonged to him or the sibling, but the fragmented body of a dead (first Annio) or a sickly—soon to joy in death the first—girl (second Annio), which—let us not forget—Mother prays to God to spare in exchange for the life of one of her boys. The texture of the void in the desire of the mother—or the mother's jouissance—George came to this world to fill is thus obvious: it is that of a dead girl.

This status for the body will not manifest for a few decades in George's life, but it will return in the psychotic breakdown that will lead him to the asylum aged forty-three. Referring to Fenichel's equation of girl to phallus, Geneviève Morel suggests that if the phallus is foreclosed, the girl comes into the foreground (2011). This will take place in the period preceding his admission to the psychiatric hospital. Yet George's sisters' bodies are not reliable fastening points to attach to through the mirror stage, as they are dead or sickly bodies. Therefore, as an adult he will attempt to make do with his life and his body without leaning on a specular identification but on his writing.

However, before we examine his adulthood I feel we need to refer to George's memories about the acquisition of language. In a few incidents from his childhood life until the age of ten, when he left his village to make a living, we can read of something we encounter in schizophrenics' words, which also gave our book its title: the subject's resistance to replace the Thing with the Word.

The Word and the Thing

What is an apple tree?

Two incidents from his childhood narrated by George as an adult show a relation to language that cannot but remind one of what Freud (1915e) wrote about schizophrenics' discourse: the cathexis of libido to word-presentations, which Lacan (1953a) linked to the Word not having murdered the Thing and all the symbolic being real (1954). What is even more useful to our reading, however, is that these events indicate the status of a particular signifier linked to the invention that will lead to the adult George's acquisition of a body.

Aged thirty-six, Vizyenos published a small short story in which he narrated an incident from his school life at Vizyi. He spoke about how particularly painful he found it to have to learn the "katharevousa" and replace with it his village's dialect (Vizyenos, 1885a). Katharevousa was an artificial form of formal Greek used before the last quarter of the twentieth century as the Greek state's official language. It was a compromise between ancient and spoken Modern Greek, the "demotic", George's original language. The name of this classicising hybrid strictly speaking means "purifying", since its role was to purify Greek by ridding it of external influences (Merry, 2004).

In this story, we can get a glimpse of a tendency to perceive the word as thing. George writes:

> "What kind of thing is this tree, sir?" I asked him, pointing toward it [the apple tree] with my finger.
>
> [...]
>
> I swear before gods and men that I did not ask about the name—I knew the name—but about the *thing*: All I wanted to know was what kind of thing that tree was, nothing else. (Vizyenos, G., [1885a] 2001, pp. 508–509)

In the same short story, George is also describing by use of a psychological theory the incapacity of proper, that is, dead and void signifiers—even more when he is obliged to learn a hybridic language—to replace the lively language he has learnt as a young boy:

> The apple tree—that is, as the psychologists say, the representation of the word apple tree entered my being simultaneously with the representation of "tree" and at a time when all my senses had their doors wide open and happily welcomed anything and everything coming from my mother or my close relatives to dwell inside my head.
>
> [...]
>
> But this one [apple tree], though dwelling securely within me for so many years now and already having acquired its household and its friends—representations with which it had cohabited for so long and which it had cultivated so many ties of kinship—one day sees Madame Apple-Bearing Tree, entering my head all of a sudden, all alone yet so arrogant, and saying to the apple tree *"Get up so I can take your place!"* "What?!" said the apple tree, "and how can that be? I have been here for so many years now, the space I occupy was free when I came and I took possession of it by right of precedence."
>
> [...]
>
> "Out, stranger! You are not one of us! We do not know you! We do not know you!" (Vizyenos, G., [1885a] 2001, p. 510)

In this narrative we seem to encounter an enlightening description of a contact with both remnants of lalangue and the language of the Other, which is the artificial classicising Greek the schoolteacher promotes. We read of George remembering having resisted letting go of the signifiers "coming from his mother or close relatives" for those coming from the side of established discourse, the strict schoolteacher's dead language, who, moreover, beats him harshly to succumb to its use. Speaking about lalangue, Lacan (1976c) specifies that it is not learnt, but "received" from the mother (p. 12). We could use this narrative as a graphic metaphor for the schizophrenic subject's resistance to dispense with lalangue (Soler, 2014), to abandon it for a language made for communication and devoid of jouissance (Lacan, 1972–1973,) or libido (Freud, 1915e).

Of course, this is a process we all go through. We all suffer the trauma of language and have to bargain hard for our abandoning its material aspect; its being closer to lalangue. I still remember my thirteen-months-old niece shouting with immense joy "woof" to every animal she saw pass on the street under the family's provincial home's balcony; dogs, cats, donkeys, and sheep. It took some time for her to abandon the use of that phoneme for every quadruped and submit to a symbolic system where dogs go "woof", cats go "meow" etc., which she later did, but at that point made absolutely no sense to her. In fact, I doubt whether she would ever be able to use the signifier again with such joy as she did at that age with "woof".

But she was only one-year-old. In contrast, George describes difficulties to do so at school age. In fact, this is not the only example at our disposal. We are offered one more from the next excerpt from his childhood life. Young George narrates encountering difficulties with the function of metaphor not only at school but in his free time too.

What is play?

This second example comes from his doctoral dissertation. There he narrates how his attempt to play generated an outcome with actual properties:

> As a ten-year-old boy, I built a small oven while playing in our yard. The incentive was given to me from the building of a similar oven in the neighbouring yard, where I had carefully observed all the stages of the work and each specific handling of the builders. When I returned from the foreign lands back home three years later, my oven was still standing there, and I was overexcited when finding out that throughout the entire period that had passed it had been used for baking bread.
>
> [...]
>
> Only when the oven had withstood the bad weather of a winter season, they learned to appreciate it and use it for practical purposes. I, however, not only had I sacrificed for its construction a part of my inclinations to these general objective purposes, but on the contrary, I had made use, above all, of my whole being, which, as in every child, was seeking for activity. The sole motive that urged me to accomplish that result was, on the one hand, this pre-existing in all beings tendency to action and, on the other hand, the tendency to imitate the adults in something. (Vizyenos, G., [1881b] 2009, pp. 159–161)

106   ABOVE THE GROUND AND BENEATH THE CLOUDS

I could not think of a better illustration of the jouissance of the child resisting being mediated by symbolic processes: George narrates how the drive was not channelled to the creation of what could have been a work of sublimation, a game, but a concrete object! Instead of creating a game, he built an actual oven, where people would bake real bread. This does not, of course, show that he is ignorant of the metaphorical character of play, but that he remembers resisting adhering to it. The oven was not built on purpose; he was carried away towards an actual creation.

This seems similar to the incident with the apple tree: the same way that the proper signifier "apple-bearing tree"—devoid of jouissance—is resisted, the process of play, preferring the symbol to the Thing, is refused too: an oven cannot be something other than an oven, similarly to the apple tree, which cannot be anything but an apple tree. "Apple-bearing tree" is nothing but a make-believe, exactly like a childish oven. In Chapter Three I have referred to the schizophrenic's resistance to make-believes, the moving forces of established discourse that make up the social bond; this will not be the last time we find this propensity in George's fiction.

As was also seen in Chapter Two, the definition of the use of the signifier—and its corresponding subjective formation—was not maintained in Lacan's teaching. In the 1960s, the concept of jouissance showed that what required regulation was not originally the field of meaning, but jouissance. From that point onwards the schizophrenic subject was not viewed as incapable of making meaning, but of dispensing with lalangue (Soler, 2014), which is linked to the corporeal effect of language on the body.

In fact, those two examples do not only speak of George's expressed peculiar relation to metaphor. Both signifiers are linked to a third one, which is of greater importance to him. It is also vital for our reading of his case, since it is linked to the status of the body, to acquire which against language that has not parted from jouissance is the challenge for the schizophrenic, as was noted in *Part I*. This signifier is the *child*.

What is a child?

Earlier it was suggested that in the fiction George writes as an adult he describes Michaliessa's children as the victims to her unnamed desire or jouissance: as her imaginary phallus or object *a* as "sheer real". Therefore, for George and apparently his siblings, "narcissistic jouissance", which is obtained thanks to the mirror stage, does not seem to fill those children's bodies, which remain attached to the primordial Other.

This happens during his childhood. Yet as an adult George will seek refuge in the signifier "child". In fact, to not let the reader in the dark, it might be written now that childhood is a concept appearing recurrently in his writing (Moulas, 1980); whether that be his poetry, his short stories or his academic writings. Every aspect of his writing career—and great parts of his life—revolve around childhood. This need of his can be explained as an attempt to detach himself from the status of Mother's imaginary phallus or object a and acquire a body of his own.

The hypothesis might be put forward now therefore that George's attempted answer to the question of his being, an answer differential to Mother's having that corresponds to his body being equated to that of a dead girl, is "child". This is a first elementary attempt for him to have a body of his own: he is not a girl; he is a child. It is an intimate and unmediated attempt at a metaphor: to replace the girl, whose body is dead, with the child. Yet as was seen in his narrations about his acquisition of language ("apple tree") and playing ("oven") George's use of signification seems rather problematic. "Child" cannot act at this point as a proper S_1. As was seen above, dispensing with the jouissance of a signifier for its symbolic aspect is not what he is best at.

"Child" in George's fiction and life could be, in fact, one more concept linked to jouissance, a version of the Thing not having been killed by the Word. We might even compare it to a "holophrase", borrowing Lacan's (1964a) reference to the solidified signifier of mentally deficient children, which consists of the absence of an interval between S_1 and S_2. In his lecture on the symptom at Geneva, Lacan (1976a) linked the autistic to the schizophrenic in that there is something in them "which freezes" (p. 20). Yet, instead of signifier and signification of the first Lacan, we prefer the freezing of signifier and jouissance of the middle and late Lacan.

Therefore, the child's body could be described not only as an image that has not entered a dialectic with a specular other's image, but also as the corporeal aspect of this signifier, its material texture in terms of the Thing: an aspect of the child's body not yet attached to its proper image. Thus, the child could be a "frozen" signifier with no clear imaginary constitution, since that is one with Mother, her $-\varphi$ or a that used to be in her belly.

As above, this hypothesis is based on George's endeavours in his adolescent and adult life, where, after building his oven by the side of the apple tree, he will leave his village and never stop writing about and researching the meaning of childhood (Moulas, 1980). We have already visited a few examples: the short stories in which he narrates his family's tragedies, the one where he speaks about his problems at school, and his thesis, in which he describes his playing as a young boy. We could summarise his research and writing—in fact, his whole life—as an attempt to answer the question: *what is it to be a child?*

It seems that during the aforementioned writing activity, analysed further below, George was capable of a breakthrough relating to the status of the body as the factor of Mother's lack, what she has and loses. In the thirty-year-long wandering that will follow his departure from the village, a different status for his body will emerge. This status, which he will create based on his writing on the One of the child, will last for more than two decades. It will not deter body phenomena in the end, but it will give him the chance to acquire the body not simply against language, which is the challenge for the "so-called schizophrenic" (Lacan, 1973a), but thanks to language. His body will be knotted to language based on an attempt to name the child's being.

CHAPTER FIVE

The beautification of the child's body

The period separating George's childhood from the outbreak of psychotic phenomena in his early forties coincides with his literary activity as "Georgios Vizyenos".

The reader might have noticed that in the previous chapter I mainly used his first name to refer to the writer. This did not happen only so that his case would resemble a psychoanalytic case history—if this was by any chance achieved, it is even better. It was because what he created to tackle the challenge to acquire a body of his own was built around, and thanks to, the signifier by which he entered Greek literature. If "George Syrmas" or "Michaelides" is a child belonging to Mother, that is, a dead girl's body, "Georgios Vizyenos" is a signifier attributing to the child's body a status different to the one it used to hold in the Michaelides family history.

Lacan writes about the psychotic subject that, detached as it is from the unconscious as the Other's discourse, it fails to give an answer to the question addressed to everyone, psychotic or not: "What am I to the Other?" (Lacan, 1958a). As was remarked earlier, in Georgios' case an elementary answer to this question is: "child". Yet his answer cannot take the form of an S_1, which will represent the subject by being articulated with other signifiers. What will happen, alternatively, is the poet and writer Vizyenos spending almost thirty years creating his own, singular "unconscious" to substantiate that signifier. This will not come about thanks to one of the established discourses, the discourse of the Other the social bond depends upon, but a discourse elaborating on the One that marks the child's body. It will create a pedestal for Georgios to stand on acquiring his body in a narcissistic rise different to the one of the mirror stage, the challenges to which were described earlier.

The subject's entrance onto the world's stage

The first steps

George left his village at the age of ten or twelve. His older brother had become a peddler, like their father and maternal grandfather, and took him on a trip to Constantinople, modern-day Istanbul (Athanasopoulos, 1992).

In Constantinople, George became an apprentice at the tailors' guild, working in a shop owned by an uncle of his. To his great discomfort, he could not go to school regularly since he had to spend long hours in the workshop (Vizyenos, 1881a). The job was harsh and the uncle was strict (Athanasopoulos, 1992; Vasiliadis, 1910). He remained there until the tailor's death, which happened after two or three years.

The adolescent George then sought the protection of a man called Yangos Georgiadis. Georgiadis was a Cypriot merchant George had probably met at his uncle's store (Athanasopoulos, 1992). Under Georgiadis' protection, he will apparently compose his first poems.

Patronage was a fading tradition in the 1860s, an effect of the advances in nineteenth-century society (Mooers, 1991). However, George benefited extensively from what it could offer him. Starting with Georgiadis, from the mid-1860s until the mid-1880s, he was never left without a patron or somebody negotiating his finding one. Georgiadis was replaced by the Cypriot Archbishop Sophronius II, and Sophronius by Bishop Lycurgus of the Greek island of Syros, the headmaster Georgios Hassiotis, Professor Elias Tandalides, and the renowned Constantinopolitan banker and philanthropist Georgios Zarifis.

It has been suggested that George was looking for a paternal substitute for his dead father in those figures (Athanasopoulos, 1992; Dimiroulis, 2009; Moulas, 1980). I am of the opinion that due to the father in George's writings and his life being a hole, these men could not have acted as substitutes for the father's symbolic function, but for his imaginary aspect. George's first and last patrons in particular, a prosperous merchant and an affluent banker, are people who give generously, instead of taking away and forbidding. They do not seem as carriers of the father's role in the sense of the oedipal myth or paternal metaphor. They do not say "no" in the sense of the Name-of-the-Father, which in French sounds identical to the no-of-the-father (*Nom du père/ non du père*).

As was remarked earlier, as an adult George does not describe a symbolic function born by a paternal figure in his writings (poems, fiction, and academic papers) but only images who own, have or lose, exactly like Mother; his poetic reference to the father is always as a bearer of poverty, whereas in his fiction the father will always be someone rich (Vizyenos, 1883c; 1895). In fact, I believe that the extent of George's "faith" in the father was so limited that, as we will see, he showed no reservations about changing his patron for a new one when he found one who could serve better his aspirations; one who could give more. Not only does he not remain attached to a paternal figure, but, as is shown below, he seems to be taking the name of the father "in vain".

In effect, since his successive patrons live in different cities and countries, George will not hesitate to change his location and profession to gain their protection. Therefore, from being a tailor's and merchant's apprentice in Constantinople, he will soon become a novice in Cyprus, under the protection of Archbishop Sophronius. There he will work as school guard and chanter and attend lessons at the secondary Greek School of Nicosia (Indianos, 1934).

Yet George writes in ground-breaking honesty—an honesty structural in the schizophrenic's resistance to the make-believe—that in spite of wearing the monk's cassock, he did not take his vows (Vizyenos, 1881b), since he had never been interested in becoming a clergyman. He simply seized the opportunity offered by his appointments to study the classics. After all, in those days and areas, the clergy were frequently the only educated people.

However, something significant seems to have taken place in Cyprus, in parallel to George's adopting the formal version of his Christian name: Georgios. The names from classical literature he meets in Nicosia will become the prototypes that will motivate his creativity. It is their brightness that he will try to assume, as will often become apparent in his writing style. They will be the matrix for his child's body's narcissistic rise, which will not depend on the other's image, but will give out a brightness stemming from their position in language, in relation to the signifier. The dead bodies of his two sisters will be overshadowed by the bright names of classic writers.

On the other hand, established discourse will only act as an instrument for George, from now on Georgios. Thus, we see him confessing with radical honesty that he did not hesitate to exploit a seemingly paternal figure like the archbishop in order to fulfil his aims.

Here we may find a parallelism, which I put forward to my full knowledge of the chance of it being absolutely erroneous, to Landru. In her reading of his case Biagi-Chai (2014) highlights the fact that this man showed absolutely no remorse for his horrible actions, which he attributed to his having to raise his family. Landru did not seem to lie in this refrain. He was dedicated to serving his "family" and could not find the reason to confess or regret his horrific conduct, since these were justified by his duty to the family. Fortunately, George did not seduce middle-aged women to drag them to their death, but only ecclesiastical masters to adopting him, in defence, in his case, of the signifier "child".

His resistance to the make-believe of the ecclesiastical version of the master's discourse is, in fact, reflected in a sentence he puts in his mother's mouth in the short story "My Mother's Sin". Mother has just confessed having smothered her baby daughter to the highest figure of religious authority in the Eastern Orthodox Church, the Patriarch of Constantinople and tells her son:

> The Patriarch is a wise and holy man. He knows all God's plans and wishes, and he pardons everybody's sins. But what can I tell you? He's a monk. He never had children, so he cannot know what a thing it is to kill one's own child! (Vizyenos, G., [1883a] 1988, p. 23)

This is one of the first times in his fiction that Georgios undresses the master of the make-believe of his authority; a monk who acts as a symbolic father (Patriarch) is very far from an actual parent.

As a result, at the age of twenty-three, Georgios does not hesitate to leave Cyprus forever for another location. A Holy Synod was summoned in Constantinople, which he returned to as part of the Cypriot archbishop's entourage. During the synod, he met Lycurgus, the Bishop of Syros and confessed to him, another member of the church with high authority (!), an aversion to becoming a monk. Lycurgus then introduced him to Georgios Hassiotis, the headmaster of the Lyceum of the Greek neighbourhood of Peran (Hassiotis, 1910). Hassiotis will become Georgios' new patron, encouraging a relocation to the Constantinople area and a change in his attire and professional status. To achieve his aim, Georgios even cited a heart-rending quatrain to Hassiotis, in which he says he is a stranger, an orphan, and a poor child and laments that he shall thus remain illiterate.

Hassiotis (1910) was deeply moved by Georgios' "honesty", which was not exactly sincere, since his mother was well and alive, he already had a patron, and had attended some classes at school. Nevertheless, Hassiotis agreed to support Georgios. The twenty-three-year old novice registered at the Theological School of Halki, one of the Princess islands. Hassiotis had to pay an extra amount so that his protégé would not be assigned to the priesthood (1910). Georgios leaves behind the signifier "novice" to become a student of theology.

Before the change in his status, however, he has changed his surname, as is observed in a letter he sends to Cyprus from the Patriarchate. Instead of Michaelides, his surname is now—and will remain so until the end—Vizyenos.

The subject's name

As was described in Chapter Four, Georgios' surname in childhood, Michaelides, which means "Michael's son", entailed no codification, but a literal meaning: that the person marked by this signifier belongs to Michael, who is an imaginary figure under Mother's shadow. "Michael's George" and "Michaliessa's tiny George", his nicknames at the village, point to exactly the same thing, as does "George", the name of his grandfather, the man who acquired the body of a girl (Michaliessa's) as his child during one of his peddling trips. These signifiers do not represent the subject for other signifiers; they simply point to the aspect of his body as the object of the Other's having.

The signifier "Vizyenos", however, the name that Georgios gives himself in Cyprus, describes a different kind of identity. This ancient Greek adjective is a signifier that, strictly speaking, means "man from Vizyi". The origin of the name by which the subject chooses to call himself resembles the brightness of the figures he found in studying classical literature.

Vizyi, the village Georgios was born in was an ancient Greek city in Thrace. In a paper he wrote a few years before his admission to the asylum, "Monks and the Worship of Dionysus in Thrace" (1888a), he described an ancient coin found in the area that read "Vizyenon", which means "of the Vizyenoi" (the plural of "Vizyenos"), the city's ancient inhabitants.

This signifier with which he renames himself seems to mark a break with the array of signifiers that were naming the child's destiny as Mother's –φ or *a*. Its use serves an attempt to diverge from that lineage of girls' bodies belonging to somebody else. It establishes his entitlement to a child's body of his own. Thus, the "child" is now properly named for the first time, as "Vizyenos". It is not at all accidental that Georgios draws this name from the village's history.

As was written in the preceding chapter, neither of Georgios' parents had come from Vizyi. Both had "adopted" that village as a residence. Therefore, as soon as he has the chance, their second son proceeds to a break with that metonymy that only points to his body belonging to somebody else. His new name is not simply that of someone who belongs to somebody; he comes from somewhere. He is a "Vizyenos", a man from Vizyi, instead of being a girl's body owned by Michael or Michaliessa, who do not have actual roots in the land of Vizyi. The signifier "Vizyenos" attempts to re-codify what Georgios *is* and helps him bring to a halt the metonymy of those who *have* the child (Grandfather Georgie, Michael, and Michaliessa). He thus attempts a naming of its body through the symbolic, different to his given name. This attempt will anchor the child's body to the Thracian soil and insert a pause in the body, its organs, and their function being anywhere "above the ground and beneath the clouds".

In effect, that signifier's origin, the ancient history of Vizyi and Thrace in general, will be a field Georgios will exploit extensively in his career as a writer, trying to raise himself to the level of the classics. If we had to sum up the body of written work that the use of the name Vizyenos will generate, we would have to talk about two themes: childhood, which has been referred to already, and Thracian heritage (history, culture, and folklore). These will constitute the topics of poems, fiction, and scientific papers and studies that he will write as Vizyenos. Thus, this new name of his will become the "Other" in the "Other" that his writing will establish. Yet this otherness is merely artificial—that is, self-made—and primarily for own consumption. Both its composites will come out of his own hands.

Georgios has already written some poems when this new name appears in his correspondence from Constantinople (Indianos, 1934). We can assume that the two appeared at the same time: the signifier "Vizyenos" is articulated with the signifier "poet". Yet the name Vizyenos will not be simply used for Georgios' representation in the field of Modern Greek literature. It will not remain a literary pseudonym. It will become the subject's name. From now on, it will represent him in his journeys, studies, and his contact with the social bond. In fact, Georgios will believe himself to be Vizyenos before that signifier is articulated to the swarm of other signifiers that will represent him: novelist, researcher, psychologist, professor, etc.

The first success and the first stumble

At the theological school, Georgios met professor Elias Tandalides, a blind poet who taught Greek (Athanasopoulos, 1992). He liked Georgios and supported him in writing poetry. Meeting Tandalides and registering at that school influenced his poetic production, bringing it under the *Phanariotes* influence.

The Phanariotes were the affluent Greek community of Constantinople, who often occupied high positions in the Ottoman Empire. They used their influence and resources to support young Greeks' studies in Constantinople, Moldavia, and Walachia (Demaras, 1972). They favoured the katharevousa, the form of Greek Georgios was refusing to learn as a young boy to replace the language he learnt from "his mother" (Vizyenos, 1885a, p. 510) (see Chapter Four). His education at Halki took place in that style. Nevertheless, whereas he was trained excessively well in it, he neither incorporated it fully, nor did he side with it wholeheartedly, as will be shown later on.

Under the supervision of Tandalides, Georgios published a first poetry collection in 1873, entitled simply "Poetic Juvenilia". Most of the five poems it consists of are written in demotic, the rival of katharevousa (Merry, 2004). Apart from one, dedicated to the theological school, Georgios' poems in "Poetic Juvenilia" are written in the first person and are about his early experiences in life, such as the death of his father. The themes of being an orphan and a poor child pervade the collection. This is his first published attempt to articulate something about the child's being in writing. He dedicates "Poetic Juvenilia" to Hassiotis (1910), his first secular patron after Georgiadis, and publishes it in Constantinople.

Its circulation makes him known to the city's Greek elite. He becomes deeply liked by the Phanariotes, since he is writing in a style this community is accustomed to. This is the first piece of evidence that, by leaning on his utilisation of the formalism of language, writing provides him with an acknowledgment, on the part of the social Other, of his being as something different from what one has: the poet of childhood Vizyenos. In fact, the researcher Vangelis Athanasopoulos (1992) had accurately suggested using the noun Poet for Vizyenos in its literal meaning. Ποιητής (poetis) in Greek literally means creator. Thus, his first poetry collection can be read as the creation of the first step of a stepladder in the sense of the *escabeau* (Lacan, 1975a). This publication distances the body from the status of what belongs to others, which we will later call a piece of merchandise with regards to the family history, and lifts it to a bright object crafted by himself.

Among his admirers in Constantinople was Iphigenia Antoniadou, a wealthy widow (Athanasopoulos, 1992). Antoniadou and Tandalides spoke about Georgios to Georgios Zarifis, a Constantinopolitan Greek banker and renowned philanthropist (Mansell, 1995). Zarifis offered him his generous patronage. The young poet and student of theology accepted it gratefully and dropped that of Hassiotis (1910) after asking his permission.

Two months after meeting Zarifis and securing his financial support, Georgios will leave Halki for his village. He stops wearing the cassock and spends the summer as the protégé of the Greek financial colossus (Athanasopoulos, 1992). He will never return to Constantinople to complete his studies there. He leaves for Athens in the autumn to register as a final-year high-school student (Papakostas, 2004).

Although his debut in the social circles of Constantinople was quite promising concerning his stepladder, in Athens things were not as easy. In fact, the first ray of light that covered his body as Vizyenos was dissolved by the cautious Athenian establishment.

Georgios arrived in the Greek capital at the age of twenty-four. He brought with him an epic-lyric poem called "Kodros", which he had started composing under the supervision of Tandalides (Athanasopoulos, 1992). Kodros is a long poem written in katharevousa. It describes in a rather pompous style the story of a mythological king of Athens. Georgios sent the poem to the Voutsinaios poetry contest the following year (Moulas, 1980). The Voutsinaios was a declining institution that had started in 1862 (Mackridge, 2009). Therefore, in his debut in the Athenian poetic establishment, the signifier "Vizyenos" is articulating the signifier of a young epic poet. The first verse of this poem are a call to the Muse for inspiration, which cannot but bring to mind the first verse of Homer's *Odyssey* (2014), a similarity for which he will be later attacked (Moulas, 1980; Varelas, 2014).

Georgios won the first prize in the contest (Athanasopoulos, 1992; Moulas, 1980). However, instead of ensuring him a recognition by the social Other similar to the one that his "Poetic Juvenilia" had achieved in Constantinople, this award became the occasion for a vacillation of the narcissistic pedestal he had started creating there.

The audience and his fellow-competitors started protesting loudly about the announcement of the results (Vasiliadis, 1910). The main reason for this response had apparently been the fact that the writer of Kodros was a "turko-meritis"—a person of Greek descent coming from a region still under Turkish rule (Barbeito, 1995)—who had not yet finished high school (Athanasopoulos, 1992). In addition, it was obvious that Kodros has been composed in complete accordance with Phanariotism, a tradition clashing with the modernistic spirit in Athenian letters of the 1870s (Alexiou, 1995).

Regardless of the protests being fair or not, Georgios does not leave them unanswered. He responds aggressively, composing a scornful quatrain describing the Athenian poets' reaction to his award (Vasiliadis, 1910). He will give an even more elaborate answer in his next poetry collection. If his writing indeed fulfilled a narcissistic function by creating the steps of a stepladder, what was at stake might have been more than his reputation as poet; falling from it could make the child's image vacillate and return the body to its prior state—that of a dead girl.

This is highlighted by another aspect of the criticism Georgios faces in Athens. A considerable part of the Athenian social and literary elite will never acknowledge the classic beauty he wishes his written works to cover him with. In contrast, their criticism will intentionally target this quality of Vizyenos's. Their polemic spirit, in fact, will denounce not only his writing but his physical appearance.

It is probably true that Georgios was not an attractive man. On the occasion of this first trip to Athens, a close friend of his gave the following detailed description of the mature high-school student's looks:

A strange guy has appeared in Athens. Having a peculiarly oriental profile, he was amongst those privileged persons that are permanently engraved in memory. His eyes were oblique as those of a Chinese, his eyebrows were jaunty, oblique, wholly black, his countenance was mignon, but with bulging cheeks of a refugee from Roumeli. (Vasiliadis, N., 1910, pp. 307–308)

The same goes for his opponents, who will often exploit this impression to justify their commentary against his character and literary production, often making particular reference to his prematurely bald head:

He will be begging again for interaction in order to display his baldness, to stretch his Chinese eyes and to push that legendary abdomen to inappropriate leaps for which we are certain that no English lady would have ever possibly accepted in her salons. (Frou-Frou, 1882, p. 4)

This scornful reaction that Georgios had to face from his first months in Athens opposes further the narcissistic effect of his writing under the signifier "Vizyenos": that is, his body's beautification against the hateful remarks of critics and the public who were attacking the imaginary. Commenting on his ugliness might have been a reminder of the equation of his body to that of a dead girl, the smothered baby he came into this world to replace or the sickly sister to whose salvation his body was offered to God by Mother (Vizyenos, 1883a).

In 1923, Freud wrote that the ego is serving three masters (see Chapter One). On this occasion, we see that the signifier "Vizyenos" must defend the acquisition of Georgios' body against three masters too: Mother and her metonymical figures, jouissance "frozen" in the signifier "child" linked to the dead girl's body, and the social Other, who is fiercely attacking the imaginary by exploiting his unattractive looks. Thus, it was at the same time hard and highly important to safeguard the subsistence of his self-made name, hitherto based on "Poetic Juvenilia" and Kodros.

After graduating from high school, Georgios became a student at the School of Philosophy of the University of Athens. This was a step toward his postgraduate studies abroad, thanks to which he would research the child's being from a new viewpoint. Soon disappointed by the conditions at the Greek university, he decided to continue his studies abroad (Vasiliadis, 1910). Satisfied with the award at the poetry contest, his patron agreed to this plan.

In October 1875, Georgios leaves the Greek-speaking world for the first time, to continue his academic studies in Germany. The distance he thus took helped him repair the temporarily damaged image of the child's body.

An ironic rectification of the stepladder

At the age of twenty-six, Georgios registers at the Royal Augustan Academy of Göttingen in Lower Saxony. He was now only a hundred miles away from Kraepelin and five hundred from Freud. Both were studying medicine, the first in Leipzig, the second in Vienna. Unlike theirs, however, Georgios' command of German was not good. Confined to his room, he was only able to speak it satisfactorily after hard work (Athanasopoulos, 1992; Sideras & Sidera-Lytra, 2009).

However, this confinement had hardly any impact on his creativity. In contrast, during that first, lonely year, he composed a new poetry collection to supplement his stepladder. It was entitled "Ares, Mares, Koukounares" (Athanasopoulos, 1992; Moulas, 1980). This is a slang expression in demotic meaning "blah-blah", "bunkum" or "rubbish".

The use of the demotic and the abandonment of the language of the Phanariotes, should not escape our attention. It shows the limited extent of Georgios' attachment to the cradle of Constantinopolitan writing. He only used literary styles in his own interest, the same thing he did with seemingly "paternal" figures: to create his own discourse that would beautify the child's body.

In fact, the collection's title, "Rubbish", is nothing but an ironic reference to the Athenian establishment, which had attacked his attempts at epic poetry with those very words and had exploited, at times, his physical appearance. The title comes from a homonymous poem in which he agrees, in a sarcastic tone, that his poetic attempts are rubbish. One might not be totally wrong in seeing in this title, next to other Vizyenos' writings, an aspect of the schizophrenic's irony, which attacks the make-believe, the moving force behind the social bond (Lacan, 1966b; Miller, 2001). Georgios then submits the collection to the same poetry contest and, truly ironically, wins the first prize again!

He studies at Göttingen for three semesters and, after a year and a half, moves to Leipzig and then Berlin. His main academic interests are the history of philosophy, aesthetics, psychology, and psychiatry (Athanasopoulos, 1992). Among his academic professors at Leipzig was

Wilhelm Wundt (Vasiliadis, 1910). It is quite likely that Georgios met two psychiatrists I referred to in Chapter One: Emil Kraepelin, also a student of Wundt's and then in his third year of medical studies, and Paul Flechsig, President Schreber's future doctor, who was appointed professor in psychiatry at Leipzig the same year Georgios registered there. A third possible encounter with a figure referred to in Chapter Two this time, was with the Swiss Ferdinand de Saussure, a student in Leipzig and Berlin (Kantzia, 2009). It is from him that Lacan would borrow terms like the "signifier" to form his theory of the symbolic.

Georgios continues composing poetry in parallel with his academic studies. He finishes another collection in 1877, called "Hesperides". Some elements from "Bosporean Breezes", a new title for "Ares, Mares, Koukounares", are apparently included in the new collection. He sends it to the next Voutsinaios, but this time his entry does not win the first prize; it is only given a plaudit.

"Hesperides" consists of three ballads whose subjects are inspired by folk songs, ancient legends, and rural tradition. It seems that Georgios' interest in folkloric themes had already appeared in the previous collection, which was never published. The admittedly short repertoire of "Hesperides" is dedicated in its totality to similar subjects (Moulas, 1980).

Like "Bosporean Breezes", "Hesperides" is never published either. Some of the poems it contains will apparently survive in a different form in his following—and last-published—poetry collection. Yet what we do know is that they were written entirely in katharevousa. Having used the demotic in a sarcastic tone in the previous collection, Georgios now returns to the language of Constantinople. This change accompanies two new signifiers "Vizyenos" is articulated to: "lyric poet" and "folklorist".

In the past it has been highlighted that there was no academic record to provide information about the duration or content of Georgios' studies in Berlin, where he went from Leipzig in 1879 (Athanasopoulos, 1992). Yet more recent research by Sideras and Sidera-Lytra (2009) has proven that not only did this happen, but also that he apparently started composing his doctoral dissertation there.

As if his wandering could not stop, in 1880, aged thirty-one, he returns to Göttingen. He registers for one more year at the Augustan Academy and finishes his thesis, which he submits in 1881. Its title was *Children's Play in Terms of Psychology and Pedagogy* (Vizyenos, 1881b).

His supervisor, Professor Herman Lotze, had expressed reservations about the topic's suitability for a doctoral thesis in philosophy. Nevertheless, Georgios insisted on doing it and the dissertation was accepted and published in Leipzig (Athanasopoulos, 1992; Moulas, 1980). This new publication articulates a new signifier to "Vizyenos": that of "child psychologist", which is, indeed, not too relevant to his studies. Yet this thesis will be referred to by a number of German and Spanish doctors within the next two decades (Varelas, 2014)! In addition, this publication will give him the chance to claim another ancient writer's brightness, following Homer. In his CV attached to it he is alluding subliminally to the Roman writer Sallust (Paschalis, 2009). Yet, more importantly, Georgios is starting to symbolise something about the jouissance in the signifier "child" under the signifier "Vizyenos".

Why, indeed, would he insist on researching the topic of children's play, when Professor Lotze was probably right in considering it irrelevant to philosophy (Sideras & Sideras-Lytra, 2009)? I believe that Georgios' determination in this matter demonstrates not only his stumbling concerning adhering properly to academic discourse, but also his need for a symbolisation of the jouissance of the signifier "child" different to that of the dead girl. An example was presented in the preceding chapter, where Georgios was trying to analyse the function of the drive in the child's activities. This is the first time after "Poetic Juvenilia" that he articulates something about the child's being under the signifier "Vizyenos". In contrast to the past, however, he does not refer to the image of the orphan child anymore, but to its physical, corporeal aspect.

For example, he describes the child's original inner force when it takes up playing: he writes that what lies inside the child before playing is a dark, intensive, and formless drive to physical-mental activity, with no measure or target (1881b, p. 178). Would one be wrong in reading in this description an aspect of the child's jouissance? In fact, with the help of a metaphor Georgios develops a guideline on how the jouissance in the child's body can be tamed. He writes that if the human body is like a machine, play can act like valve mechanisms, which can defuse the vapour running inside it (Vizyenos, 1881b, p. 126). He also offers advice on how to avoid unwanted disturbances in the child's growing body. He writes that parents should not suddenly shake the baby's body when playing with it, in fear of causing them spams; as for adolescents, they should avoid rotating cars or swings in fear of sexual over-excitation (!) (Vizyenos, 1881b, pp. 174, 183).

Georgios also refers to a number of incidents from his own childhood—like the one with the oven described in Chapter Four—and writes something that can highlight more than anything his own status as a child. He argues that one will be able to understand his arguments if they were, like him, *a child in body and soul* (Vizyenos, 1881b, p. 150). Indeed, next to his thesis, his attempt to elaborate something on the child's "body and soul" will take place in the next two literary genres he will deal with.

His next claim to bring the jouissance of the child under the signifier "Vizyenos" will take place in his poetry and fiction. In them, a new feature of his use of language will appear. This will be the highest point in the rise of Georgios' body on the stepladder, including a direct relation to the real: his exploitation of elements from lalangue that will bring "Vizyenos" closer than ever to a name for the speaking being. Unfortunately, he will never recover from the downfall that will follow this.

The zenith of Vizyenos

A small turn back

1881 was Georgios' last year in Germany. He visited Greece twice within a year. In May he visited Samakovo, another Greek village in Thrace, near the modern-day Turkish-Bulgarian border. His maternal family owned land in that area, which used to have an iron mine. He had the idea of exploiting its abandoned mine, which had been destroyed by the Russian army after war with Turkey (Athanasopoulos, 1992; Koutrianou, 2003). Probably due to the ill health of his patron, he was looking for funds to safeguard the publication of his works (Chrysanthopoulos, 1994), which were vital for his beautification. For the moment, this idea would not occupy his interest for long, but this would change—with detrimental effects—in the near future.

His next trip was to Athens in January 1882, aged thirty-three. He might have tried to dwell there, with no success. Yet his social life was not as marginal as in the past. He read poems at Parnassus, the oldest and most prestigious Greek cultural club (Athanasopoulos, 1992; Moulas, 1980) as well as at the royal palace. There, he also took part, as the leading character, in the performance of an original theatrical play called *The Bad Time* (Koutrianou, 2003; Varelas, 2014). His participation generated a mocking caricature published in the periodical *Asmodeus* with the headline "a good hero in a bad time!" (Varelas, 2014, p. 5). "Amateur actor" is now a new signifier articulated to the signifier "Vizyenos".

Yet Georgios soon announces he is leaving for Paris. On the occasion of his departure, a column in the periodical *Mi Hanesai* writes about his presence in the Greek capital. The comment revives the polemic spirit of the Athenian press that had made his narcissistic pedestal vacillate seven years earlier:

> Unfortunately, on the other hand, Mr. Vizyenos has been born to play this role of the beggar. Having passed—and we are not saying this in order to humiliate him, but in order to write history— through all the stages of brutalisation, i.e. those of the grocery servant, of the chanter, of the tailor, of the altar boy, of the seminarist, and having been suddenly abducted from the strata of his origin thanks to Mr. Zarifis of Constantinople, he did not have enough soul to change his character as much he changed his fortune, but instead he has preserved the properties of vulgarity and lack of honour intact and after a staying in Germany for possibly seven years—for all his small poetic worth and due to the deprivation of Mr. Zarifis' material resources, having sadly suffered in his health, he has carried these properties of the grocer's boy to all the salons of Athens, where he has been humiliated, he has flattered, he has been a parasite, and he has been laughed at everyone, even by the young royal prodigy, having been forced into all these—for the sole purpose, as he himself has been modestly claiming, to secure subscriptions for himself for the future publication of his books.
>
> [...]
>
> He has been subverted to such great humiliation in Athens that from a Poet—as he would wish to be—he has ended up being a salon clown. (Frou-Frou, 1882, pp. 3–4)

Despite the idea that Vizyenos had been a poet and writer marginalised by the Athenian literary establishment, more recent research has shown that this was probably due to competing political and personal interests, and that he was in fact liked by a part of Athenian social circles (Mavrelos, 2009; Varelas, 2014). How can one ignore the fact that he is invited to read and perform at the royal palace? However, regardless of the interests behind this harsh criticism, one cannot but note that the journalist is pointing out accurately the swarm of professional identities

Georgios has held. It is also worth bearing in mind that after his theatrical debut, he announces he is leaving for yet another European tour to raise funds for his publications and live the life of … who knows what?

His subsequent stay in Paris did not last long. He was introduced as a poet to French philhellenes (Athanasopoulos, 1992). In November he left for London. Three years after his departure, a young neurologist called Sigmund Freud will visit Paris to study nervous diseases with Jean-Martin Charcot (Freud, 1893f).

London will be the last Western metropolis Georgios will stay in before his final return to Greece. Thanks to the evolution of his writing, his narcissistic rise will attain its greatest height there.

The Greek ambassador will introduce him to the Greek community of London, which "almost adored him" (Vasiliadis, 1910, p. 310). This is the second time this happens in his life. Ten years earlier, he had become the Greek elite's favourite as a young poet in Constantinople. In London he will supplement his stepladder with a new poetry collection, short stories and children's stories, and start a second dissertation, which he will finish in Athens.

The peak

Georgios' poetry collection published in November 1883 is written once again in the demotic, like "Bosporean Breezes", putting an end to the use of the katharevousa of "Hesperides". It is called "Attic Breezes". In its first edition, he announces the forthcoming publication of three more works: "Bosporean Breezes", a collection of a hundred and fifty children's poems, and "Modern Greek Short Stories" (Moulas, 1980).

The topics of most of the "Attic Breezes" come from the same source that inspired "Hesperides": folk tradition, mainly from Thrace. His poems are about folk beliefs, legends, Greek myths, and, in general, popular mythical perceptions of the world, life, nature, and history (Athanasopoulos, 1992). What should not escape our attention, however, is that in some of those poems he makes a seemingly superficial use of sounds from nature or animal cries that he will also use in his children's poems.

Like his children's poetry, those poems are written in the demotic. This seems reasonable, since this version of Greek is simpler and easier, and therefore more accessible to children, than katharevousa. Yet this alone does not make them different from what he has written in the past. What does make them different is the material they are made of.

In those poems, Georgios turns, for the first time, to onomatopoeia. He uses monosyllabic words that imitate animal cries and sounds from nature or inanimate objects. Sometimes those words are used in their common form, like "woof-woof" or "splish-splash". In other instances, he modifies them, or invents original ones. Two examples follow: a poem from "Attic Breezes" and one of his children's poems:

The Thracians' chant

Out of Thrace, my dear friends,
Tra-la, tra-la, tra-la la-la,
Out of Pieria,
This is where Religion was born.

And the auras of the Thracian wind have drawn,
Tra-la, tra-la, tra-la la-la,
Out of her golden torch
A spark to Greece.

And they sowed it close-
Tra-la, tra-la, tra-la la-la,
To the old Athens,
To the first Eleusis.

And light came to the darkness,
Tra-la, tra-la, tra-la la-la,
And down there has appeared
Zeus and his race.

Hence each one should strive
Tra-la, tra-la, tra-la la-la,
To carry the light now
Back to its first land.
(Vizyenos, G., [1884] 2003, p. 494)

The blacksmith

Ding dang the fast
The dirty blacksmith
Ding-dang all day long
What do you think he is doing down there?

Ding dang narrow-wide,
Iron plates he has on fire,
Ding dang and on the anvil
He shapes them as he pleases.

Ding dang a share
For the ploughs he pounds,
Ding dang a shovel
He makes for a farmer.

Ding dang a solid
He is now making a lock.
Ding dang a plow,
For the unplowed vineyard.

Ding dang he pounds
Horseshoes for the beasts
Ding dang nails he blunts
For the builder that nails.

Ding dang the fast
The rough blacksmith,
Ding dang down there,
Such things he does all day.
(Vizyenos, G., 1997, p. 214)

Of course, one could note that in those poems Georgios is imitating children's language to suit the signifier of "child psychologist" or "educator" the signifier "Vizyenos" is articulated to. This could have been indeed his intention. Yet what seems to also take place, especially in poems for the younger children, is a utilisation of lalangue more than in any other case of his use of language.

The poem "The blacksmith" was not chosen randomly to translate and present above. In this, along other children's poems of this period, we can view Georgios inserting in his writing fragments from his traumatic experience of the encounter between the body—this time, an animal's and his own—and the signifier, which is represented in this poem by the signifiers "ding dang". This experience is described in another childhood memory from his doctoral dissertation on children's play; a memory that offers us access to the spectrum through which George as a child himself experiences the impact of the signifier upon the living body that cries while falling. He writes:

> When I was a child, I used to stand in front of the forge of a black-smith who was making horseshoes and I used to feel great pleasure hearing the peculiarly rhythmic pounding of those working at the place. Each time I managed to find a bent nail and a flat piece of iron, I used to pound incessantly, imitating the blacksmith, even in bed.
>
> [...]
>
> A little later, however, when I was obliged to see how they tied each other the legs of an ox and lied it down violently in order to shoe it and when I heard its moaning and its groaning, I disappeared as soon as I could, without ever daring going back to the forge or remembering my tools again. (Vizyenos, G., [1881b] 2009, p. 188)

I believe that the reading of this childhood memory along the above-mentioned poem offers us a first-class example of the utilisation of the remnants of one of the signifier's first encounters with the body. Of course, the deciphered parts of lalangue cannot but be hypothetical (Soler, 2014). It seems, however, that in this particular example we can trace something of the One's impact—which needn't even be a proper word, like "ding dang"—on the child's "body and soul"—to use Vizyenos' own words—before its encounter with the discourse of the Other.

Yet Georgios will not stop there. He will not simply transliterate those fragments into poems. Consonant to what he would write about the apple tree and the oven of his childhood, he cannot create poetry for its own sake. What he constructs must serve an actual objective, similar to an oven not being an oven unless it is actually used to bake bread and the signifier "apple-bearing tree" being unable to fully represent the thing apple tree. Thus, he will try to assemble those poems in a comprehensive system that will act as an educational tool for children through poetry; from nursery to adolescence (Koutrianou, 2003). Its architecture will, surprise-surprise, resemble a ladder with four steps, which will guide the child on the gradual acquisition of language over lalangue.

It seems that at this point in his creation, Georgios achieves an isolation and a utilisation of the real that strikes the corporeal aspect of the signifier "child" in him, instead of his dead sisters. Moreover, he is constructing a stepladder for this to be raised upon, which couldn't but remind the Lacanian reader of the concept of the *escabeau*.

This ascending route concerning the rise of Georgios' child's body on the stepladder will be carried on, and reach its peak, in his next writing endeavour. In fact, something of a similar nature concerning lalangue can be also found in Georgios' other literary activity in London, which is his acknowledged original invention of a genre in Greek literature: the "Modern Greek short story". In the British capital, he will compose five of the famous six short stories that he will publish between April 1883 and November 1884.

His first published short story was "My Mother's Sin", referred to earlier. This is considered his best short story (Wyatt, 1988a). Indeed, it is the most famous and widely read among the six stories, constituting today part of the curriculum in Greece's public senior high schools (Akrivos et al., 2010). Yet he had written two other stories before it (Moulas, 1980). Those do not seem to generate something equally genuine, apart from articulating the signifier "Vizyenos" to the signifier "novelist" for the first time.

The two short stories apparently written before "My Mother's Sin" (1883a) but published after it are "Between Piraeus and Naples" (1883c) and "The Consequences of the Old Story" (1884b). They seem to be Georgios' weaker short stories (Moulas, 1980). I believe it not accidental that in both stories he is imitating pre-existing literary genres. The first is written in the style of travelogue, the second in that of a romantic novel influenced deeply by the German tradition (Alexiou, 1995; Chrysanthopoulos, 1994; Moulas, 1980). In fact, it includes references to Goethe, Wagner, and Heine, and it even takes place in Germany.

The "travelogue" "Between Piraeus and Naples" (1883c) is about the flirtatious encounter between an adolescent girl and a travelling poet taking place on a maritime journey from Piraeus to Naples. The poet aspires to join the girl's rich family in a diplomatic appointment to Calcutta, where he is invited by her father, a wealthy businessman but incompetent poet. When the main character is informed of the girl's father's intentions—to make him a unique audience for his own meagre poetic endeavours and to ensure that the girl will be left behind—he decides to turn down the invitation (Vizyenos, 1883c).

"The Consequences of the Old Story" (1884b) is about the unfortunate platonic affair between a friend of the narrator, who is a Greek student of psychology in Germany, and a German girl. The narrator's friend considers himself unworthy of the girl's pure feelings due to a traumatic past love affair. He therefore resists her. In the end, due to a manipulative intervention by the girl's father, a well-respected professor, the two lovers separate, the girl goes mad, and both die the same day.

What we will keep from the two aforementioned stories, since their originality is somehow questionable, is the rich and prestigious father characters; as was remarked earlier, this is the kind of father that exists in Vizyenos' cosmos. Yet if in those stories, which were probably written first, Georgios is imitating other writing genres and styles, in the other four—three of them written in London—he seems to do something similar to what he did in some poems in "Attic Breezes" and his children's poetry: utilising, in an original style, elements from lalangue.

The remaining London stories—following "My Mother's Sin" (Vizyenos, 1883a), in which he is exposing Mother's tragic secret—are "Who Was My Brother's Killer?" (Vizyenos, 1883b) and "The Only Journey of His Life" (Vizyenos, 1884a).

In "Who Was My Brother's Killer?" Georgios writes about his older brother's obscure murder and the quest for his murderer, who proves to be someone Mother had nursed in the past. When this man finds out he has killed his saviour's older son without knowing it, the unintentional murderer goes mad. The narrator is left wondering whether it is him or the abettor who should be regarded as his brother's killer (Vizyenos, 1883b). It has been suggested that Vizyenos wrote this story following the patterns of Sophocles' *Oedipus Rex* (Hemrich, 1985).

"The Only Journey of His Life" (Vizyenos, 1884a) will become, along with "My Mother's Sin", the most favourite short story in Greece. It has been turned into a film and staged as a theatrical play more than once (Kyriakos, 2009). In this story, the narrator is George, a ten-year-old boy working in a Constantinople-based tailor's workshop. He complains of the fake stories that had enticed him to become a tailor, which his grandfather had brought him up with when he was younger—and which are, in fact, myths, legends, and fairy tales. Yet he is later given the opportunity to find out that his grandfather had himself been tricked by those stories, believing them to be true when, to avoid compulsory recruitment into the Ottoman army (Nicolle & Hook, 1995), he was brought up by his parents as a girl (Vizyenos, 1884a). The same peculiar event in the family history, of a boy being raised as a girl, will characterise Vizyenos' last leading character in the homonymous short-story "Moscov-Selim" (1895), which will, however, be written two or three years after his departure from London.

Therefore, the five short stories written in London, next to "Moscov-Selim", can be viewed as a thematic elaboration upon the being of the child. In fact, this goes as far as researching the question of the child's confusion of gender identity, which takes place in the two last short stories. This subject seems significant not only because it examines an aspect of childhood, but because it touches upon the subjective history of his author, a boy who was expected a girl and whose body was offered to God by Mother in exchange for the salvation of his sickly sister's body (Vizyenos, 1883a).

But Georgios' research of childhood in his magnum opus, which is his short stories, is not only thematic. Like his children's poetry, his use of language in them also presents a status we have not met before; a status that could be linked to the real that touches the child's body.

On the one hand, he illustrates a versatile use of language style in his fiction, as he had also done in his poetry. In fact, instead of choosing to use katharevousa or the demotic, this time he is using both! He uses katharevousa for his narration and for the discourse of people in high positions, and the demotic for the discourse of people like his family and peasants from Thrace. Yet along with this skilled use of formalism, in the three autobiographical stories, as well as in "Moscov-Selim", he includes something of a different form but similar nature to the sounds he used in children's poems and "Attic Breezes": Thracian monosyllabic exclamations and, more importantly, words in Turkish.

Next to the combined use of elements from both katharevousa and the demotic, in those four short stories Georgios adds units from the language of the Turks, which, for Greeks, is not just another foreign language. It is the language of the people whom Greeks saw as violently occupying Greek lands, like Georgios' village. It is, moreover, the language he and his family had to learn in spite of being Greek. Turkish words used in those stories are given a critical part in the plot

(Dimasi, 2013). Yet what seems to be most important about their function is that they are left untranslated:

> It was the cries of the *eféntis'* wives, children, and babes, who leaped up and fled to their *harem* in disorderly haste out of fear I might see them without their *yasmáki*. Kyamíl, in his small, show-white *saríki*, his long, green *tsubé*, with his pale and likeable expression, almost as tall as the wall of the forecourt, regularly opened the gate for me with that sweet, sad smile on his lips as he bent to the ground in the deep and heartfelt *temenás* of welcome. (Vizyenos, G., [1883c] 1988, p. 71)
>
> Because every so often, my dear," said Grandfather still more gloomily, "the *Yanitsarió* came out—huge, terrifying Turks with their high *kavúkia* and their red *kavádia*—and they made the round of the villages under arms with the *imám* in front and the *tseláti* behind, and they gathered up the best-looking and smartest Christian boys and made Turks out of them. (Vizyenos, G., [1884a] 1988, p. 178)

As an effect, in their only existing English version until 2014, William Wyatt (1988b), the translator, had to include a few pages before each story giving definitions for those words, which he left untranslated to retain a bit of the colour of the original (p. 54). It would seem, indeed, pointless to subtract these elements from Vizyenos' fiction.

Georgios' use of the language of the people who were believed to brutally occupy Greece makes his writing unique in a twofold way: it generates something new both for literature and for himself.

Concerning Modern Greek literature, this use of Turkish is unique because in a place and an era when nationalism was thriving (Moulas, 1980), Vizyenos did not hesitate to use the language of foreign occupation in his short stories. Of course, after five centuries of Ottoman occupation in Thrace, Turkish words were already a part of the Greek vocabulary. Yet recent research showed that only half out of the 232 Turkish words found in Vizyenos' short stories are part of the actual common vocabulary of the two languages (Dimasi, 2013). The majority of the rest must be Georgios' own introductions. This clashes once more with the supporters of katharevousa, who considered foreign words, let alone Turkish ones, as units that polluted Greek.

The Greek language therefore would never be as free as it was from foreign, let alone hostile, influences, after the publication of those short stories. In them, Georgios does the exact opposite of what was aimed at by katharevousa, i.e., to "purify" Greek from foreign influences. He uses Turkish to vaccinate Greek with words that carry something of a different nature to signifiers that lead to signification; one that ex-sists for Greeks and their language. Imagine how the Greek literary audience, coming across those words in highly esteemed periodicals, must have felt when the spirit of the era was to eliminate not only the Turkish language but the yoke of the Ottomans from Greek lands still under occupation. Indifferent to the expectations of the social and literary Other, Georgios reinserts into Greek literature what others wanted to expel.

Yet this operation also carries a subjective weight for him, which is directly related to his need to bring the real of the child under the aegis of the symbolic, and therefore to localise the jouissance inherent in it, which is pulling his body to the side of the dead girl. Similar to the sounds from nature inserted into his children's poetry, words in Turkish, which was of course spoken in Vizyi, where he passed his childhood, might have been experienced by him as units of lalangue that do not carry a meaning in Greek, the language of communication. They could have been experienced as the language of Greece's persecutors, its real, which marked his child's body. Thus, his use of them untranslated at critical points in his fiction constitutes his practice similar to that of Joyce's epiphanies, phrases that link the real to the unconscious (Lacan, 1975–1976). Like, Joyce, whose answer to the hole of paternity generated utterances like "Riverrun, past Eve and Adam's, from swerve of shore to bend of bay" (1939, p. 3), Vizyenos' answer to what a child is was "with their high kavúkia and their red kavádia" (1884c, p. 178).

It might not be accidental that the aforementioned forms of actively treating lalangue that Georgios proceeds to—the use of sounds from nature in children's poetry and Turkish words and Thracian exclamations in his short stories—are found in the last stages of his composition of poetry and fiction. His children's poems are the last signs of mainstream poetry of his of which we know, whereas the aforementioned short stories were apparently the last of the big six written, despite "Between Piraeus and Naples" and "The Consequences of the Old Story" having been published as second and fourth.

Those works could be the pillars of his stepladder, the narcissistic pedestal that lifted the child's body far above scornful remarks about the genuineness of his writing and the beauty of his face and placed him by the side of those names from classic literature he was alluding to. In effect, his biographer and friend Nicolas Vasiliadis (1910) narrates that in Georgios' flat in Athens there was a library filled with luxurious publications from classical literature, and in a shelve there was his own small pile of expensive publications.

Georgios appeared indeed passionate about his collections being published in luxurious editions. He partly achieved this thanks not to Zarifis' expenses (Athanasopoulos, 1992; Moulas, 1980) but to donations from the Greek community in London (Papakostas, 2004; Varelas, 2014) to the Trübner publishing house. The Greek poet Kostis Palamas (1994) recalls the thick and well-printed volume Vizyenos carried with him, making those who saw him feel jealous.

Even if that had been indeed Georgios' intention, the beautifying function of his publications cannot be ignored; they raised his body, the body of a child, upon a pedestal that kept it away from known dangers. I think that what we find before us is the knotting of a body and its organs to a beautified child's image based on the signifier, an achievement generated thanks to a personal invention that reached its peak after leaving Athens in 1875 and before his return there in 1884.

Unfortunately, leaving London and stopping that elaboration made his edifice—and, consequently, his body image—vacillate and eventually collapse.

Leaving London was not Georgios' own choice. He was forced to do so by a sudden event that would make things very difficult for him. An end was put to his bright rise by the death of his patron on March 17th, 1884 (Athanasopoulos, 1992). He thus had to return unprepared to Athens and make a living for the first time after many years.

A sudden downfall

The remnants of Vizyenos

In Athens Georgios will strive to maintain what remained of his stepladder, which would not prove an easy business. Zarifis' funds were suddenly no longer available, so no expensive publications were safeguarded for the pillars of his edifice. Resources had to be found not simply for his publications, as he did when he first researched the mines of Samakovo, but for his living too.

However, Athens was never a friendly environment for him. This was a place where literary and social circles did not welcome him whole-heartedly; neither did they affirm his having a bright body. For the next few years, he would try to maintain his old glory, but his creation, which reached its peak in London, was now vacillating dangerously.

He will publish three much shorter stories up until the beginning of 1885: "May Day" in the newspaper *Acropolis*, the children's story "Tromaras" in the children's periodical *The Edification of Children*, and "Why the Apple Tree Did Not Become the Apple-Bearing Tree" in *Estia*. It seems that in the last one, fragments from which were presented in Chapter Four, Georgios is purposely exploiting his reading of Plato. In it we find resonances with the Platonic dialogues *Euthyphro* and *Cratylus* (Kantzia, 2009). With one exception, his known fiction ends then (Beaton, 1988). He seems to have written two more short stories, "The Destroyed [or Damaged] Festival" and "Corneras", but they did not survive (Varelas, 2014). Therefore, we do not know if in them he continued the instrumentalisation of elements that resonate with the One.

The same happened with an older, lost theatrical play in five acts, called "Diamanto" (Moulas, 1980; Papadopoulou, 2009; Varelas, 2014). This points to another signifier, "playwright", of whose content and quality, unfortunately, we have no evidence either. What we do know is that Vizyenos admired deeply Henrik Ibsen, for whom he would write a paper after a few years (1892). It might not be totally wrong to assume that there may have been allusions to the Norwegian playwright in his own drama, as there were in his short stories (Papadopoulou, 2009).

During this period, Georgios turns to teaching at Athenian high schools and occasionally writing for periodicals to make a living, while in the meantime he deals with the theoretical subjects he studied in Germany. He submits a second thesis in philosophy, which he has started in London, for a fellowship at the University of Athens, entitled: "The philosophy of beauty according to Plotinus". One cannot but highlight his interest in the neo-Platonic philosopher's approach to beauty, which he was so passionate about (Vasiliadis, 1910). Georgios is appointed an assistant professor of history of philosophy but never teaches at the university (Athanasopoulos, 1992; Beaton, 1988; Varelas, 2014). The signifier "professor", however, will linger, since it will be noted as his profession in the documents accompanying his admission to the psychiatric hospital.

Another opportunity for him to earn a living under the signifier "folklorist" was missed during the first months of 1885. The Ministry of Foreign Affairs had decided to commission him to write a study of the folk tradition of Greek lands under occupation, like Thrace. Yet Charilaos Trikoupis, the incumbent Prime Minister, lost the parliamentary elections of April (Keridis, 2009). The plan was abandoned and Trikoupis' supporters, like Georgios, were then removed from positions in the public sector by the supporters of his rival, new Prime Minister Theodore Diligiannis (Clogg, 2013).

Thus, next to the sudden collapse of Trikoupis' foreign minister's initiative, Georgios was also removed from the Athenian high school where he was teaching (Xireas, 1949). He was appointed to the high school in the island of Syros, but he never went there (Koutrianou, 2003; Varelas, 2014). For some time, he managed to get paid by taking sick leave, confirmed by medical reports. According to Varelas (2014), this is when the first signs of the disease that would result in his admission to the asylum appear.

One year later, and while in the meantime Trikoupis has resumed power, Vizyenos' interest in the abandoned mine of Samakovo revived (Koutrianou, 2003). He made a few trips to Thrace to pursue that opportunity. He would dive in the mines with his brother and fellow-villagers to gather samples for foreign mining companies. It seems that the name "Vizyenos" was no longer enough for knotting his body to the Thracian soil. The former had to dive actually beneath the ground.

His occupation with the mine gradually became an obsession. He even made poor Michael, his only surviving brother, sell land he owned in order to fund the expedition (Athanasopoulos, 1992). Yet this new signifier of "businessman" will gradually overshadow and replace the others. The Athenian press did not hesitate to mock that endeavour writing that "Mr. Vizyenos' mines must be mines of rhymes!" (Kaneis Allos, 1886).

Between 1886 and 1888, Georgios will, indeed, publish nothing, occupied as he is with the mining business. Whereas the outbreak of his psychosis is usually placed in 1892, the year of his admission, we might not be wrong in identifying it a few years earlier, in his new occupation with the mine, which is linked to a signifier that will become delusional.

Yet he writes a few papers and books up until the early 1890s, under the signifiers "professor in philosophy" ("Elements of Logic" (Vizyenos, 1885b)), "psychologist" ("Elements of Psychology" (Vizyenos, 1888b)), "folklorist" ("Monks and the Worship of Dionysus in Thrace" (Vizyenos, 1888a)), and "scholar" ("Fine arts during the first quarter century of the reign of George I" (Vizyenos, 1888c)), and entries in the *Bart & Hirst Encyclopaedic Dictionary* (Vizyenos, 1889–1892).

Very few poems of his—and no poetry collection—survive from that period. Although it had been repeatedly suggested (Athanasopoulos, 1992; Moulas, 1980) that he participated in the Philadelphian poetry contest in 1889, it was recently proved that he did not (Varelas, 2014), which explains why he was also ignored by critics.

On the other hand, between 1888 and 1889 another signifier related to art will be articulated to the signifier "Vizyenos": that of "trainer of actors/amateur director": he will be asked to help performers staging Sophocles' *Antigone* and Aeschylus' *Persians* to adjust to the ancient Greek text (Koutrianou, 2003; Papadopoulou, 2009).

A dissolving swarm of signifiers

An impressive amount of signifiers is therefore observed becoming articulated to the signifier "Vizyenos" in Georgios' almost thirty-year-long wandering. They are not limited to the ones Frou-Frou (1882) counted in his scornful article: "grocery servant; altar boy; tailor …" Georgios has also been a novice, a student of theology, an epic poet, a student of philosophy, a lyric poet, a children's psychologist, a folklorist, a writer of children's poetry, a fictionist, a professor in philosophy, a children's storyteller, an actor, a playwright, a high-school teacher, an encyclopaedic writer, and others. What is more, those signifiers often intentionally resonate with the styles of names whose heights he wishes to reach upon his stepladder: Homer, Sophocles, Plato, Plotinus, Sallust, Goethe, Ibsen, the Romantics, the Phanariotes, and others.

One might rightfully suggest seeing here a touch of what Lacan (1956a) highlighted about the symptomatology of many schizophrenic subjects: the personality that is copying some else's in obvious lack of genuineness, that is, Helene Deutsch's "as-if" (1942). However, it seems to me that in Georgios' case there are at least two major differences to Deutsch's concept.

First, this does not happen in everything Vizyenos writes: his children's poems, children's stories, and the majority of his short stories, in which language takes a particular form that was analysed above, are unanimously praised and recognised as original and genuine works (Moulas, 1980; 2013; Varelas, 2014). Second, and concurrently, next to this array of signifiers that might indeed show a propensity toward the "as-if", there is the master signifier "Vizyenos", which is articulated with them in a transcendental way. This invented signifier seems to link together all the composites of the swarm linked to professions, writing activities, and pre-existing writers, and to represent the subject for them.

In effect, this aspect of Georgios' life might be of use as a good illustration of the schizophrenic subject when it is being represented by a swarm of signifiers (Miller, 2001; Sauvagnat, 2000; Soler, 1999; Zenoni, 2012). This is another effect—analysed in Chapter Three—of the schizophrenic's inability to inhabit established discourse and abode by the make-believe, for which an S_1 is a prerequisite. However, the writing activity of our author, a man who did not seem to mind about being represented by an impressive array of identities—neither many schizophrenics seem to, due to their resistance to abide by established discourse—did not stop there. He proceeded, quite early, to an act of naming: he gave himself the name "Vizyenos". As was suggested above, that signifier achieved to some extent to circumscribe the One that, for Lacan (1972–1973) is the "signifying order" (p. 143) made up from the swarm of signifiers.

In fact, the beginning of his end would be accompanied by the contamination of this swarm by the delusional signifier "businessman", which would gradually overshadow all others and replace Georgios' representation by the signifier "Vizyenos". This will happen concurrently with the detachment of the body image from the subject; the body will then fall prey to the real aspect of language.

CHAPTER SIX

The psychotic breakdown

In the preceding chapters, we examined two periods in Georgios' life: his childhood and his adolescence and adulthood. In the first, we saw his starting point, the equation of "child" to a dead girl's body in the family history, a body that fell under the shadow of Mother's desire or jouissance. In the second, we examined the invention that raised that body on a narcissistic pedestal, a stepladder related to the signifier "child" that was renamed "Vizyenos".

However, there came a point when this master signifier could not keep the return of jouissance in the child's body at bay. After the 1880s, signifiers linked to the "having" rather than the "being" of the child took over Georgios' signifying representation. In the end, the outbreak of body phenomena flooding the child's body with jouissance was not avoided.

The end of signification and the beginning of delusion

The fragmentation of the body

As noted earlier, in the late 1880s the signifier "businessman" had started overshadowing the other signifiers in the swarm that the signifier

"Vizyenos" was articulated to. Georgios sustained some of his other identities, like "scholar" and "folklorist", whereas at the same time he spent long hours pursuing his mining business. In 1889 he travelled to Thrace for the last time, to pursue its realisation.

After his return to Athens he was offered a new position and the chance to articulate a new signifier to the signifier "Vizyenos": that of professor of Rhythmic and Dramaturgy at the Athens Conservatoire. He accepted it happily, but his teaching suddenly stopped. He had to leave Athens temporarily for the last time.

A "mysterious" disease had appeared. It would be attributed to an unfortunate sexual encounter in Germany, a venereal disease (Athanasopoulos, 1992; Papakostas, 2004; Varelas, 2014). Georgios will use the times' formal term, "a disease of the marrow" (Moulas, 1980; Papakostas, 2004). From the diagnosis of general paralysis that he will be given upon his admission, we deduce that it was considered a manifestation of a syphilitic infection.

Having probably presented symptoms from the mid-1880s already (Varelas, 2014), Georgios was prescribed a visit to the Austrian spa city of Gastein for shower-therapy. He did so in August 1890. He did not stay in Gastein for longer than a month and a half, due to the high cost of therapy and accommodation (Vizyenos, 1890). A very enlightening document survives from his stay in Gastein, where he describes his condition before returning to Athens. It is a letter to his brother, Michael, from which the part where he refers to his condition is presented below:

> But the bad news is that I am feeling the presence of the disease each and every moment not only because I often feel a sense of heat throughout the entire length of the backbone in both sides, but also because it has now been some time that my lower legs have been as if they have become numb from the cold and they cannot get easily warmed. Moreover, this weakness of the legs puts me in despair. I cannot and I am not allowed to walk for more than one quarter of the hour, without a need to rest for at least as much time. On the other hand, each time I try to walk for more time and to enjoy the beauty of this place right here, my condition is getting worse, and I cannot sleep at night due to the suffering I have in my back. Nonetheless, during my walking the disease is definitely not displayed as a walking disorder, as is the case with others who suffer

worse. Only from time to time and according to the fatigue my knee suddenly bends without noticing it in order to prevent it. I have already made 17 baths here; the doctor has not allowed me to do more than that. Since the nature of the baths is such as to weaken in the beginning, I am presently found in a very weak condition during these days, and consequently I am very nervous and sensitive, a thing on which I did not want to write you so as not to behave to you as well more roughly than appropriate about your errors and so as not to appear too much of a complainer. However, I could not restrain myself and, now that I have said everything, I see that the thing has upset me and has moved me more than I was afraid of. My tears have been running ceaselessly for no other reason than because the weakness of my nerves has been greater. (Vizyenos, G., [1890] 2004, pp. 73–75)

Reading these lines, one cannot but put forward the hypothesis that at this stage Georgios has started experiencing not being the master of his body: his legs, his knees, and even his eyes move without his being able to control them. In contrast to the acquisition of the body image that is established in the mirror stage, which gives to the infant a jubilant sentiment thanks to it being viewed as a *Gestalt* (Lacan, 1949), Georgios is here feeling the effects of the fragmented body, which precedes this and in his case is related to the dead girl's body. Those symptoms might have indeed been caused by a syphilitic infection, yet their effect upon the imaginary constitution of the subject is unquestionable; the body image, which he had struggled for years to dress with a narcissistic brightness, is being experienced as fragmented, like the decaying bodies of his smothered first and his sickly second sister. The child's body is not under his control any more. The stepladder's beauty is lost. Georgios returns to the condition where someone else is the master of his body.

When he returns from Austria in late 1890, he is seen in an excited mood and mobility, characterised by nervousness and overwhelming productivity (Athanasopoulos, 1992). He only speaks about the old iron mine in Samakovo. Needless to say, this has in the meantime been deemed a worthless investment by estimators, which shows clearly his indifference to the Other's judgment. Hassiotis, his penultimate patron, writes about having met Georgios again in Paris, where the latter has apparently travelled despite his meagre finances to promote the mining business. Hassiotis is surprised to hear that instead of spiritual works and laurers, Vizyenos is continuously speaking of a mining business, to exploit which he is seeking for capitals (1910).

Georgios' old patron is describing accurately the predominance of this new signifier over Vizyenos' old endeavours. It seems that the body's coherence, which must have been seriously damaged by the illness, was no longer linked to the creation of his singular discourse but to the acquisition of resources. Yet this will only realise in his delusion.

His agitated mood and nervousness after his return from Gastein was channelled into the mining business and some theoretical work. He returned to teaching at the Conservatoire, he started composing a study of Zeller's philosophy and translated famous European ballads for a study published a few years later, "On Helicon: Ballads" (Vizyenos, 1894). However, within that fruitful activity he also presented signs of inappropriate language and behaviour, which are linked to a new, delusional, signifier: "patron".

The body prey to language

Georgios once behaved inappropriately after a long night's study. He started shouting and throwing stones at the neighbours' roosters, upsetting the neighbourhood (Athanasopoulos, 1992). This was testified to by his landlady, Sofia Fravasilis, who would play a critical part in his final breakdown and admission to hospital.

After his return from London, Georgios had rented two rooms at the house of Antonio Fravasilis, a Hellenised Italian merchant who had two daughters, Bettina and Itala. They lived in a neoclassical building that still stands in the centre of Athens. Georgios had converted one of its floors to a study and living space (Athanasopoulos, 1992).

Georgios had gradually become a family friend of the Fravasilis'. He would take their girls to the park when they were younger. He had even negotiated for Bettina to be offered a scholarship at the Conservatoire, as she was a talented pianist (Athanasopoulos, 1992). After Fravasilis' death, his widow decided to rent the floor of the luxurious building where the family resided. She moved with her daughters and mother-in-law to a smaller house. This happened in early 1892, a year after Georgios' return from Austria. However, the forty-three-year-old man's feelings for Bettina had changed. Formerly a family friend who wanted to stand in her father's place, he now became an aspiring suitor.

In a series of visits to the Fravasilis' new household, Georgios offered flowers to Bettina, expressing his admiration for her beauty, purity, and artistic talent. These first visits did not worry her mother (Athanasopoulos, 1992). In the meantime, he visited his old friends to ask for money to hold the wedding. Georgios spoke about it as an agreed business and offered as guarantee shares from the exploitation of the worthless iron mine. None of his friends lent him the money. This made him extremely angry. People were refusing to recognise him by the identity of "wealthy businessman". Yet the problem with the wedding was not only that there was no money with which to hold it, but that the bride knew absolutely nothing about it.

Georgios visited Bettina's mother to ask for her hand in marriage some days later. He first talked to her about his recent success in making hugely profitable agreements with foreign businessmen about the Samakovo mine. Sofia responded to the news with joy, believing them to be true. Then Georgios shocked her by announcing that he intended to marry her fourteen- or sixteen-year-old daughter—there have been testimonies about her being even younger (Athanasopoulos, 1992)—and make her queen of a rich household. Sofia tried to buy time, asking of him to return after three days for her final answer. Georgios did so, but her answer was still negative.

Georgios tried to change Sofia's mind, speaking of the immense wealth with which he supposedly supported an orphan girl in Constantinople. The latter was not true of course. In fact, it adds to the delusional signifier "businessman" that of "patron". Georgios seems to be aspiring to occupy a place similar to that of Georgiades (his first patron), Zarifis, or even his foster-grandfather, all of whom treated children like merchandise. Georgios is now the aspiring owner of children, more specifically, the master of girls' bodies, via a nonexistent treasure.

Bettina's mother tries to calm Georgios down, saying he should wait for her daughter to grow up. Yet he can only see her response as a final and absolute refusal. He leaves the Fravasilis' angry, but his wish to marry Bettina does not cease. He returns in an unkempt appearance at five o'clock in the morning to try persuade her run away with him. After having paced nervously up and down in front of Bettina's window, her mother tells him to leave. He leaves after many hours, calling her names and using words that he was never before known to use (Athanasopoulos, 1992).

This is not the only time during this period that he employs inappropriate language. During a friend's visit to his apartment in early April, an impressive amount of unreadable and incomplete poems, full of inappropriate language and vulgar expressions, were seen on his desk (Valettas, 1892). Athanasopoulos (1992) suggests that they must look like other titles Valettas notes like: "On my lonely mattress", "Open your pure thighs", and "Don't pull yourself away in bed, my light!" The same witness narrates that Vizyenos had turned into a speedy verse-writing machine (Valettas, 1892)!

This testimony seems exemplary of the organ of language having taken over the body. Georgios' body does not belong to him any more—but he is it. He belongs to the Other of language. We see manifesting what Zenoni (2012) describes as language and body passing in the real.

The incident involving Sofia Fravasilis took place during the first days of April 1892. On April 11th, the newspaper *Acropolis* announced that Vizyenos lost his mind. He apparently attempted to kill himself twice (Athanasopoulos, 1992). His admission to an institution was imminent. It took place two days after the second alleged suicide attempt. There are two different descriptions of how this happened.

According to the first version, Georgios went with his friends on an excursion to the western suburbs of Athens. They had enticed him by promising to abduct Bettina and hold the wedding in the country. On their return, he was led to the Dromokaiteion hospital (Athanasopoulos, 1992).

According to another version, which seems less likely, since this biographer of his is not always reliable (Athanasopoulos, 1992; Moulas, 1980), when returning from the university one day Vasiliadis found Georgios in a small beer tavern, after being informed that the poet had gone mad. He was sitting between two friends and murmuring verse incessantly, inspired by passers-by or anything he was told. According to his friend, "that was not poetry; it was a poetic stream of the moment" (Vasiliadis, 1910, p. 321). We observe once again therefore his body having fallen prey to the organ of language. Even if this incident did not happen one day before Georgios' admission, it confirms the impression given by Valettas (1892). The following day, after a tormenting night full of freak-outs, moaning, and groaning, Georgios was escorted to the asylum (Vasiliadis, 1910, p. 322)

We see therefore two testimonies where poetry is being imposed upon our poet. He has become its direct medium; it is being enforced upon him. In his state in those testimonies we can read Lacan's (1956a, p. 250) remark that the psychotic is "inhabited, possessed by language". In what comes out of Georgios' mouth and hand in those incidents—and what will occur in the asylum—he is indeed being "spoken rather than speaking" (Lacan, 1953a: 234). The schizophrenic becoming an instrument of language, of which the "speedy machine" can be a graphic illustration, describes a crucial moment for the subject: its disappearance.

If this is indeed a manifestation of language having taken over the subject's body, it is not hard to explain Georgios' attempts to flee from the stage by trying to kill himself. The passage to the act, during which the subject disappears, is viewed in psychoanalysis as a radical attempt to separate from the Other (Miller, 1986; Verhaeghe, 2008). Of course, the Other that Georgios is trying to detach himself from is language unresolved from the signifier, the symbolic unseparated from the real, which, for the schizophrenic, is the only Other (Miller, 2001).

There is no detailed information available on how Georgios exactly attempts to put an end to his life. Yet the fact that he is reported to have tried this twice shows how unbearable the return of jouissance to the body must have been for him. This intolerable condition probably triggers those unsuccessful attempts at a separation. Yet they do not result in the subject's absolute disappearance. Georgios does not die, although the subject does not appear in the same condition as before. Like those of Caesar, who is a new subject after crossing the Rubicon (Lacan, 1955b; Miller, 1986; Stevens, 2009), Georgios' acts also have an effect on the subject. The picture he presents after his suicide attempts is much different to that presented in the past.

In the asylum

General paralysis of the insane

Also known as general paresis, Georgios' diagnosis upon his admission, general paralysis of the insane, was a not infrequent psychiatric disorder in Europe (Hare, 1959). It was attributed to syphilis. It is nowadays conceived as a neuropsychiatric disorder. A sub-chapter was later dedicated to it in Kraepelin's (1913) psychiatric textbook as "dementia paralytica" or "general paresis". It has now been extinguished in the Western world thanks to the invention of antibiotics.

There is very scarce evidence of Georgios' love life and, consequently, of whether he could have contracted a venereal disease. Nevertheless, his symptomatology, the age at which it usually appeared, and its progressive character agree with his diagnosis. General paralysis is considered as mainly affecting men between twenty-five and forty-five and occurring ten to thirty years after infection. It manifests in fatigue, dizziness, loss of social inhibitions, asocial behaviour, gradual impairment of judgment, euphoria, mania, depression or apathy. It is also characterised by mental deterioration and personality changes as the disease progresses (Beck, 2008; Koshy, 2012).

On the other hand, suffering from general paralysis does not change much concerning our reading of his subjectivity. In fact, as notes Leader (2011), Paul Schilder's studies of the 1920s proved that the psychotic symptoms of patients suffering from syphilitic infections were "grounded in their pre-infection personalities, disproving the idea that the area of the brain that had been damaged would determine the person's symptomology" (p. 567). Verhaeghe (2008) also points out that a somatically etiological approach does not suffice to explain the fact that very few patients affected by syphilitic infections in the end presented paralytic dementia.

Therefore, even if the outbreak of some of Georgios' physical symptoms can be explained by the diagnosis of general paralysis, their content, as well as the patient's subjective relation to reality, cannot be attributed to, or at least fully explained by it. But even if it was, this would be of minor importance to a psychoanalytic case history, since, as Lacan also writes about psychosis:

> The only organicity that is essentially involved in this process [is] the organicity that motivates the structure of signification. (Lacan, J., [1958a] 2006, p. 477)

On the other hand, as was assumed above, the symptoms of general paralysis could be related to the outbreak of schizophrenic symptomatology with regards to making Georgios feel he is not the master of his body, a condition he described graphically in his letter to his brother.

It seems that the experience, probably caused by general paralysis, that he had in Gastein—and which he portrays in detail—must have triggered the derangement of the child's body's narcissistic covering and its return to the status of a dead girl's body.

Master of children's bodies

Georgios' condition in the asylum is described as deteriorating gradually, confirming the psychiatric diagnosis of general paralysis. During his friends' first visits, he is able to maintain lengthy conversations, whereas less than four years later he has completely withdrawn from any contact with the hospital's small community.

He will initially treat a number of visitors and other figures in the asylum the same way he had treated Bettina: as children's bodies he lays claim to thanks to immense wealth. During this period, his appearance will be closer than ever to late-nineteenth-century psychiatric patients, like the ones described in Kraepelin's textbooks.

When, during walks in the woods, he is escorted by a guard, Georgios confuses his own identity and that of the guard. He tries to comfort the guard, telling him that he will get well soon and advising him to turn to Georgios as soon as he is released from the asylum. Georgios declares that he will employ him at his mining business (Athanasopoulos, 1992).

In the aforementioned example, one can clearly see the confusion between Georgios and others' images, a recurrent phenomenon in the asylum, indicative of the precarious character of specular relations for him. As was noted in *Part I*, paranoid delusions use this as a starting point.

Yet in Georgios' life in the asylum the Other's evil in the form of jouissance is not limited to certain figures, as happens in paranoia (Deffieux, 2014; Miller, 2001). Let us not forget to note that nothing like this had happened before his admission to the asylum; despite his clash with the Athenian social and literary establishment, Georgios never presented any propensity to localise jouissance in the field of the Other (Lacan, 1975b), as he attempted in his unstructured delusions in the hospital. In there, jouissance could be attributed to any figure. For example, Georgios confessed to another visitor that he found it important for King George to be convinced that Vizyenos did not intend to give 700 million to Prime Minister Diligiannis ("Kiris", 1895).

Another testimony comes from another friend and former high school student, Stephen Stefanou, who visited Georgios during his first year at the Dromokaiteion. He wrote that the poet did not initially seem insane to him and that he felt that Georgios should not be in the asylum. However, Georgios then tells him that he can help Stefanou study abroad by assisting him financially, the same way he himself has been helped by others in the past. The student becomes worried and slightly scared. Georgios then takes a business card out of his wallet and writes in French to Credit-Lyonnais to pay Stefanou 100,000 francs for him to spend it wherever he fancies (Stefanou, 1936).

Three years after Georgios' admission, the same guest to whom he spoke about the King and the Prime Minister visits the ward's doctor. He wants to ask for more information about Georgios' condition and his prognosis. The medical expectations in his forty-sixth year were that there was not a single glimpse of hope and, since he was suffering from general paralysis, that Georgios' life was now only a matter of days ("Kiris", 1895).

The absolute abandonment of Narcissus

The end of Georgios' life proved not to be mere days away, but this did not change much. He died in April 1896, eleven months after his friend's visit in May 1895.

He gradually withdrew from the asylum's community. From the early days of April, he stayed in bed, being unable to move around, even when helped by others. He did not eat and his facial features became deformed. Things became more serious on April the 12th, when he could not feel anything and was only fed with milk and some broth (Athanasopoulos, 1992). This might remind one of catatonia, which is also the most severe manifestation of schizophrenia, the "collapse of psychic reality'" (Redmond, 2013). In schizophrenic psychosis, catatonic episodes show that the body is diminished to an empty bag (Biagi-Chai, 2014).

The complete detachment of the imaginary itself leads to the picture Georgios presents in his last days in the asylum. Confined to his room, he is unable to walk, move or speak. Jouissance has taken complete control of the body; the real and reality, subject and object, are one (Biagi-Chai, 2014). Any remaining subjective mark has been erased and Georgios will, very soon, pass away. The Other has been removed from his place and the subject cannot even sustain himself at the position of Narcissus (Lacan, 1958a). It seems that at this final point Georgios is not even capable of identifying precariously with the specular other's image.

On the morning of April, the 15th, it is obvious that death is imminent, so they try give Georgios his last communion. He resists it, refusing to open his mouth. He is refusing to consent to a ritual of a discourse—itself an established one—in which he has long ago expressed his disbelief. Finally, he concedes in the evening and dies after a few hours, exactly four years after his admission on April 14th, 1892 (Athanasopoulos, 1992).

Two days after the closing ceremony of the first modern Olympic Games, the Athenian elite, which had treated him rather harshly, attends his funeral taking place at public expense at the church of Saint George Karytsis in central Athens. Stripped of the narcissistic brightness it had held for more than two decades, the mature child's body is interned at the First Cemetery of Athens (Moulas, 1980). It has now met the destity of Georgios' other deceased siblings: that of Mother's –φ or a.

CHAPTER SEVEN

"Knotting it up": a topological approach to Vizyenos

s was explained in Chapter Three, in Lacan's later teaching subjectivity is maintained by the real, the symbolic, and the imaginary holding to each other through either a Borromean knot or a supplementary fourth ring, the sinthome. If Georgios' writing as Vizyenos achieved a temporal subsistence of the subject—the effects of whose disappearance were discussed above—could this have come about by a fourth ring that knotted the detached real, symbolic, and imaginary?

His case was analysed in the three preceding chapters. Chapter Four examined the status of the child's body as Mother's $-\varphi$ or a—a destiny also shared by his two dead sisters, the one preceding him and the one following him—and the resistance to symbolisation. Chapter Five investigated Georgios' writing endeavour, which attributed a different aspect to his body. Under the invented signifier "Vizyenos" a stepladder was constructed for the child's body, which was covered with narcissistic brightness that put it next to names from classical literature, aiming at the same time at elements from lalangue. His body was thus won over against language. Finally, Chapter Six concerned the dissolution of this edifice, the breakdown that led to the outbreak of psychotic symptoms of the return of jouissance to the body, and Georgios' admission to the lunatic asylum.

If those parts were brought together to summarise his life from birth to death, we could come up with a linear sequence that would look like this:

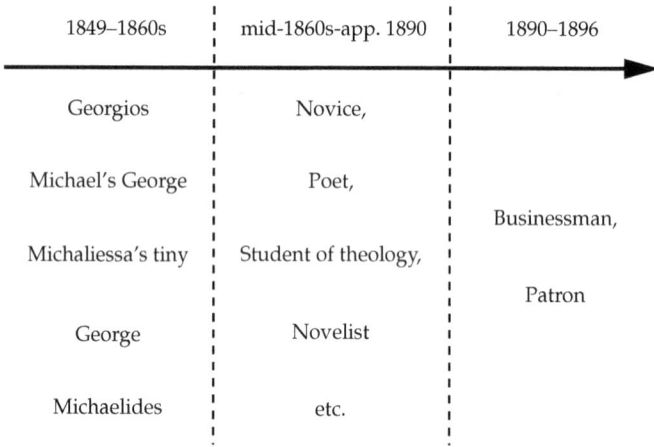

1849–1860s	mid-1860s-app. 1890	1890–1896
Georgios	Novice,	
Michael's George	Poet,	
		Businessman,
Michaliessa's tiny	Student of theology,	
		Patron
George	Novelist	
Michaelides	etc.	

Figure 5. Linear approach to Vizyenos.

Under the three separate periods, I have noted the subject's respective signifying representation: on the left hand side we read "Georgios", "Michael's George", "Michaliessa's tiny George", and "Michaelides", and on the right the delusional signifiers "patron" and "businessman".

Those groups of signifiers come from different periods. Yet they have something in common with regards to the signifier "child", which is interrupted by the second period, when the signifier "Vizyenos" is adopted in naming the "child". They both describe the child as an item that belongs to a master; they limit the being of this signifier to the level of having; the having that in the family history concerns girls'—dead—bodies. In Georgios' childhood, signifiers show that he belongs to a lineage of motherly figures who simply have and lose children, primarily girls (Grandfather Georgie, Michael, and Michaliessa). This is turned upside down in the early 1890s, when Vizyenos becomes that master's figure to whom as "patron" and "businessman" other children's bodies belong (we first saw two girls, Bettina and an inexistent orphan girl in Constantinople, and then his former high-school students visiting him in the asylum and the hospital guard).

On the other hand, the swarm of signifiers that represent the subject during the second period are articulated to the signifier "Vizyenos". Those signifiers do not represent the child as a body belonging to someone, but say something about its being and circumscribe the real of the signifier "child" under the writer's invented name. During this period, Georgios leads a life with no manifest psychotic symptoms and achieves a minimal insertion into a part of the social bond based on the narcissistic effect of this edifice.

However, to substantiate the hypothesis that this invention has the effects of a sinthomatic knotting, we must leave behind the preceding chapters' chronological perspective and move towards a topological approach. Miller (2011) suggests that for Lacan, in the end, the real—which is our compass in the study of subjectivity—is topology.

Such a direction will highlight one of the reasons for which there is one more clinical lesson to be drawn from this case for the "secretary to the insane". The sinthomatic study of Georgios' case can form a paradigm of a subject having been able to compensate for the lack of help from the established discourses by achieving a temporary but subjective treatment of the major risk that schizophrenic subjects run: of jouissance, detached as it may be from the body image, returning to the body. Understanding how some subjects achieve this can make us think about directions in which to orient work with subjects with a triggered psychosis (Leader, 2011). This is further suggested in *Part III*.

In the topological approach to his case below, it is argued that what Georgios creates seems to contribute to the acquisition of his body thanks to the change it brings with regards to its spatial constitution. His case therefore will now be studied in light of topology (τόπος [topos] = "locus") rather than chronology (χρόνος [chronos] = "time"), as happened in the pages above. Chronology, writes Soler (2014, p. 3) is inert itself, presenting a "drawback that is not entirely innocent", since it "elides the One that links all the textual variations," which we have suggested being linked, in Georgios' case, to the signifier "child".

Thus, in the following discussion, Lacan's topological approach to the real, the symbolic, and the imaginary is employed. The preceding chapters' linear approach is left behind.

The omnipresence of the Thing (real and symbolic)

The One

To depict the interconnection of the real and the symbolic in Georgios, I start with two rings directly linked to each other; the one on the left stands for the real (R) and the one on the right stands for the symbolic (S). Thus, the following shape is produced:

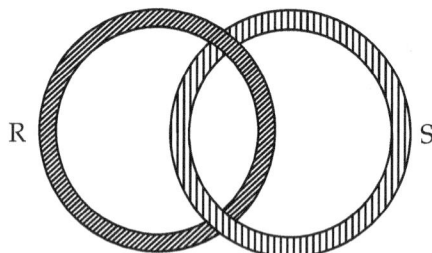

Figure 6. The real and the symbolic in Vizyenos.

This is not my original idea. I have borrowed it from the figure Lacan used to illustrate Joyce's case and, more specifically, the sinthome in the last lecture of *Seminar XXIII* (1975–1976). In fact, this is only one part of the figure Lacan drew on the board that day. The remaining part, not used here, shows how the imaginary is hooked onto the intertwined real and symbolic by use of the fourth ring, the *sinthome*. The reader can return to Chapter Three for the full image. The function of the imaginary in Georgios' case is discussed further below, after the present examination of the connection of the real to the symbolic.

One cannot overlook in this part of Lacan's suggested shape that the real and the symbolic, in spite of the undisputed absence of a Borromean knot, are already linked to each other. I believe this illustration portrays clearly what Freud describes when he writes that in schizophrenia word- and thing-presentations are not separated (1915e), which Lacan (1954) translates as all the symbolic being real for such subjects.

In the figure above, we can see a depiction of the status of some elements from language that the subject is confronted with regardless of time, i.e., if he is "Michael's George", the poet Vizyenos or the affluent businessman, a delusional identity. A few examples of what this formation consists of were presented earlier, such as "apple tree" and "children's play", both of which are linked to a signifier of vital importance for Georgios that we should also imagine in the intersection of the real and the symbolic: "child". This signifier is not void of jouissance. The corporeal aspect of the child has not been fully symbolised; it is in fact linked to the jouissance of dead girls' bodies.

In *Part I*, it was highlighted that the non-advent of separation, which refuses the schizophrenic subject the capacity to inhabit the established discourses, leaves jouissance inhabiting this space despite the success in the process of alienation. The small concentrations where phallic jouissance is found in neurotics, like the Freudian libidinal zones, have not been created. Subject and drive remain one "uncanny and always incomplete totality" (Verhaeghe, 2008, p. 210). Thus, in some signifiers jouissance lingers. Soler calls these signifiers—like "child" in this case—that alienation has not fully touched "real signifiers" (Soler, 1999).

However, it must be specified once more that this does not concern all signifiers. Not all words are like this for the schizophrenic. Not every signifier is a real signifier, whereas there might be cases where this never manifests (Leader, 2011). In Georgios' case, despite the particular status of the signifier "child", the subject was capable of making skilful use of the signifier's formalism. Many schizophrenics can under certain circumstances use language correctly (De Waelhens, 2001b). What we should imagine therefore as filling the two interrelated rings above is not only S_1s that have not parted from S_2s, "real signifiers" or holophrases, which are caught in the intersection, but also signifiers that have been assimilated by the symbolic.

On the other hand, it seems that the direct relation to language's real aspect never stops bearing a corresponding risk for the schizophrenic subject: to take over its body. If we read Freud's (1915e) examples in "The Unconscious" with the help of Lacan (1973a), schizophrenic body phenomena can be explained based on the fact that the body organs are signifiers that, as real, run the risk of allowing jouissance to run through them; to speak (Morel, 2011). Something of the same nature happened to Georgios, whose body, after the dissolution of his edifice, was handed back to language, the schizophrenic's only Other (Miller, 2001). Thus, even when he managed to enter a marginal part of the social bond under a narcissistic brightness that involved an instrumental use of lalangue, the two rings did not stop being intertwined. Jouissance, which inhabits some words more than others, was never properly distanced, although an aspect of it was certainly utilised by him for some time.

This is what a topological reading of cases like that of Georgios shows us: the interrelation of elements from the real and the symbolic does not vacillate. The constitution of parts from the real and the symbolic, the Thing, as directly linked to each other, is not therefore chronological. It never ends. With time, a new effect on how the imaginary is anchored to the real and the symbolic will emerge and Georgios will take a distance from it. Yet their interrelation per se will not change.

Therefore, when one takes up working with schizophrenics, they should not neglect this kind of relation between the patient and the amalgam of jouissance and language depicted in the figure above. This is one of the first lessons one must learn as "secretary to the schizophrenic" and of which the topological approach to Georgios' case reminds us.

As was noted in Chapter Two, Lacan clarifies that he is using the term "secretary" to encourage clinicians to take the words of the person they work with literally (Lacan, 1956a). In effect, one of the consequences of incomplete separation is that the person himself or herself is the first to take their words literally. Therefore, good secretarial skills require fine-tuning with the schizophrenic's own approach and relation to words, even when that is not fully or actively manifesting. This is, after all, one of the causes of body phenomena in schizophrenia: that the subject is acquiring its body and organs with no mediation from the make-believe. Remember Paul, who, in order to stop speaking drew an actual full stop on his tongue.

Taking things literally

I am sure that clinicians who work with schizophrenics will have many examples to remember regarding the argument that the schizophrenic takes things literally. We have already noted an early remark by Victor Tausk about his patient with the "twisted eyes" (Freud, 1915e), which moreover shows the impact of this condition on the patient's body.

Leaving aside clinical observations for a moment, this condition reminds me of a fascinating dialogue from a beautiful and acclaimed Greek documentary film by Filippos Koutsaftis, produced in 2000, from which I was inspired for the title of this book. Its name is *Αγέλαστος Πέτρα* (Agelastos Petra), which means "mourning rock". It was the outcome of ten years of filming in Eleusis, an ancient Greek shrine where the Eleusinian mysteries took place. Today it is a rather underprivileged industrial area near the western suburbs of Athens.

Among the city residents parading in the documentary, we frequently see a man called Panayiotis Farmakis, who is now deceased. Panayiotis Farmakis was a wandering figure whom one could describe as the good-old village fool; he walks incessantly, covering long distances, he sometimes wears his jacket over his head, and he is looking for ancient fragments among industrial debris. There comes a point when this figure disappears for some time from the film. When he shows himself again, we hear the director asking him: "where do you live? Where is your address?" He receives the following radically literal reply from the wandering amateur archaeologist, who is anything but fool: "above the ground and beneath the clouds!" Koutsaftis asks him again, but Panayiotis Farmakis does not elaborate further than this; he simply repeats the sentence, which seems to be his life's moto.

Beyond its being humorous, in this beautiful example we can see the moving force behind schizophrenic irony, whose role is exactly to show the fraudulent nature of established discourse and the make-believe (Miller, 2001), and is linked to the status of the schizophrenic's body. We have noted that irony comes from the subject and goes against the Other (Biagi-Chai, 2014), striking at the root of every social relation (Lacan, 1966b). Indeed, what the schizophrenic teaches us is that the place to find one's body—schizophrenic or not—can only be above the ground and beneath the clouds.

This aphorism describes the two aspects of the body in schizophrenia, which we saw in both *Part I* and in our reading of Georgios' case in the present part.

The first one is its corporeal aspect, its being a material. This is an effect of the subject's refusal to abide by the artificial constructions functioning within the networks of the social Other. In Georgios' case, this was a body of pure flesh belonging to Mother or her metonymical figures; more specifically, a corpse, a girl's body with no name of its own, whose jouissance was not appeased by the signifier. As we see in Panayiotis Farmaki's aphorism, signifiers, addresses, names of streets, and postcodes are nothing but make-believes, forgeries for the schizo-phrenic: above the ground and beneath the clouds is the only location we can find one's body. In fact, if we pay attention to what the schizo-phrenic says, to what he or she can teach us, as Miller suggests in his truly didactic paper "Ironic Clinic" (2001), we would have known that this is, in the end, the only place where our bodies are found too.

The second aspect of the body in schizophrenia illustrated in this ground-breaking phrase is described below, but we might as well give out a touch of it at this point: its imaginary status, which is floating. As far as the imaginary aspect of the schizophrenic's body is concerned, "above the ground and beneath the clouds" may as well mean any-where; not localised.

I believe that the first aspect of the schizophrenic body, which is linked to a structural status of the schizophrenic subject, is also portrayed in the two rings of the figure above, illustrating the real and the symbolic as being intertwined. Since make-believes, the products and generators of otherness, hit a wall in schizophrenia, words do not achieve a purely representing quality but have fused with the Thing in its sense as sensorial, vocal or material (Soler, 1999). The location for one's body is above the ground and beneath the clouds, the same way that an oven is an oven, an apple tree is an apple tree, and a child is a body belonging to Mother; period.

However, despite this formation's omnipresence, that is, with the real only "tamed" to a superficial degree by the symbolic thanks to alienation and away from the benefits of the established discourses, a schizophrenic might be somehow able to live a tolerable life, avoiding the real overwhelming the stage.

Let us return to Georgios: leaving behind his first years at the village, during his early adulthood he proceeds to a titanic attempt to tackle the fundamental deficits inherited from that condition, and gains a considerable amount of time before the return of the non-symbolised in the real of the body. This seems to have happened during the crafting of his writing, which partly achieved to bring the real of the child under a signifying construction that gave a narcissistic value to the body. On his stepladder, he went as far as the instrumentalisation of elements from lalangue, the mark on the One, the "vast reverse" from which only some fragments can be extracted (Soler, 2014, p. 23).

An open window?

In effect, if moving from alienation to separation is impossible, the direction that can take place to somehow regulate the eternal interconnection of the real and the symbolic seen in S_1s and jouissance being "frozen" is a utilisation of the imaginary, which Georgios partly succeeded in by creating a stepladder for the child's body to stand on.

In fact, the Thing not having been murdered by the Word does not leave everything else fixed or predetermined. Lacan (1973b) writes that structure does not define meaning. What took place with the imaginary, the domain of meaning, emotion, and the body image in Georgios' case shows the place where flexibility can lie in working with schizophrenics. If the interrelation of the real and symbolic is non-negotiable yet tractable, the same does not go for the imaginary.

In fact, as has been remarked a few times, Georgios' body's imaginary covering did not derive from the mirror stage. It did not pass through otherness that is established via the mirror stage or discourse, as paranoid and neurotic subjects do, but through a utilisation of the One, the debris of the subject's first encounter with language. Let us now examine its status.

The flexibility of the imaginary

Being = having

As was suggested earlier, whereas the interconnection of the real and the symbolic is the *sine qua non* in schizophrenia, the imaginary is characterised by a different status. It is a register *in statu nascendi*, unfixed and for this reason flexible; a register that must anchor the other two intertwined registers for the subject to acquire the feeling of their body. As above, in this respect the phrase "above the ground and beneath the clouds" does not describe the body's radically "material" aspect, but the fact that this can find itself anywhere; and this generates an infinite number of places where the body can be localised—remember Paul, the nineteen-year-old man who sometimes saw his body crawling on the ceiling. Whereas concerning the real and the symbolic "above the ground and beneath the clouds" regards rigidity, concerning the imaginary it is linked to flexibility.

In the subject who is not schizophrenic, the localisation of the body takes place thanks to the intervention of otherness that starts with the mirror stage and continues with separation—via the help of established discourse—that generates an ordinary symptom; what is described, in other words, as the belief in the father. On the other hand, schizophrenics must overcome this obstacle without that aid, even through an extraordinary anchoring of the floating imaginary on the intertwined real and symbolic.

In Chapter Four I described the condition George narrated experiencing in childhood as that of Mother's imaginary phallus or *a*, which localised no meaning about his being as "child" thanks to a signifying use of signifiers. "Being" and "having" were not separated, a condition that happens thanks to the successful paternal metaphor that gives subjects the chance to assume their body through established discourse. George's being was not named in some way different to what belonged to Mother, which would have been a symbolic rather than an imaginary constitution. The neurotic subject can, thanks to the phallic dialectic between being and having, move from the one side to the other without much trouble (Morel, 2015). Yet in psychosis, where the phallus is absent, things are not that simple.

In his writings we read of the identification of George's being to Michaliessa—and her metonymical figures'- having. He can be what can answer her enigmatic desire. Unfortunately, this left no body for the subject to have, apart from that of a dead girl, which belongs to the primary Other—in Lacan's even earlier period, it is a part of the maternal imago. An imaginary constitution is not therefore anchored to the real of the body via a mediation by the symbolic that will name this subject's being. In George's childhood the signifier did not create a link between the imaginary and the real.

In effect, the signifiers he is named with during childhood only come to confirm this status for the body that belongs to the Other. Therefore, the link between the imaginary and the symbolic could be portrayed thus:

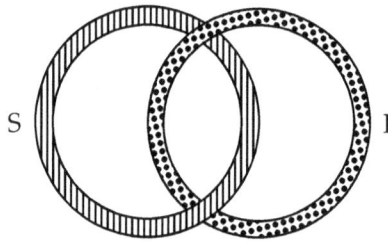

Figure 7. The symbolic and the imaginary in Vizyenos.

Peddler and piece of merchandise

In the figure above, the ring on the right (I) represents the imaginary and that on the left, like in the preceding figure, the symbolic (S). The two registers are intertwined in the case of Georgios, depicting the fact that signifiers are only serving this elementary status of a body that belongs to Mother, of which his father was another figure: Georgios, "Michael's George", "Michaliessa's tiny George", Michaelides, businessman, and patron.

This status could be summarised in calling those basic formations, of the child and the field in which this belongs, as "piece of merchandise" and "peddler", since in his family history children—with his own Mother as the first of them—are treated like merchandise that someone acquires. A simpler formula could be "proprietor" and "property", which seems to be the quintessence of the relation between child (girl) and parent (Mother) in his family history for at least two generations.

Therefore, with the symbolic serving the imaginary instead of bringing it under the yoke of signification, the child's body belongs to Mother like a piece of property. The jouissance of the signifier "child", which bears a material quality described above, is thus not attributed an imaginary identity of its own. Its imaginary constitution is not yet named or localised via the help from the symbolic.

The topological approach to Georgios' case shows us that the imaginary does not stop bearing this texture for this subject. In effect, it is not only before, but also after Georgios' writing activity as "Vizyenos"—which achieved the connection of the real and the imaginary aspect of the child's body—that the child's unnamed being remains the other's having.

This is observed after the gradual dissolution of his edifice, discussed below, when his motherly patron died and his body's beauty vacillated due to his neurological disease.

Unsurprisingly, in the last decade of his life, in his growing delusion as businessman and patron, we saw prevailing an imaginary constitution of himself as a maternal figure, which, for Georgios, means one thing: the proprietor of children's bodies. Therefore, in his delusion he became someone whose property were children's bodies. We observe that what changed was not the texture of the imaginary, but the position of its coordinates did: it was now him "Mother" and others (Bettina, the inexistent orphan girl in Constantinople, his former high-school students, and the hospital guard) the children.

This illustrates for us once more the dysfunction of the mirror stage and the establishment of otherness. In the lack of the speaking being's stepladder, which established his own "Other", Georgios could not even sustain himself at the position of Narcissus, whose significance Lacan noted in 1958. The imaginary was no longer mediated by the symbolic in its link to the real. Madness, which is synonymous with complete freedom in Lacan's cosmos (1967b), appeared in phenomena showing the disconnection of the three registers (Lacan, 1973–1974). Thus we saw a body, stripped of its narcissistic brightness, turn into an empty bag (Biagi-Chai, 2014).

It seems therefore that the type of narcissism that characterises those precarious specular relations shortly before and in the asylum is not the same as the one deriving from the edifice constructed during his almost thirty-year-long writing endeavour. In it, the narcissistic covering of the body that equated him with Plato, Sophocles, etc. did not depend on a specular image, but on the signifier, which circumscribed the real aspect of the signifier "child" inherent in the language of childhood, Turkish, Thracian exclamations, etc.

We might therefore have to speak of a different status for the imaginary, similar to Joyce's ego, which does not replace the imaginary, but does anchor a side of it to the real and the symbolic. This might be related to Laurent's (2015a) suggested "modified narcissism". The stepladder that raised Georgios to the level of bright names from literature was in no way similar to his megalomaniac and erotomaniac delusions of the early 1890s, which derived from a precarious relation to what is at stake at the mirror stage. Thanks to his writing, the body image was hooked to the real because of the mediation of a titanic fight with the signifier that generated Vizyenos' speaking being.

Vizyenos as sinthome

Joyce and Vizyenos

As was analysed in Chapter Three, the sinthome is a fourth factor, a knot, which connects the three registers: real, symbolic, and imaginary. The subject, whose subsistence depends on the sinthome when an ordinary symptom is not formed, must emerge in the symbolic (Vanheule & Geldof, 2012).

As above, in Joyce's case this happened thanks to the belief in the identity of "The artist". This identity was the *ego* that, thanks to the writing activity supporting it and based on the dissolution of language it produced, created a fourth ring that knotted the imaginary to the symbolic and the real. If we return to Joyce's case, we will see that one of the effects of his sinthome was that the imaginary, which was slipping away—remember the scene where he is beaten up while tied to a fence—was hooked upon the intertwined real and symbolic. Thus the body that could alternatively lie anywhere "above the ground and beneath the clouds" was anchored.

Having mentioned Joyce, I would like to refer for a moment to the way Lacan (1975–1976) illustrates the sinthome topologically, used a few pages above. On this occasion, I would like to highlight once more the argument that, as far as his relation to language is concerned, Joyce's psychosis is characterised by a schizophrenic texture. Soler (1999; 2014) writes that in Joyce's writing Lacan finds what Freud had remarked about schizophrenics' discourse. Morel (2003) puts it as Joyce's trouble being "closer to schizophrenia than paranoia" (p. 143).

Why would Lacan choose to portray Joyce's case in this way—the real and the symbolic as directly intertwined—rather than simply show the three registers as unconnected and interrelated only thanks to the sinthome? Probably due to Joyce's direct relation to language in its texture of jouissance. I am not suggesting that Joyce was schizophrenic in the way that patients to whom I referred in *Part I* were. Yet, as was also suggested in Chapter Three in relation to the dipole of paranoia and schizophrenia, one would not be totally wrong in bringing to mind the latter rather than the former when it comes to Joyce. Lacan himself (1975–1976) differentiated the Joycean solution from the paranoid invention topologically by referring to the three registers as having merged into one in paranoia. In addition, as I have also stressed in *Part I*, Joyce's ego has nothing to do with specular relations, the matrix for the paranoiac and neurotic's identification. On the other hand, it certainly cannot be argued that Joyce *is* schizophrenic.

Nevertheless, as has been already remarked, Georgios describes a starting point that seems to be similar to Joyce's: the fact that the father was not a father for him. Yet Joyce remains, as Lacan writes (1975–1976, p. 70), "rooted" (*enraciné*) in the father, and this motivates his solution, the sinthome. Joyce's symptom, especially as viewed in *Ulysses*, is fatherhood. It seems that even if for Georgios the father constitutes a hole too, he is not looking for him; he is only taking the father's name in vain in order to realise the pursuit that motivates him: to anchor a bright body to the signifier "child", which otherwise is only equated with a girl's corpse.

Therefore, there are two unconnected aspects in the signifier "child": the signifier in which corporeal jouissance is "frozen", hence, its characterisation as "real signifier", and the image of its body, which, *in statu nascendi*, is fastened to Mother. What will change thanks to Georgios' edifice is a temporary anchoring of the body's image to the real of the signifier "child" via the intervention of the symbolic. Thanks to this anchoring Georgios will be able to exploit the resonances of the One, which precede the advent of the Other's discourse, and which exist in everybody, schizophrenic or not; he will thus use in his poetry and fiction phonemes and meaningless units of language like "tra-la, la-la", "ding dang", "ai-hak", and "temenás", aspects of jouissance that are not uttered by a dead girl's body but by a body that is alive, a body enjoyed in its narcissistic rise; an outcome that might remind one of Joyce.

In fact, based on a topological illustration of Georgios' aforementioned invention, we can portray how, as Lacan suggested in 1976, we can surpass the father by using him in an alternative way to Joyce. The following depiction of the writing of Vizyenos is suggested:

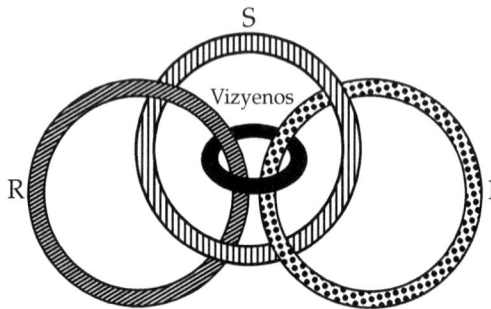

Figure 8. Sinthomatic approach to Vizyenos.

Vizyenos as a knot

In the figure above, the black ring in the middle stands for the signifier "Vizyenos", which appears in the symbolic and links the child's body image (imaginary) to the real signifier "child" (real and symbolic). Rooted in the symbolic, borrowed, as it is, from Vizyi's heritage, the name "Vizyenos" is articulated to the swarm of signifiers representing the subject for the "Other" that his writing establishes. At the same time, it links the body image to the real of the child thanks to an exploitation of language through the "incarnated effects of lalangue" (Soler, 2014, p. 61): "tra-la, lala", "woof-woof" etc. This is the period when, thanks to the utilisation of language, Georgios feels this body that benefits from a narcissistic rise different from the one owed to otherness; specular or related to established discourse.

I suggest that the pedestal he created by alluding to Homer, Plato, Sophocles, etc. successfully aimed at borrowing something from the brightness of those names. It was with that brightness that he dressed his body, both metaphorically and actually (in the middle of that period

Georgios wore archaic clothes that made him look so bizarre that he was arrested in Berlin because the imperial guard took him for a mad assassin aspiring to kill the Kaiser (Xireas, 1949)!).

Therefore, the subject was not any more simply "Michael's George" etc.; its body now belonged to Vizyenos, a subject that emerged from the depths of the symbolic. When he thus defends his doctoral thesis, enters aristocratic and literary salons, strolls dressed oddly in Berlin, Paris, and London, and reads his poems at the Athens palace, his body is enjoyed upon the stepladder and acknowledged, moreover, by some parts of the social bond.

Yet this distorted symbolic that helps the subject become represented by the signifier "Vizyenos" is not the Other's discourse. It is a self-made discourse that does not link to the half-said truth of the unconscious. It is closer to Lacan's speaking being, which Lacan suggested in replacement of the unconscious, as was noted in Chapter Three. "Vizyenos" may be a better illustration of a name "subjected" to the speaking being than a signifier for a subject dependent on the Other's discourse: it is a name stemming from a discourse on the One, the debris of the real (Soler, 2014).

If the aim of treatment in psychosis could in some cases be indeed the construction of a name (Leader, 2011; Verhaeghe, 2008), the function of the invented master signifier "Vizyenos" in Georgios' case shows us a link between the body image and the jouissance of the body, both of which are related to the concept of "child". In the absence of an inherited name on the side of the father, Georgios manages to name the child's being "Vizyenos", a name that does have a—temporary—effect on jouissance: his ability to play with and enjoy language to the extent that he manages to utilise its units belonging to lalangue in his written works. The instrumentalisation of the *jouissance* of language—linked to the body *image*—which will persecute him in his early forties, was possible thanks to that *name*.

As I have suggested frequently, another appropriate way to study the function of Vizyenos' writing is in connection to Lacan's (1975a) other way to approach Joyce's extraordinary construction: the stepladder or *escabeau*: the pedestal that offers the speaking being a narcissistic boost, which is what fascinated Lacan in Joyce's case (Miller, 2015).

I find this concept particularly suitable to his case especially when we think of the root of beauty it contains. This is expressly contrasted with the continuous reproaches in the Athenian press about Georgios' ugly face, his repulsive voice, and his uniquely bald head! It seems that Vizyenos' writing crafted the stepladder upon which his flesh—a potentially decaying dead girl's body—rose for more than two decades and helped him assume an image through a link with shining names from classical literature.

To use in an arbitrary manner the coordinates of established discourse, it seems that the emergence of the master signifier (S_1) "Vizyenos", in representing the subject (S) for a swarm of signifiers (S_2), utilised Georgios' direct relation to lalangue that subsists instead of an absent object a–condenser of jouissance. If this is so, then it seems that the four components of an established discourse—albeit distorted, as Soler suggests regarding schizophrenia (1999)—can be all located in the discourse George Syrmas or Michaelides created under the name "Vizyenos". In the place of discourse that passed through otherness, however, we find a singular discourse on the One, with sinthomatic architecture and effects.

Treatment

Thanks to his creation, Georgios was therefore able to utilise language, the first of the body's organs someone must obtain (Lacan, 1973a) and, thanks to this, enjoy—and thus acquire—the child's body.

In addition, in spite of the radical difficulties with the social Other that the writer continued experiencing, Georgios also, albeit marginally, entered some parts of a social bond; the stage of contemporary Greek-speaking literature or the circles of Greek socialites and scholars in London. The same had happened in Constantinople, when he wrote his first poems. As has been remarked already, although the sinthome does not refer to an Other in terms of the unconscious, it does establish a relation to the social bond. Thus we can explain how, standing on his stepladder, Georgios achieved a partial insertion into some parts of the social bond in spite of his lacking the coordinates of established discourses. Not everyone considered him an arrogant and impertinent outsider in Modern Greek literature, although his looks and conduct showed his refusal to abide strictly by the social standards.

To sum up in use of more clinical terms, thanks to this invention Georgios achieved, with relatively lasting effects, what Zenoni (2008; 2012) sets as the aim of work with schizophrenics: to find the connections between the body and the symbolic instead of a direct attachment of the imaginary to the organs and to restore the subject's relation to the world's order, to be followed by an insertion into the social bond. If we consider the acquisition of the body in terms of a symbolic anchoring of the imaginary to the real as making up the first part, then it goes without saying that his writing can be considered an invention that succeeded in such a task. Based on the fact that it allowed him, moreover, to develop a marginal relation to parts of the social bond, in Constantinople, London, and partly in Athens, we may be entitled to attribute to it sinthomatic effects. This can be also argued based on one final achievement of his creation that has not been hitherto mentioned.

It seems to me that one of the accomplishments of Georgios' writing that we can learn a lot from in the clinic of schizophrenia was the cut it introduced to in one of the fundamental characteristics of this condition: the resistance to believing.

As has been highlighted already, one of the fundamentals in schizophrenia is the resistance to make-believes, which was beautifully summarised in Panayiotis Farmakis' answer that his address was "above the ground and beneath the clouds". Lacan had highlighted this very early, although he had not yet suggested this approach to the make-believe. A relative comment can be found, for example, in *Family Complexes* (1938), where Lacan wrote that in schizophrenia a discordance can be observed between "conduct and belief" (p. 62). In paranoia, belief also occupies a different status, yet not the "not believing in it" (Lacan, 1964a, p. 238).

I find that the schizophrenic's resistance to adhere to otherness in any way—of the specular other or the big Other—is where this refusal to "believe" stems from. This is what schizophrenic irony denounces (Lacan, 1966d). This implies therefore that the attempt to make the schizophrenic believe in a pre-regulated Other is pointless. This is why, for example, Lacan (1976) remarks that Joyce—and we must add Georgios as well—has cancelled his subscription to the unconscious. Joyce does not need an analysis, because he has achieved what analysis does through his writing.

Of course, what Georgios eventually created did not annihilate the above-mentioned condition. His writing did not establish a relation to an Other in its sense either as the unconscious or as established discourse, nor in a paranoid specular or big Other. He did not believe in such a formation. He did not do so either after his admission or before it. On the other hand, he created something else to make the signifier "Vizyenos" subsist. He crafted a "subject" subjected not to the Other of the unconscious, the regulated Other of the signifier in which he could not believe, but the corpus of his writing, which went as far as exploiting the jouissance of lalangue (babbling, sounds from nature, Thracian exclamations, and words in Turkish). The fact that the schizophrenic cannot believe in otherness does not mean that he cannot believe in or even "adore" his body (in terms of a sinthome or stepladder). In *Seminar XXIII*, there is reference to the speaking being adoring his body because he believes he has one (Laurent, 2015a). After all, ever since Freud, *auto-eroticism* has been the stage the schizophrenic is condemned to in absence of a capacity to establish otherness.

Returning therefore to the early psychoanalytic suggestion of working with schizophrenics based on the strengthening of the ego, we can confirm an orientation toward narcissism, but not in the way this was being encouraged in the past, that is, through promoting the establishment of otherness, either specular or related to discourse. A "modified" narcissism that may resemble Vizyenos's, might bring about "auto-eroticism's" beneficial effects.

Summary to Part II

The life of George Syrmas or Michaelides can be represented by an ascending and descending curve that corresponds to the status of the body, whose direct attachment to language is a recurrent phenomenon in the clinic of schizophrenic subjects.

The man who passed the greatest part of his life as the writer, poet, and scholar Georgios Vizyenos spent his childhood incarnating Mother's imaginary phallus or a, a status that was also invested by the first signifiers that named him. Yet in his adult life he escaped that condition—the challenge was similar for Schreber and Joyce (Morel, 2003)—by constructing a stepladder based on an instrumentalisation of language that went as far as utilising lalangue. This bipod stepladder, with one leg in the symbolic and the other in the real, gave his body narcissistic brightness by equating him to names from classical literature. However, the apparent manifestation of a syphilitic infection brought this construction down by indicating that he was not his body's master. Psychotic symptoms broke out and language took over.

Vizyenos' narcissistic creation did not generate a neurotic or paranoiac's delusional ego, which have their roots in the mirror stage. Hence, no Other was created by him in the fashion of the paranoid metaphor or neurotic symptom. Its ballast was rather the material from lalangue, the amalgam of real and symbolic, through which his body was enjoyed. This reminds me of Freud's (1915e) remark that the schizophrenic ends up with the libido being cathected to words instead of objects or an ego and this being one of the first steps at a recovery or cure. The case of Vizyenos seems to show how we can carry forward this cure, which has not got to do with the discourse of the Other, but with that of the One. The Thracian writer did so by digging deep not in the abandoned iron mines of his homeland but in his childhood memory and extracting elements such as "ding dang", "tra-la, la-la", etc.

PART III

AFTER A HUNDRED YEARS:
THE CONTEMPORARY LACANIAN
CLINIC OF SCHIZOPHRENIA

Introduction to Part III

It has now been more than a century since Bleuler transformed Kraepelin's dementia praecox (1899) into schizophrenia (1911). The vocabulary of mental disorders has undergone many more changes ever since.

During the twentieth century, once-prevalent psychiatric terms were abandoned or replaced (e.g., *conversion disorder* in place of *hysteria*), whereas new clinical concepts appeared due to social, historical, and scientific changes (e.g., *gender dysphoria*, *PTSD*, and *stimulant-related disorder*) (APA, 2013). Yet it is not only names that have changed but the symptoms that we encounter too (Verhaeghe, 2015).

The concept of schizophrenia underwent significant changes in the past century as well and suffered severe criticism (Arieti, 1974; Laing, 1990; Szasz, 1976). However, this signifier is still widely used in the twentieth century by psychiatrists, psychologists, and psychotherapists who wish to treat people diagnosed as schizophrenics.

Psychoanalysis is not an exception either. The short history of Freud's conceptualisation of paraphrenia is exemplary of schizophrenia's persistence in this field.

As was noted in Chapter One, when schizophrenia was introduced by Bleuler, Freud (1908; 1911c; 1914c) partly disapproved of it and promoted in its place the term "paraphrenia", which represented a more generalised aspect of this concept. Yet soon enough and despite those initial reservations, he abandoned this idea himself, returning to the use of the signifier "schizophrenia" without accounting for that change (Freud, 1915e; 1924b). It is thus still used by many psychoanalytic schools and institutions, including Lacanians.

Indeed, Lacan's significantly minimal use of this term—especially following the 1960s—and his use of indirect language (1957b; 1973a; 1975–1976) when he talked about schizophrenics has not deterred Lacanians from using this signifier extensively in theory and in the clinic.

Why is schizophrenia so popular a psychiatric and psychoanalytic term today, a hundred years after its invention by Bleuler, in spite of the multilateral criticism and changes it has encountered?

Its persistence in both fields could be a sign of schizophrenia's topicality. If psychiatrists and psychoanalysts cannot abandon this signifier, it could be serving some purpose. Psychiatry and psychoanalysis started using the term "schizophrenia" so that clinicians could recognise and discuss a treatment direction for patients who did not fall within the existing categories of mental diseases. Their shared use of schizophrenia therefore could still be serving the purpose of diagnosing and treating the forms of this type of psychosis.

Is, however, the utilisation of schizophrenia still common in the two fields? Where do we stand today, more than a century after the lively dialogue between Freud, Jung, and Bleuler? I attempt to answer those questions in the following two—and final—chapters.

If the reader expects to find that the gap distinguishing psychiatry from psychoanalysis has widened after a century, they will not be surprised. It seems, indeed, that we are past the era when the same case example—President Schreber—was used by scholars from both disciplines in support of their respective arguments (Bleuler, 1911; Freud, 1911c). In contrast, it is argued that there are substantial differences between them concerning the clinical use of the term "schizophrenia". Whereas psychiatry is led by classification and suggests treatments for symptoms as these are affirmed by the Other, psychoanalysis is led by diagnosis, which serves first and foremost an investigation of the subject's constitution that is linked to the One. It seems that their only remaining common reference to schizophrenia is the use of the same signifier, whose significations seem to differ greatly.

CHAPTER EIGHT

Diagnosis: the schizophrenic subject and the real

In spite of the gap between the two disciplines having widened during the past century, both psychoanalysis and psychiatry still need to form a diagnosis when faced with a psychotic subject, although not for the same reasons. In psychoanalysis, the establishment of diagnosis must be linked to an orientation for the treatment, whereas, as is shown below, the same does not necessarily apply to modern psychiatry.

This difference is depicted in the two disciplines functioning within different discourses, a development in Lacanian theory analysed in Chapter Three: on the one hand there is psychoanalytic discourse, and, on the other, the master's and university's discourse (Verhaeghe, 2008).

In the present chapter, it is suggested that in order to form a diagnosis of schizophrenia that can orient treatment in Lacanian psychoanalysis, two basic steps must be taken: first, to perform a differential diagnosis between schizophrenia and the other two psychotic subtypes identified by Freud and Lacan; secondly, to investigate the subject's singular relation to the real. The second step is a direct effect of the first, which confirms the absence of a specific orientation of jouissance.

Psychoanalytic diagnosis in two steps

Phenomenon and structure

There is a typical phenomenon that Lacanian psychoanalysts agree on when it comes to schizophrenia: the return of jouissance to the subject's body (Laurent, 2012; Leader, 2011; Miller, 1983; 2012; Soler, 2014; Vanheule, 2011; Zenoni, 2012). The presence of this phenomenon, analysed extensively in the preceding chapters, could be viewed as a diagnostic indication for schizophrenic structure.

In the preceding chapters, it was described that the return of the dead girl's jouissance to the child's body in Georgios Vizyenos' case happened during his breakdown of the early 1890s. It was suggested that, probably in reaction to physical phenomena caused by an apparent syphilitic infection, the body image was detached from the speaking being and the body was taken over by the organ of language, as was observed in incidents preceding the writer's admission to the Dromokaiteion hospital (see *Part II*). It had become itself, now, a body lying above the ground and beneath the clouds.

As was described in *Part I*, a common way in which this appears in the clinic of schizophrenia is subjects complaining about the state of their body or organs (Leader, 2011). They say, for example, that they feel them floating, missing or having been replaced. Remember the patient of Jung's (1906) who complained that her spinal cord had been torn out, a remark so frequent we also find it in a contemporary patient of Kraepelin's (1904); Peter, the schizophrenic patient I met during my undergraduate placement, who located his mother's genitalia in his throat; and Paul, the young man who saw his body crawling on the ceiling and had to draw a full stop on his tongue to stop talking. Two other characteristic examples that come to mind are Jane and Susan. The first was a middle-aged woman who visited the aforementioned mental health centre complaining that the blood in her veins had been replaced by little green people who were floating in them. The second was a young woman in psychoanalytic therapy who kept her thighs tightly together for fear that her intestines would flow out from her vulva or anus.

As above, this common symptom—shared by the delusional seamstress, Jane, Susan, Peter, and Paul—refers to the fragmented body that precedes the mirror stage. This is the danger those individuals run following any vacillation of the body image that is precariously anchored to the subjective constitution: the body and the organs can be found anywhere above the ground and beneath the clouds (see Chapter Seven).

Yet this sign, which can lead us to suggest the presence of schizophrenia, is merely a phenomenon. As was highlighted in *Part I*, Lacan suggested (1956a) going beyond the phenomenon, the visible, and heading for the structure when working with psychosis, which points to the relation between subject and signifier (Lacan, 1958a).

It seems that two things must be specified in forming a psychoanalytic diagnosis based on the observation of phenomena: a) establishing the underlying structure causing the phenomena and b) designating a treatment direction. Addressing those aspects corresponds to the case of schizophrenia too.

Differential diagnosis: crossing out the third factor

As was remarked earlier, the twentieth and early-twenty-first centuries saw a continuous evolution of the psychiatric vocabulary, leading to an expansion of diagnostic categories, including the ones used to diagnose psychotic subjects. Those are discussed extensively further below. In contrast to psychiatry, the vocabulary of psychotic categories in psychoanalysis has been kept rather minimal for the last hundred years.

The main psychotic sub-types recognised in Lacanian psychoanalysis are three. All of them are encountered in Freud. Lacan never added a fourth. He elaborated on the existing three based on his own interpretation of Freud's writings. This happened during his second theoretical elaboration, in the 1950s, which established a structural theory based on two concepts of major importance that he introduced to the field of psychoanalysis: the subject and the Other.

The subject was, of course, the cornerstone of the era of the predominance of the symbolic. Lacan, who introduced it meticulously in that first period of his open teaching, never concealed that Freud had been the first to locate it in Schreber's *Memoirs* (1966a). It seems that psychosis cannot be examined without reference to the subject (Miller, 2003b). The theoretical "counterpart" of the subject, the locus from which it arises, the regulated big Other, was the second major concept introduced by Lacan that we need in order to form a differential diagnosis. Both were discussed in detail in *Part I*.

The three psychotic sub-types described by Freud and still at use in the Lacanian orientation are paranoia, schizophrenia, and melancholia.

Apart from those three, a fourth category, which is encountered in this form in neither Freud nor Lacan, has relatively recently appeared in Lacanian psychoanalysis: "ordinary psychosis" (Miller, 1997; 2009a). This concept is not discussed in the present chapter, but in the following one, because I believe it to be of greater assistance in the study of treatment rather than diagnosis. There is also the question of mania, which Freud places on the side of melancholia, but it has been suggested that it might be advisable to think of it in relation to schizophrenia (Leader, 2015). In the present chapter, I deal with differential diagnosis between the three Freudo-Lacanian psychotic sub-types.

The question of the subject's relation to the Other is an instrument for performing differential diagnosis between psychosis and neurosis (Verhaeghe, 2008; 2015). Unlike the neurotic subject, the psychotic subject is subjected to the Other "without mediation" (Gherovici & Steinkoler, 2015, p. 3).

However, it seems that the same question can be used for differential diagnosis among the psychotic sub-types, since this "absence of mediation" itself presents a number of modalities. In fact, addressing the question of the subject's relation to otherness is bound to put schizophrenia on the one side and the other two sub-types on the other. It seems that the other two differentiating variables noted by Leader (2015), meaning and the localisation of the libido, derive from the respective status of the distance from the Other (Verhaeghe, 2015). Let us remind ourselves briefly of the subject's relation to otherness in paranoia and melancholia.

In the mid-1950s Lacan said that Freud had had justifiable reasons for differentiating paranoia from schizophrenia (1955a). In our reading of his synopsis of the seminar on the psychoses (Lacan, 1958a), as well as his earlier theories on human development (Lacan, 1938), it was implied that those reasons were summarised in the presence of the subject and an "Other" in the paranoid writing of a case like President Schreber's, which was built around the specular relation like a pearl formed around a grain of sand. The core of a belief in the figure of an Other exists in paranoia (Wachsberger, 2007), despite only as evil (Miller, 2010).

Lacan rarely spoke about the other psychotic sub-type, melancholia (Freud, 1917e). When he did, this also happened in the late 1950s to early 1960s. In melancholia, the subject occupies a different position in relation to the Other, that of embodying its rejected object, its waste (Lacan, 1957b); in melancholia the object "takes the helm", "triumphs" (Lacan, 1962–1963, p. 335). In this case the Other is thus the agent from which the subject qua object wants to part; yet Lacan writes that in his or her self-accusations, the melancholic is entirely in the domain of the symbolic (1961).

In both sub-types, therefore, there seems to be a minimal belief in a figure of otherness who enjoys (paranoiac) or rejects (melancholic) the subject. This indicates the presence of some kind of link between subject and Other.

Of course, as was noted in Chapter Two, the psychotic subject does not emerge from the successful paternal metaphor or the completion of alienation and separation. Thus, the big Other as a regulated "battery of signifiers" (Lacan, 1960a, p. 682) is not established. Yet it seems that the belief in otherness in paranoia and melancholia—albeit an unregulated agent in comparison to the neurotic's regulated Other of the signifier—is linked to a limited subjective constitution.

In paranoia, the subject is in accord with the presence of the evil Other, built around the processed mirror stage. It is him or her that this Other is missing, to whom the Other's evil is directed, as President Schreber is to God. Similarly, in melancholia, the subject is not what the Other wants, but what it is not worth having, what is guilty of being rejected, fundamentally excluded from the Other (Lacan, 1962).

The subsistence of those subjective formations is related to the emergence of respective signifiers from within this unregulated field of signifiers to represent the subject. Being "God's wife" (Schreber, 1903) or something relevant to "piece of shit" (Grigg, 2015) are signifiers that represent uniquely this subject who is, respectively, either wanted or thrown away.

To sum up, in paranoia and melancholia there seem to be an otherness and a subjective formation which, linked to that agent or field, is represented by a signifier. The subject and Other's status is not the same in the two modalities, of course. Yet the presence of a link between subject and Other makes them to some extent consonant. In both modalities, subjects are related to an otherness established and regulated to some extent by its bad will or contempt for the subject.

These beliefs correspond to a particular status for transference. For the paranoiac, the belief in this Other was the prerequisite for "any possible treatment of psychosis" (1958a). For the melancholic, transference is—for reasons explained below—impossible (Miller, 2012). Nevertheless, this still makes it different from schizophrenia, where transference is impotent.

In effect, otherness does not seem present in such a way in schizophrenia. The schizophrenic's disbelief in the Other and his or her incapacity for transference have been already discussed in detail. The schizophrenic knows that no such thing as an Other exists, due to the absence of the Other's Other (Lacan, 1958b). In *Part II*, I noted how this appears in schizophrenics' discourse, which denounces with ground-breaking irony make-believes like addresses by replying that one's address is simply "above the ground and beneath the clouds". This was a quality I also attributed to Georgios' writing when he named his poetry collection *Rubbish*.

The absence of a belief in an Other, which is inherited from the failed processing of the mirror stage, prevents the installation of a regulatory agent for the subject's emergence, as happens in paranoia and melancholia. There is no mediation between the subject and the real (Ver Eecke, 2001a). Instead of a signifying chain, we encounter a field where signifiers and jouissance, word- and thing-presentations (Freud, 1915e), the real and the symbolic (Lacan, 1954), have not been separated. Hence, the schizophrenic is represented by a swarm of signifiers (Miller, 2001; Sauvagnat, 2000; Soler, 1999; Zenoni, 2012).

To understand how this condition leads to the body phenomena described above, we must remind ourselves of an important shift in Lacan's teaching—from the focus on the subject and the Other (1950s) to the reformulation of jouissance and its connection to the real (1960s).

As was discussed in Chapter Three, from the early 1960s onwards the unregulated field of the Other is not simply the field of signifiers but of jouissance that inhabits the body, corresponding to a new relation to it in psychosis (Ribolsi, Feyaerts & Vanheule, 2015). It seems that the subject's precarious subscription to an evil or rejecting Other in the two aforementioned psychotic sub-types offers them a factor for channelling jouissance: on the one side (paranoia) there is identification of jouissance in the field of the Other (Lacan, 1975b) and on the other (melancholia) there is the subject's embodiment of the object that wants to kill itself, being unworthy of the Other (Lacan, 1961). In both cases, a cut is produced in the primary field of jouissance that precedes the subject's emergence, which is channelled to the body image. In paranoia, this is the body in its narcissistic dependence on the mirror stage, whereas in melancholia it is the object selected also through a narcissistic identification (Freud, 1917e; Lacan, 1962–1963). A void in jouissance is thus created and the subject with a body subsists, although in melancholia that is prone to fall from its beauty and be experienced as the Other's waste (hence, the earlier comment about the impossibility of transference), similarly to the situation in paranoia, where it can become the target of persecution.

In fact, no one claims that this channelling of jouissance to the body's image is something the subject experiences as benign. Paranoid and melancholic subjects often need to put an end to that relation either by striking the evil in the Other (Lacan, 1946) or by committing a passage to the act, which in the second takes place frequently in a logical way like throwing oneself from the window (Lacan, 1962–1963). There is a price to be paid for identification of jouissance in a field of otherness too.

On the other hand, the schizophrenic's lack of belief in an Other and of a substantial subjective constitution leaves no channel open for jouissance. This cannot be attributed to a specular other, an Other or its object, because such formations are not established in schizophrenia. There is no third factor to direct jouissance to. The boundary between the self and the Other is "continually in jeopardy" (Leader, 2015, p. 137). There are no imaginary gaps in the relation between the subject and language, their only Other (Miller, 2001). As Freud (1911c) and the early Lacan (1938) noted, the schizophrenic has a problematic relation to the other's image. The ego does not work as in paranoia. Consequently, having no established otherness to be projected to, jouissance is channelled to signifiers. This can happen in two ways; either in the form of enjoyment or in that of a vehicle of mortifying intrusion (Leader, 2015). And the organs or the body are also signifiers.

Therefore, the structural criterion that can explain the characteristic body phenomena in schizophrenia is the absence of a mediating factor, in the form of an other, Other or its object, between the subject and the real, which will offer it a target to channel a part of the libido or bodily jouissance. If such a factor of otherness was established, then we would not encounter phenomena of the return of jouissance to the subject's body. It is not the phenomenon therefore but its structural foundation that leads to the differential diagnosis of schizophrenia (De Waelhens, 2001b). It is the confirmation of that relation to the Other, or rather its absence, which must be viewed as a diagnostic criterion. This seems to be summarised in "L'Étourdit" (Lacan, 1973a), where Lacan explains the challenge, for the schizophrenic, of obtaining its body and organs without the help of the established discourses; that is, the way to relate to the Other of the social bond and regulate jouissance.

Nevertheless, even after excluding the presence of an established factor of otherness and the diagnosis of paranoia and melancholia, it seems that no orientation for treatment can be designated by the mere diagnosis of the schizophrenic sub-type. This is so precisely because of the absence of a predefined orientation for jouissance.

To form the diagnosis in the other two psychotic sub-types, the clinician must have an idea of the otherness circumscribing the subject's relation to the real; the form of an evil Other (paranoia) or its rejected object, the object-waste (melancholia). They can therefore be prepared to orient or support the subject in defending himself or herself against the jouissance that is coming from that direction.

In schizophrenia, in contrast, there is only language as the subject's only Other (Miller, 2001). There is no specificity for jouissance, neither in its narcissistic nor in its corporeal aspect. Its return to the subject's body must certainly be avoided, yet the clinician does not have a clear indication as to where to orient jouissance apart from the body. Judging that a subject is not paranoid or melancholic therefore does not complete the diagnosis of schizophrenia.

A clinician must not forget that there are as many forms of the subject's constitution in relation to the real as there are cases (Biagi-Chai, 2014). Pursuing this, as I tried to do for Georgios Vizyenos in *Part II*, may indeed be one of the first steps for orienting treatment (Freud, 1915e) the clinician can follow. For Miller (2011), the question of the real—and, consequently, of the subject's relation to it—is posed for every action we call therapeutic.

Quest for the subject's relation to the real

If there is no Other for the schizophrenic subject to relate to, there is its unmediated relation to the real. How can this be approached, however, when the real is what escapes symbolisation? In 1924, Freud described the status of the subject's relation to reality in psychosis to contrast it to neurosis. Yet the subject's relation to reality should not be confused with their relation to the real.

Reality could be equated to the make-believe, the creations formed by the imaginary and the symbolic (Lacan, 1973a; 1975–1976) acting as the neurotic subject's defence against the real (see *Part I*). The real, on the other hand, seems to be closer to one's being before their complete adherence to discourse and the make-believe, which is marked by the One.

It is a subjective translation of one's first experiences of sensation, of the words and looks coming from the other that accompanied the subject's coming to life (Biagi-Chai, 2014). That first meeting with the other's words and looks is described as the encounter with lalangue, which Lacan (1972–1973; 1976a) described, among others, as "moterialism" (see Chapter Three). One's moterialism is more archaic compared to one's relation to reality. Regardless of one's relation to the make-believe, we cannot neglect that moterialism bears subjective weight as it carries the mark of the One.

What Freud describes as the psychotic's relation to reality, could therefore summarise what happens in paranoia and melancholia, in which a minimal belief in the Other exists: it is the Other as evil or rejecting the subject established upon a corresponding imaginary constitution. Of course, a type of reality exists for the schizophrenic subject too, yet his relation to it resembles neither that of the neurotic nor that of the paranoiac or melancholic.

In *Part II*, I attempted to show the difference between the two in the case of Georgios Vizyenos. We saw body phenomena, signs of the return of jouissance to the body, which carried a different subjective weight compared to that of his invention. In them the subject was, as was suggested in Chapter Seven, fading. On the one hand, such phenomena could have indeed helped a clinician diagnose a schizophrenic subject. Yet this would not be the specific subject in question. Moreover, even though the exclusion of the third, mediating factor and the diagnosis of schizophrenia would be probably safe, that would lead to no guidance for treatment.

What circumscribed Georgios' relation to the real was not his irony, his body becoming the object of the organ of language or his metonymic representation by signifiers, but his relation to signifiers linking to the concept of childhood. Without focusing on the subject's relation to the signifier "child", a hypothetical clinician who would meet Vizyenos would be lost in orienting support for this subject in his relation to the body. Let us not forget that Georgios' stepladder, his narcissistic construction, tackled the lack of a body image for the child, which was destined to be a dead girl's corpse. A coherent and "orthopaedic" (Lacan, 1949) image was missed for the "child"—not any signifier.

The clinician's work is thus to support subjects in defending themselves against this singular texture of jouissance, as Vizyenos did thanks to his writing activity by creating for the child's body a narcissistic covering that attributed to it the brightness of classic writers who occupied a significant position in language. This is discussed further below, in the chapter examining treatment. The clinician cannot overlook the importance of the subject's singular relation to the real, the quest for which I suggest as the second, essential, step in diagnosis.

On the other hand, this is not a direction that everyone working clinically with schizophrenic subjects adheres to. The schizophrenic's relation to the real, which can be found highlighted in Freud and Lacan's texts, is exactly what modern psychiatry is ignoring. Before moving to how Lacanian psychoanalysis supports the schizophrenic based on it, I would like to refer to the contemporary treatment of schizophrenia from the field of the discipline which first configured it, a hundred years ago: psychiatry.

Psychiatric classification: a parallel pathway?

DSM-5: friend or foe?

In the pages above, I suggested what a clinician informed by Lacanian psychoanalysis could look for in order to form a complete diagnosis of schizophrenia. If one asked a psychiatrist in the Western world the same question today, they would probably receive an answer implicating the initials "DSM", three letters standing for the *Diagnostic and Statistical Manual for Mental Disorders*, the American Psychiatric Association's diagnostic manual, now in its fifth edition (2013).

To form a diagnosis on the day of Vizyenos' admission, his doctors could have consulted the third edition of Kraepelin's textbooks. The same could have continued happening in psychiatric hospitals for a few more decades. In contrast, in the second half of the twentieth century, and now, in the twenty-first century, people in similar positions cannot avoid consulting DSM (Verhaeghe, 2008).

DSM is unanimously characterised by Lacanian psychoanalysts as the contemporary "bible" of psychiatry (Gherovici & Steinkoler, 2015; Leader, 2011; Vanheule, 2014). Its popularisation during the twentieth century (Guéguen, 2013) was assisted by academic and psychiatric institutions where evaluation in the form promoted by the cognitive-behavioural paradigm in the mental-health domain is prevalent (Aflalo, 2015).

The latest edition of DSM has been criticised widely from a variety of perspectives (Vanheule, 2012; 2014), a critique coming even from people once in charge of its publication (Laurent, 2015b). The significant changes this edition brought to the psychiatric diagnostic manuals seem to have had a twofold effect on the approach to mental illnesses like schizophrenia.

On the one hand, DSM-5 continues the tradition of preceding editions in advocating an approach focusing on phenomenology. Diagnosis works upon what is visible, what the classifier can see (Leader, 2011). Phenomena are read as quantifiable symptoms (Aflalo, 2015; Morel, 2011). In addition, despite the break with the meticulousness of the early-twentieth-century psychiatric clinic, it remains in the Kraepelinian tradition of suggesting a biological origin of mental disorders.

Lacan had already stated his disagreement with both approaches to the study of psychosis in the 1950s. He had argued that a) the only organicity at play is "the organicity that motivates the structure of signification" (1958a, p. 477) and that b) phenomenon and structure should not be confused (1956a). Thus, if we add biological determinism to the emphasis on phenomena, DSM-5 leaves absolutely no space for the diagnosable person's subjective relation to the real: what makes subjects schizophrenic is a biological cause and what helps practitioners diagnose them as such are phenomena labelled as symptoms.

This biological and symptomological approach in the psychiatric conception of psychosis might seem, by itself, far from Lacanian psychoanalysis stemming from Lacan's theories of the 1950s. On the other hand, at first sight the spirit of DSM seems closer to a later Lacanian thesis, the so-called theory of "generalised foreclosure" (Miller, 1993).

DSM's newest edition generated a multiplication and simplification of diagnostic terms deriving from the approach described above; we have arrived at a number of disorders five times bigger than the 106 of the first DSM (Maleval, 2015)! This impressive number is not innocent. It has come about by describing as disorders what were hitherto largely perceived as everyday activities, such as "tobacco-related disorder" and "caffeine-related disorder". Moreover, we see research being encouraged in the field of other very frequent activities in our time, "internet gaming disorder", next to "caffeine-use disorder" itself (APA, 2013).

This array of signifiers that aim at guiding psychiatric diagnosis seems to serve a propensity to label as a mental disorder almost every type of behaviour (Aflalo, 2015) and thus diagnose everybody: smokers, coffee-drinkers, internet gamers—and who knows who will come next. This tendency toward hyper-diagnosis might initially seem to echo the most famous of Lacan's final aphorisms (Laurent, 2015b), that "everyone is mad, that is, delusional" (Lacan, 1979, p. 3).

This final shift in Lacan's theory was discussed to some extent in Chapter Three. It was somehow foretold already in the 1960s, when Lacan declared that there is no Other of the Other (1958c) and multiplied thence the Name-of-the-Father (1963). This idea, which came to its peak in the mid-1970s thanks to the theory of knotting, has led Miller (1993) to formulate "generalised foreclosure".

Miller (2001) suggests that we can learn from the schizophrenic subject that make-believes are nothing but artificial creations that help us defend ourselves against the real. We are all schizophrenic, he writes elsewhere (Miller, 2012), because the body and its organs present us with problems. To solve the problems posed by the real, we have to invent something singular, like schizophrenics do, since the Other of the Other, a ready-made regulator, does not exist (Lacan, 1958c). Yet it must be clarified that this theory does not make schizophrenia as a psychosis disappear. "Generic madness" is not psychosis (Miller, 2008, p. 39). As for schizophrenia, it remains, according to Miller (2001) and Zenoni (2012) the "measure" for psychosis.

I suggest giving the aforementioned approach the working label of an "ordinarisation of delusion". To be schizophrenic in the sense of attempting to defend oneself against the real with a singular creation has something of the ordinary about it—hence, "everybody" is delusional (Lacan, 1979). This seems to be the spirit of the later Lacan as Miller (1987; 2001) reads him.

What is encountered in DSM-5's aforementioned propensity to diagnose everyone seems to be the exact opposite. By labelling behaviours such as the consumption of caffeine, smoking, internet gaming, etc., as disorders, this manual does not promote what I suggested calling an "ordinarisation of delusion", but a tendency to make being ordinary a delusion, what we could label, respectively, as "delusionalisation of ordinariness".

The result might somehow seem similar: everybody is considered delusional. Yet whereas in Lacanian psychoanalysis this means that everyone can occupy the position of exception, in modern psychiatry's propensity to hyper-diagnosis no such position is left; everyone must fall within a category. No one can escape diagnosis.

In fact, it seems that the latter has become modern psychiatry's main objective, which, in contrast to psychoanalytic diagnosis, leaves treatment outside. Although we read that DSM-5's long-term aim is "the accurate diagnosis and treatment of mental disorders" (APA, 2013, p. xii), this is not found among its short-term objectives:

> The ultimate goal of a clinical case formulation is to use the available contextual and diagnostic information in developing a comprehensive treatment plan that is informed by the individual's cultural and social context. However, recommendations for the selection and use of the most appropriate evidence-based treatment options for each disorder are beyond the scope of this manual. (APA, 2013, p. 19)

The user therefore must limit his or her expectations, in consulting DSM, to the formulation of an accurate and reliable diagnosis, which is set as its actual scope. Fair enough, one might think. What is wrong with a diagnostic manual limiting its own power to diagnosis? Yet a few pages later come what illustrates the actual status of diagnosis. Its authors highlight that "the diagnosis of a mental disorder is not equivalent to a need for treatment" (APA, 2013, p. 21). This excerpt does not simply state that diagnosis does not correspond to a specific treatment orientation, as is written elsewhere, but to a need for treatment.

APA's diagnostic manual therefore does not designate treatment not because its authors do not feel capable of it, but because they feel there might not be any necessity for one. This seems to be the quintessence of diagnosis that the contemporary psychiatric establishment promotes in the Western world: diagnosis for its own sake, in other words, *classification* (Vanheule, 2012).

Psychoanalyst Paul Verhaeghe (2008) discusses the differences between psychoanalytically oriented diagnosis, which, as was seen above, can be viewed on the axis subject–Other, and the type of diagnosis promoted by today's psychiatric discourse. Unlike psychoanalytic discourse, the second seems to derive from what Lacan described as the master's and university's discourse (Lacan, 1969–1970).

The theory of discourses was described in Chapter Three. In the depiction of the four discourses offered there the reader can see that psychoanalytic discourse seems to be the only one where the divided subject and the concept condensing its jouissance are articulated (in the upper level), whereas in the remaining three it is barred. In psychoanalytic discourse, although it cannot be spoken or written, the subject's relation to the real of its jouissance is focused in an attempt to grasp a logical part of it (Aflalo, 2015). In the master's and university's discourse, which are represented not only by psychiatry but the scientifism-oriented model promoted by the cognitive-behavioural paradigm, there is an attempt to objectify, measure, and evaluate that quality, eradicating thus its singular character. Only psychoanalytic discourse is the discourse "of the particular, even of the singular" (Miller, 2008, p. 29). Hence, Morel's apt description of the distance between psychoanalytic and contemporary medical discourse as a "no man's land" (2011, p. 41).

This difference between the two approaches is not irrelevant to historical change. Psychoanalysis emerged from giving expression to subjects—the hysterics—rebelling against the master's discourse with their bodies. Today, the master does not simply want things to run smoothly—he wants to impose an implementation of evaluation (Aflalo, 2015). This is carried forward by the university's discourse, which contemporary psychiatry and a number of psychotherapeutic and even psychoanalytic schools (the IPA) adhere to. In it, in the place of agent—and, later on, make-believe in Lacan's teaching (1971)—we find S_2, that is, knowledge. However, as happens in the master's discourse too, the truth of knowledge (S_2) lying underneath it is the master signifier (S_1). The make-believe of knowledge therefore is conditioned by the—unconscious—wish to govern, incarnated in the zeal for evaluation that excludes the One.

Therefore, DSM-5-led diagnosis is not oriented at recognising and acknowledging one's subjectivity, which pertains to the subject's relation to the real. It aims at classifying subjects according to a number of criteria that separate the subject from its jouissance, since in the master's and university's discourses the two concepts are always separated (Lacan, 1969–1970; see Chapter Three). To classify everyone is not the same as diagnosing them (Vanheule, 2012). The essence of psychiatric diagnosis is, on the other hand, the erasure of subjectivity (Guéguen, 2013). What matters is the label, regardless of how that is used. As psychoanalyst Agnès Aflalo (2015) puts it, the knowledge set out in manuals like DSM produces every day more "victims", on whose suffering silence is imposed (p. 12).

This is the general framework of the contemporary psychiatric diagnosis of mental disorders. Let us now turn to someone's classification—or "victimisation"—as schizophrenic. We are bound to discover few similarities and many differences not only with psychoanalysis, but also with DSM's late-nineteenth- and twentieth-century precursors.

Classifying ... schizophrenias

DSM treats schizophrenia, which has been included in it ever since its first edition (APA, 1952), as a syndrome—in other words, a group of concurrent symptoms (APA, 2013, p. 87). Of course, this is not a new approach. The idea of schizophrenia being a syndrome was established as early as its introduction by Bleuler's (1911) in his monograph that spoke of the "group of schizophrenias".

For DSM-5, for a group of symptoms to be labelled as schizophrenia, it must last "for at least six months" and involve "a range of cognitive, behavioural, and emotional dysfunctions" (APA, 2013, pp. 89, 99). More specifically, cases that can be classified within the spectrum of schizophrenia must present abnormalities in one or more of five main domains: "delusions", "hallucinations", "disorganised thinking (speech)", "grossly disorganised or abnormal motor behaviour (including catatonia)", and "negative symptoms" (APA, 2013, p. 87). To be classified as schizophrenic requires the presence of at least one of the first three domains of symptoms during a minimum amount of time, i.e., one month.

In this list of symptom domains we meet some of Bleuler's (1911) criteria, more specifically a mixture of his fundamental and accompanying symptoms. On the other hand, there is a major difference between the latest version of DSM and the Bleulerian (and Kraepelinian) tradition that had been maintained in its previous editions. In DSM's recent version, the differentiation of the classic sub-types—which in its penultimate version were the paranoid, the disorganised, the residual, the undifferentiated, and the catatonic one (APA, 2000)—is eliminated. This innovation took place because it was considered that sub-types could neither capture the heterogeneity of schizophrenia nor designate reliable treatment orientations (Tandon et al., 2013).

On the one hand, this innovation might initially seem correlative to the psychoanalytic approach to schizophrenia. Psychoanalysis never attributed structural status to the schizophrenic sub-types either. As was highlighted earlier, the specification that psychoanalysis must establish beyond recognising the absence of a third factor is what is at stake in the subject's relation to the real. This orientation cannot lead to a further categorisation, since from that point onwards everybody is a distinct category, an exception.

In contrast, it seems that the elimination of schizophrenic sub-types hardly put an end to DSM's propensity for classification. The fact that one stops being classified as "paranoid", "catatonic" or "residual" schizophrenic does not mean that a more general diagnosis aims at their subjective constitution. In contrast, it seems that the lifting of the barriers within a label like schizophrenia serves the aim of one being able to be classified as schizophrenic without the prerequisite of falling into a sub-category, which Kraepelin and Bleuler introduced based on meticulous clinical observations. The multiplication of categories in the successive editions of DSM seems to hide the most fundamental distinctions between clinical entities (Grigg, 2015). Similar to the way it treats other disorders, DSM-5 seems to be seeking, indeed, to label someone as schizophrenic meticulously and with great rigour, yet it pays only marginal attention to that individual (Vanheule, 2014).

It therefore tends to conceive of schizophrenia as a category of criteria to be filled regardless of the diagnosed person's contribution to their condition, which lies in their relation to the real; an empty bag, like discourse, where the person is required to fit. Doesn't this comprise an attempt to make the schizophrenic enter ready-made criteria set by established discourse, whose resistance to which has been extensively highlighted thus far?

We might not be wrong in concluding therefore that the focus of psychiatric diagnosis is not a subject, but a disorder, and that its objective is not to designate treatment, but to recognise a syndrome's presence. For example, let us ask ourselves for a moment whether Georgios would have been classified as schizophrenic according to contemporary psychiatric classification. The answer must probably be in the negative for two distinct reasons.

On the one hand, one would have to turn to another diagnosis, since the presence of other mental disorders or disorders owed to medical conditions (in his case, an apparent syphilitic infection) fall within the criteria for a differential diagnosis of schizophrenia (APA, 2013, p. 104). On the other, and this seems more important, even if the signifier "schizophrenia" was used for his case, in the end this would not make a great difference when judged from the psychoanalytic perspective. DSM-5 presents a rigorous desire to confirm the presence of a condition, a syndrome that fulfils a number of criteria, rather than a subject. The idea behind one's classification as schizophrenic is that as long as this takes place, then we have a case of schizophrenia; this does not mean that the presence of a schizophrenic subject can be confirmed too.

Therefore, it is not only Georgios who could not have been diagnosed as a schizophrenic subject according to DSM-5; no one is, apparently. Contemporary psychiatric classification does not diagnose subjects, but syndromes. The syndrome is the aim (Klotz, 2009). In fact, it seems that diagnostic concepts derive from the effects that medication tackles, without establishing an undisputed etiology (Aflalo, 2015). In other words, schizophrenia for psychiatry is what is tackled via the use of antipsychotic medication.

There might not be much thus in a psychoanalytic approach, as the present aspires to be, standing opposite contemporary psychiatry's ability or wish to identify an objective entity as schizophrenia. This approach seems to abide perfectly by medical semiotics where symptoms, complaints, and behaviours are viewed as objective indicators of a dysfunction that can be classified in a syndrome, regardless of the subject's contribution to it (Vanheule, 2012).

It seems thus that the two disciplines are describing different aspects of the same condition. They might seem to be running in parallel but their respective objectives are vastly different: on the one side, we find classification and the clinical addressing of symptoms. On the other, we find diagnosis and the treatment of jouissance, both linking to the subject's relation to the real. On the one hand we find established discourse and the Other, and on the other we embark on a quest for the One.

However, although wiping out psychoanalysis may not be among the objectives of contemporary psychiatry, the predominance of its instruments and its scientific cover-up have been used by various institutions, psychoanalytic ones not excluded, to eradicate the praxis of Lacanian orientation.

One such example is a relatively recent attempt by the French Ministry of Health to cast aside psychoanalysis in favour of cognitive-behavioural therapy (CBT), assisted by the predominant biopsychosocial model in psychiatry and even by "orthodox" psychoanalytic institutions like the French branches of the IPA (Aflalo, 2015). Psychiatry today may not see itself as a rival to psychoanalysis, but it may be used as a Trojan horse by others. Although this does not seem to be the rule in contemporary psychiatry, one cannot overlook this prospect. Alternatively, voices have been raised, such as that of the psychoanalyst and psychiatrist Jean-Claude Maleval (2015), who suggests that psychoanalysis can bring about a break with the DSM modality in psychiatry and pull it toward a discipline characterised by "humanisation" (p. 109).

~~Schizophrenia~~

In contrast to current DSM- and CBT-led psychiatric classification, the psychoanalytic approach to psychosis focuses on the subject instead of the disorder. This seems to be the most significant property of the contemporary psychoanalytic approach to schizophrenia, as is shown by contrasting it with prevalent contemporary psychiatry.

We should not thus overlook the fact that apart from using the descriptive "so-called" (1973a; 1975–1976), Lacan talks about schizophrenics rather than schizophrenia. There might be a lesson for psychoanalysis to be drawn from looking at how psychiatry views schizophrenics: what makes someone schizophrenic is each and every subject's direct relation to the real instead of his or her fitting specific pre-set criteria that ignore their subjectivity. What makes one schizophrenic for psychoanalysis is what makes them an exception, the One, instead of what classifies them in a category to confirm a set of rules constructed by the Other of the social bond. It seems that one could be led to conclude that one schizophrenia does not exist and to cross that word out.

This formulation might remind the reader of the later Lacan's style, as this has been transmitted in a few infamous and extensively misinterpreted remarks from his later teaching, such as that "the woman" or "the sexual relationship" do not exist (Lacan, 1972–1973).

The second has been discussed in Chapter Three. In relation to the first negation, many seem to focus on the noun in that phrase, "woman", and overlook the definite article, "the". Lacan (1976a) never said that women do not exist. In that phrase, he does not refer to the existence of women as speaking beings, but to the absence of the signifier for woman in the unconscious. The being of the woman can only be found outside the symbolic (Morel, 2011). Thus in his renowned seminar on feminine sexuality, love, and knowledge entitled *Encore*, Lacan writes Woman in the formulae of sexuation with a bar: ~~Woman~~ (in the French version it is ~~La~~ femme; the bar strikes the definite article) (1973b).

Similarly, taking Lacan's references from "L'Étourdit" (1973a) and *Seminar XXIII* (1975–1976) a step further, along with his minimal references to schizophrenia, we could suggest that schizophrenia does not exist. Thus, the psychoanalytic diagnosis of schizophrenia might coincide with the logic of the fierce commentary this concept met with during the second half of the twentieth century, suggesting that there is no such thing as schizophrenia; we therefore may choose to strike it with a bar too: ~~schizophrenia~~. Apart from the word's unfortunate connotations, which Freud had also highlighted from an early stage (1908; 1911c), it seems that the descriptive "so-called" or "what is called" can be referring to the singularity of each case. At some point Miller (1987) playfully suggested that psychosis, in terms of a unified field, does not exist either.

Yet if schizophrenia may not exist for psychoanalysis, schizophrenics do. These are subjects like Peter, Amelia, Paul, Jane, and Susan, who are all marked by an unmediated relation to the real and who have found—or not found—some way to deal with it by knotting to the One an imaginary constitution for the body, like Georgios did by elaborating on the being and the language of the "child".

Finding such a way is vital for the subject's subsistence. As was noted above, its orientation can be already designated by a psychoanalytic diagnosis, which can give the clinician an idea of the direction where treatment must start or take place. This was demonstrated in Georgios' case, in a knotting of the child's body and language evident in his multidimensional writing activity.

Some subjects, like him, are capable of finding such a way alone. His writing lasted for almost thirty years. Joyce's probably lasted for his entire life. Clinicians can use those paradigms as examples to help, like skilled "secretaries", subjects who are not themselves sufficiently fortunate or capable to find such an orientation in their struggle with the failures of the make-believe. In the following chapter, there is an investigation of ways in which schizophrenic subjects can be encouraged to attempt this.

CHAPTER NINE

The range of schizophrenic inventions

As was noted above, if psychoanalysis is still in need of diagnosis, this is so that the clinician can orient treatment (Guéguen, 2013; Leader, 2011; Verhaeghe, 2008). The objective of contemporary psychiatric diagnosis, on the other hand, seems to be limited to classification (Vanheule, 2012).

In the following pages, I describe how the link between psychoanalytic diagnosis and treatment applies to the case of schizophrenia by studying the range of various attempts by schizophrenic subjects to tackle the challenges stemming from the body's direct relation to the real, unmediated by the symbolic.

Before presenting those, I discuss the origins of the rationale of a Lacanian orientation in the treatment of schizophrenic subjects found in Freud. Yet to explain one of its coordinates it seems appropriate to start with a short reference to the point where the preceding chapter stopped: the psychiatric approach to schizophrenia.

The logic of the psychoanalytic treatment
of schizophrenia

Stabilisation at any cost?

The medical treatment of schizophrenia seems to be taking the approach to psychiatric diagnosis one step further: from ignoring the subject's relation to the real to attacking its manifestation with no second thoughts.

Contemporary pharmaceutical treatment of schizophrenia is considered successful in reducing "positive" schizophrenic symptoms (Tandon, Keshavan, & Nasrallah, 2008a; Tandon et al., 2008b; Leucht et al., 2009). This approach, however, seems to be running totally opposite to the treatment suggested by Lacanian psychoanalysis.

We do not need to look at Lacan's later teaching on the sinthome to grasp this (1975–1976). We can stick to the simple remark from *Seminar III* (1955a) that those phenomena are linked to the reappearance of the non-symbolised in the real. In psychoanalytic treatment we are interested in the subject's relation to the real because the impact of the One on the body, the unary trait, can be found in the interim. Thus, the pharmaceutical addressing of those symptoms is attacking some of the few instruments available to the clinician for accessing the singular character of every subject, schizophrenic or not.

Lacan has criticised an attack like this, which resonates with what was advocated by his friend, French organicist psychiatrist Henri Ey, arguing that being delusional may be indeed an "error" but this does not correspond to any deficit of belief (1946). That something might not be "objectively" acknowledged as true has absolutely no effect on the subject believing it. In the 1940s Lacan treats this as "truth", whereas in the 1960s he will rather see the real in it. This attack to the truth or real is what is assisted by the excessive use of medication.

Modern psychiatry thus seems to prefer silencing the real and working with what seems like reality; in other words, attacking the One for the sake of the make-believe, the forgery stemming from the Other of the social bond, which the schizophrenic encounters structural problems believing in. Of course it must be clarified once more and with no further ado that no one is in any case advocating to encourage subjects to become delusional; what is encouraged is a quest for the subjective resonances in those phenomena, as Lacan suggested in *Seminar III*.

Yet despite the gap between the two disciplines it seems that the psychiatric addressing of mental disorders has transmitted a signifier to the field of the study of psychosis in psychoanalytic literature: "stabilisation".

Lacanians (Grasser, 1998; Leader, 2011; Maleval, 2015; Soler, 1988) frequently use this term to describe the objective or effects of treatment with psychotic subjects. Stabilisation was a term I had also used when I first wondered about Georgios' case. One of the questions I was asking myself was what helped this man remain "stable" before his admission to a psychiatric institution and despite the fundamental challenges he was facing with regards to his body (see *Part II*).

In her paper "Stabilisation of Psychosis", Soler (1992a) remarks that this signifier may as well refer to cases of sedation, often observed in clinical work with psychotic subjects. Nothing can be said of instability in their case. What is more stable, wonders Soler, than the subject who rests deep in its bed (1992a, p. 195)? To see how unrelated to psychoanalysis stabilisation at any cost is, we can remind ourselves of the only period of utter "stability" in Georgios' case: his last months at the Dromokaiteion hospital, when he was unable to move, speak or write. We can hardly claim that from his life's various endeavours and experiences described in *Part II*, this one had a treatment effect just because it kept the material aspect of his body stable.

In contrast, instead of asking what helped him remain "stable" I could have asked myself what helped the *subject* subsist in Georgios's case. Chapter Seven concluded that the adopted name "Vizyenos" and the writing this accompanied had effects of treatment because they corresponded to the acquisition of the body and its organs by the subject or the speaking being. This helped Georgios tackle for more than two decades the fundamental challenges to knot one's body and organs to language. On the other hand, one cannot suggest that he was the master of his body after his narcissistic pedestal vacillated, with the beginning of the end being located somewhere in the late 1880s.

No acquisition of the body image is guaranteed by sedation or stabilisation, which is among the effects of psychiatric medication. No matter how stabilising its effects might be, the pharmaceutical eradication of symptoms does not focus upon the subject's constitution but tackles it. If there is an aspect of the subject's relation to the real hidden in those symptoms, attempting to silence them with no second thoughts ignores one of the few subjective elements in the schizophrenic condition.

This approach reminds me of my employment for some months at a central London supported-housing facility for people with severe and enduring mental disorders. Ten residents, among them many schizo-phrenics, were supported in keeping a household, paying their bills, and maintaining a seemingly "stable" mental condition. Consonant to the contemporary psychiatric establishment, where evaluation depends on what the evaluator can see, if those people were able to demonstrate that they could live on their own—by showing, for instance, that they could cook once a week—they were considered as progressing and were soon encouraged to rent an apartment of their own. Moreover, the company's policy was for tenants' frequently expressed delusional beliefs to be attacked in a rather disregarding—and in my opinion, dis-respectful—manner: "whenever they are sharing those thoughts, you should tell them that this is nonsense and it is not helping them", was the guidance to staff members like myself. Needless to say, coming from a psychoanalytic perspective, I found it very difficult to abide by such guidelines and very soon saw the way out. Yet I still hold that no mat-ter how "stable" those people appeared to the eyes of the evaluator, the silencing of the subjective resonances hiding behind thoughts like "I am JFK's fiancé" or "I am the Queen's cousin" was leading nowhere, due to its total lack of respect for the above-mentioned subjective reso-nances. And relapses, which were not infrequent—and which speak of anything but stability—were witnesses to that failure.

Consequently, "stabilisation" is a term about whose use psychoana-lysts must be very careful (Soler, 1992a). The same happens with another term employed by psychiatry and even used by Freud: "recovery". Aflalo (2015) wonders how one can define a state as "normal" if recovery is con-sidered as the return to such an original condition (p. 65).

Those terms will thus be avoided in the following analysis of schizo-phrenic inventions that can constitute a treatment direction. A clinician should not in any way aim necessarily for stabilisation, since that can often cost the subject's presence, or a recovery, when a "normal" state to which the subject is called to return is precarious.

What, then, can be the objective of psychoanalytic treatment with schizophrenics, which must investigate the subject's relation to the real and is not identical to stabilisation or recovery at any cost?

An objective rooted in Freud

In the first half of the 1910s, Freud would suggest that for the para-noid aspect of the paraphrenic subject, "victory" lay with a secondary projection of libido to the self and similar others, as an effect of the loss of object-love, a theory he formulated in his first major study of the psychoses (1911c; 1914c). In contrast, for the proper paraphrenic (schizophrenic), "victory" at a first stage in Freud's theory lay in hallucination, and then the projection of libido to words, since otherness in the form of similar figures cannot be established, as Lacan confirmed in the 1930s and 1950s.

The subject's incapacity to recover the object is maintained in Lacan's teaching too, yet in a different rationale. As was noted in Chapter Three, for Lacan the object is never lost in psychosis. The madman has it in his pocket (Lacan, 1967a). Alienation (Lacan, 1964a), the first operation of the causation of subjectivity (Miller, 2009b), may have taken place to some extent, but separation, which generates the extraction of the object *a*, has not. As was discussed a few pages above, the object does not exist as a third, mediating factor, between the subject and the Other of language.

Georgios' invention was neither linked to an attachment to otherness, specular or related to discourse, or in recapturing any lost object, but to an acquisition of the subject's body. In Chapter Seven, I analysed the anchoring of the imaginary to the real through the symbolic based on Lacan's theory of knotting. There was no word about regaining any lost object, because no object was ever lost. What was regained was not the subject's relation to an object, but the body image.

Thus, this direction for a treatment for the schizophrenic subject has its roots not in the Freud of the 1910s, but of the 1920s. A few years after "The Unconscious", where Freud (1915e) clarifies that the object is never actually recaptured in schizophrenia, the founder of psychoanalysis suggested as the differential mark between neurosis and psychosis not any more the loss of the object, but the nature of the subject's withdrawal from a piece of reality (Freud, 1924e). This is the way that a Lacanian clinician can assist the subject to continue with one of the schizophrenic's "first steps" at a recovery (Freud, 1915e): to address the clash with reality.

Earlier, it was argued that in the later Lacan reality is a composite of make-believes. It is the junction of symbolic and the imaginary, which Miller (2006) writes as: S ◊ I—the rhombus standing for all relations in Lacan's cosmos, as in his formula for fantasy: $ ◊ *a* (Evans, 1996). The schizophrenic constitution is characterised by a detachment of the imaginary (which, apart from the body image, also includes emotion and meaning) from the real.

In "The Loss of Reality in Neurosis and Psychosis", Freud (1924e, p. 187) argues that the loss of reality is "made good" in psychosis through a replacement of that external reality by a "new, imaginary external world". A new imaginary external world instead of a new relation to the object, as he had argued concerning Schreber and had excluded for the schizophrenic (Freud, 1911c). Thus, the factor to which jouissance will be channelled is not an object, but a new imaginary agent. The third, mediating, factor needed between subject and the real therefore must be introduced in the domain of the subject's own imaginary external world, rather than in the form of an external object.

To show how this happens for the subject who cannot establish otherness like paranoiacs, neurotic and—partially—melancholic subjects (that is, all those that are not "so-called schizophrenics"), we need to turn to Lacan's later teaching. The later Lacan's (1975–1976) view of how to support the subject's subsistence—from the interconnection of the real, the symbolic, and the imaginary, with no reference to a factor such as the Other's Other—does not seem too far from this suggestion.

If we wanted to apply this objective of the treatment to schizophrenic subjects—since in 1924 Freud writes about psychosis in general—in light of the later Lacan's reading, we could, indeed, set it as the anchoring of the imaginary, which is floating above the ground and beneath the clouds, to the subject's constitution, which initially corresponds to their direct relation to the real attached to the symbolic. This will introduce a third factor, where jouissance will be channelled and help him or her "acquire" the body and its organs.

If we still want therefore to employ the term "stabilisation" in the treatment of schizophrenics, we might use this term for the status of the flexible imaginary in relation to the other two registers. The body image must be grasped so that it can anchor the jouissance inherent in the real (and the symbolic).

Yet, as was written earlier, the clinician does not have to invent the field in which the body image must anchor the subject's relation to the real. He or she can benefit from the subject's direct relation to the real, as in Georgios' relation to the real signifier "child". They can, then, encourage the psychotic subject's "capacity for invention" (Maleval, 2015, p. 101) in a welcoming setting where he or she leads the work, rather than in a place of a transferential relation guided by the subject-supposed-to-know, which may suit other subjective constitutions (Allouch, 2015).

Below, I present a number of treatment directions for schizophrenics that have been suggested by psychoanalysts from the second half of the twentieth century until today, picking up the thread from where this was left in *Part I*. Potential "secretaries to the insane" are given the chance to judge if the one stemming from Lacan's later teaching seems suitable for the schizophrenic subject, as I tried to show by examining the case of Georgios Vizyenos.

Capturing the imaginary through … the imaginary

a-a': Fastening to a small other's image

Working with schizophrenic subjects via an exclusive mobilisation of the imaginary is one of the oldest orientations in the psychoanalytic treatment of this psychotic sub-type. It is based on the idea that the subject's imaginary constitution, the ego, established during the mirror stage, rests upon the infant's identification with the complete image of its body (Lacan, 1949).

It is thus based on localising the imaginary of the body through the image of the other. Consequently, in the theories and techniques enlisted in this category, an anchoring of the body to the subject is achieved thanks to the use of the imaginary, with only secondary references to the symbolic.

A schizophrenic subject's simplest, and at the same time, most precarious attempt to acquire their body image comes from one's sole dependence on the imaginary axis. In the previous chapters, there has been reference to its theoretical foundations, Freud's narcissism (1914c) and Lacan's mirror stage (1949), from which paranoid constructions begin: the body image is captured thanks to the image of the body of someone else, a specular, small other, represented in the *schema L* by the axis as *a-a'*.

This is, however, an elementary and precarious anchoring of the body, exactly due to the fact that the subject is expected to depend upon something they have not been able to fully establish: the intrusion of otherness (Lacan, 1938). Thus, its fragile character is frequently observed in hospitalised schizophrenic subjects, that is, after its vacillation. How often do we not meet in the clinic people suffering a breakdown after a friend, a colleague or even a pet disappears from the stage? In Chapter Two, I referred to the example of Amelia.

A similar case was that of a hospitalised young man, Stephen. Stephen was a twenty-seven-year-old man admitted for a third time to a public psychiatric institution. Manifest symptoms had started in his late adolescence, when he met a young woman at a bar. That woman supposedly resembled another girl, whom he had been talking about as his puppy love. He described the incident thus:

> I met a woman whom ... A woman ... a small girl rather, I was four and she was six. I hugged her, she hugged me, we danced a blues, I lost myself in that aura, in her aura, she asked me to marry her, she told me *"do you love me? Will you marry me?"* and I said yes. [...] That girl was put in an orphanage because her mother had no money, she could not raise her, and *"will you marry me?"* she said [...] then, when I was sixteen, I went into a bar and I saw that beautiful girl dancing and I thought to myself *"I know her from somewhere".*

Before the incident in the bar Stephen had not presented symptoms of the return of jouissance to the body. The image of the woman dancing sensually was the occasion for his first breakdown and subsequent hospitalisations. After that event, he would frequently get involved in fights, make excessive use of drugs and alcohol, and suffer severe fractures. What had happened?

It seems that the young girl's image was functioning as a specular other for Stephen, helping him fasten to his own body. Hence, his reference to hugs, dance, and auras when he recounted meeting her. Yet it seems that this fastening lacked the gravity of an identification confirmed by the Other, which is the matrix for narcissism in paranoia as well as in "normal" human development. Thus, the image of the girl dancing in the bar annulled the innocence of the image of the six-year-old "orphan" girl's body, contaminating it with hints of sexuality or femininity stemming from the hole created by the real of the inexistent sexual relationship (Lacan, 1973a). Stephen collapsed. In lack of a "third factor", this happened by breaking his body parts or sedating himself via an excessive consumption of drugs. All these were attempts to localise his body image somewhere; to stop it from being anywhere above the ground and beneath the clouds. This anchoring was necessary, since his body had stopped being supported precariously by the "orphan" girl's image, to which he had not identified, but simply "fastened".

At the end of the day, both Freud (1911c; 1914c; 1915e) and Lacan (1938; 1955–1956) highlighted the schizophrenic's incapacity to adhere to the imaginary steadily by establishing otherness. Nevertheless, despite its precarious character, we must not neglect the minimal gain by the subject's being maintained at the position of Narcissus, as Lacan puts it in "On a Question Prior to Any Possible Treatment of Psychosis" (1958a): a position like this, in the end, is better than no position, as we can deduce from Freud's reading of Schreber's case (1911c) and as was seen in Georgios' first years in the asylum. Of course, Georgios' and Schreber's solutions implied much more than fastening to a small other's body image, like Stephen.

The potential "secretary to the insane" may encounter such relations to others' images when working with schizophrenic subjects. However, this is not a practice that can be intentionally employed by the clinician. He or she can encourage the patient to maintain them, if those are help-ful to the subject, yet always bearing in mind their precarious status. The same seems to happen for a more complex variation of the attachment of the schizophrenic subject's body image thanks to imaginary means.

Lent ordinariness

Lacan referred to this still precarious but more complicated treatment in his seminar on the psychoses (1955–1956). It was summarised by Helene Deutsch's "as-if" personality, describing cases where, by copy-ing others, the schizophrenic creates an artificial personality that lacks genuineness (Deutsch, 1942). One can clearly see in this reference the mirror stage at work too: a subject who lacks or has a poor ego forms a false ego by adhering to images of others (Leader, 2011, p. 198).

In this case the small other's body that still helps the imaginary sta-bilise is not simply where the subject fastens as a specular image, as was described above. Subjects are copying more than the other's image, although there is still minimal connection between the imaginary and the amalgam of real and symbolic, if there is one. Borrowing the other's personality is more complicated than the simple specular adhesion to someone on the basis of *a-a'*.

It might not be wrong discussing an aspect of what appears in the phenomenology of Deutsch's "as-ifs" under the signifier "ordinary psychosis", which was rather recently introduced as a category for the study and treatment of psychosis in the schools of the Freudian Field (Miller, 1997).

This signifier emerged when Lacanian psychoanalysts asked themselves about non-triggered psychoses (Laurent, 2012), patients whom the clinician hesitated to diagnose as neurotic, although they presented no manifest signs of psychosis. Something did not really fit in (the same observation had led Deutsch to formulate the "as-if"). This clinical category is not characterised by a rigid definition; it is "more of an epistemic than an objective category" (Miller, 2009a, p. 149). In the almost two decades that have passed since its introduction, Lacanians have not seen eye to eye about exactly what ordinary psychosis is (Brousse, 2009; Klotz, 2009; Miller, 2009a; Stevens, 2009).

Jacques-Alain Miller (2009a), who coined the term, suggests that schizophrenia "may well be the reality of the subject, which may appear as an ordinary psychosis because it's not self-evident" (p. 153). He thus encourages clinicians not to restrict themselves at the level of ordinary psychosis, if such a diagnosis is being thought of, but to go beyond that and find the classical sub-type of psychosis behind it (paranoia, schizophrenia or melancholia) (Miller, 2009a). Therefore, instead of crossing out schizophrenia, this epistemic category seems to be showing exactly one of the treatment directions that a subject can create: those that fall within the spectrum of the ordinary, like the "as-if."

Take for example Philip, a twenty-five-year old man who came to see me complaining about his unconsummated love life. Philip has never had sex, despite his expressed wish to do so; we might already pose the hypothesis of a problematic relation to phallic jouissance. Whenever Philip was attempting to have intercourse he felt his body "petrified". His marginal social life comprised a couple of friends, a girl and a boy, whom he was describing as his *"enfants terribles"*, in a neologistic use of this phrase. While he was in therapy, Philip avoided any sexual activity and things were running fine when suddenly a cousin of his wanted to have an affair with the female friend. That was more devastating to him than the failures in his sexual life, since his dependence on the girl's image was one of the subject's few imaginary constitutions. My therapeutic direction at that point was to support its maintenance—with no impressive results, I must admit.

I believe this was due to a clinician having frequently very limited power over those ordinary but relatively more elaborate "solutions", since they are often already established—or vacillated—when subjects meet him or her.

In contrast, cases that have achieved an anchoring of the imaginary thanks to an operation emphasising the symbolic or the real, such as Joyce, merit the characterisation of "extraordinary psychosis!" (Miller, 2009a), even if that never triggers. I believe that inventions like Georgios' must be also considered among the extraordinary ones, if only for the volume of his creations through writing.

Regardless of how we approach this orientation, as a form of "as-if" or as "ordinary psychoses" where the imaginary prevails, the clinician has limited power over this treatment too, since it relates to where the schizophrenic is not a master: processing otherness. This is probably why Lacan (1956a) calls them "conformist imaginary identifications". We cannot do much more than help sustain it, if that is for the subject's benefit, as in Philip's case. Therefore, this creation can be also listed among the ones a "secretary to the insane" might encounter, although they might have no power in introducing one.

Of course, this does not mean that such a solution cannot be a temporary functional treatment for a schizophrenic subject, be that viewed as a rather simple creation compared to Georgios or Joyce's. Despite being a relatively simple creation, the "as-if" can still provide the subject with a support mechanism (Leader, 2011). After all, when we discuss ordinary psychosis, don't we place emphasis on the absence of loud manifest psychotic phenomena? "Lent ordinariness" can provide a relatively functional treatment for a schizophrenic—and not only, since paranoia and melancholia may also be its foundation.

However, the establishment of imaginary relations so that the schizo-phrenic subject can acquire a feeling of their body is not something that psychoanalysts have not tried to initiate. According to such approaches, the clinician must not simply support the introduced small other or alle-viate the effects of its vacillation, but they can introduce practices to help the subject acquire their body image via other parts of the imaginary.

One of the first to suggest such an approach was the German-born psychoanalyst Gisela Pankow, a contemporary of Lacan's, to whom he refers in his seminar. Her work is presented below as exemplary of practices where clinicians attempt to generate a treatment for the schizophrenic subject based on the introduction of an imaginary agent rather than supporting the presence of an already established one, like the *a-a'* or the "as-if".

Active introduction of the body image

Pankow was among the few clinicians of her time to accept for psychoanalysis psychotic patients with severe problems (Gaudillière &

Davoine, 2009). In her clinical work called "dynamic structurisation", it was considered essential to give the person a chance to integrate the dissociated images of his or her body (Pankow, 1958). This happened by integrating the "amplified" counterparts of Lacan's mirror stage (*a* and *a'*) to give rise to a *Gestalt* (1949).

Pankow encouraged the establishment of an imaginary relation to the subject's body through the forced introduction of an external, third factor which other subjects might create thanks to a small other's specular image or by copying their personality.

She would ask schizophrenics to create models with clay. Pankow believed that this material could act as an equivalent to the subject's body image (1961). She maintained that working on it could help the schizophrenic discover the external layout of his or her body image. Thanks to clay-modelling and speech during therapy, the subject was believed to be given the chance to discover the boundaries between the external and the internal world of their body, recognising it thus as a unified form. After that was achieved, interpersonal relations would come into play to introduce the dialectics of being and having. When a patient, for example, created a shoe, Pankow (1985) would ask them "Whose shoe might that be?" or "if you were this shoe, what might you do with my body?" (p. 443) depending on whether she wanted to introduce the potential of an object-relation or the identification of the schizophrenic's body with the model. This activity aimed at helping the subject to establish what was inside his or her body and what was not, and even paved the way for psychoanalytic work in the style of the school of object-relations (Pankow, 1961).

This theoretical position and therapeutic direction can therefore be counted among the treatment directions that implicate introducing a third, imaginary factor to the subject's world with no reference to the existing subjective constitution with regards to the real. Ver Eecke (2001b) describes it as "work aimed at repairing the body image by means of imaginary products" (p. 99).

Yet the lack of focus on the symbolic or real does not in any way mean that Pankow's work and analogous approaches are of minimal use or value for schizophrenic subjects. Sometimes identifications can assist the subject to maintain a fragile equilibrium (Morel, 2011). In effect, the idea of anchoring the body image by means of other imaginary parts as well as specular relationships has even been used in institutional work with schizophrenics that claims to be successful (Dana, 2015; Ver Eecke,

2001b). An example from the United Kingdom is the therapeutic communities that arose in the 1960s and 1970s inspired by Klein's work (Hinshelwood, 2001); these are communities of non-authoritative interpersonal relations, where the subject is invited to function in a setting where a democratic relation between residents and staff is encouraged; according to Leader (2011, p. 295) this is nothing but another way to involve imaginary relations in therapy.

Such approaches may indeed succeed in an objective like this, offering the subject a new "imaginary external world". Yet they seem to overlook two significant remarks by Lacan: first, that the schizophrenic is not a master of establishing otherness and, secondly, that the first body organ that can help acquire the rest is the language-organ (Lacan, 1973a). In Pankow's work language does play a role, yet a supportive one, rather than being at the core of the treatment. Moreover, the language whose use she encourages is not the one where the symbolic is closer to lalangue and the subject's relation to the real. This approach seems to be in discord with Freud's (1915e) remark about one of the first attempts at a recovery being the cathexis of libido to word-presentations instead of images of the self or others.

Lacan implied this even before his theoretical shift towards the real linked to the living being, in *Seminar V, The Formations of the Unconscious*. He referred there to Pankow's approach to the "subject when he is schizophrenic" (note, once more, the indirect reference to schizophrenia) (Lacan, 1957b). He argued that approaches like that ignore the primary character of the signifier and law, the Other in other words, and privilege meaning and figure, a personality (1957c); in other words, the imaginary.

Pankow's neglect of the real at this stage can be viewed in the neglect of the symbolic, which Lacan had already identified to the former in schizophrenia (1954). For her part, Pankow (1958) insisted that her suggested employment of the body-image was assisted by the intervention of "symbolising functions" (recognition of a dynamic relation between the whole body and one of its parts and recognition of the content and meaning of that tie that transcends the form). Yet she still seemed to be describing the imaginary, in which lay body image and meaning. Pankow is summarising her work as "a creative process based on the dialectics of forms" (1985, p. 441), which is nothing but imaginary in Lacan's thinking, established in the mirror stage. Yet narcissism, which lies on the mirror stage, was considered a breakthrough for the paranoiac, rather than the schizophrenic.

It seems therefore that placing emphasis on the imaginary part of reality pays little attention to the part of the person's subjectivity entangled between real and symbolic, where jouissance lies. Thus, although Lacanians do not overlook the potential of a therapeutic quality in "acquiring" the body through the use of parts from the imaginary, their approach seems to focus more on the side of the symbolic, which is already linked to the real. The orientation in treatment they promote, contrasting with the preceding one, is discussed below.

From the symbolic to the real

Paranoid pseudo-metaphor/symbolic suppléance/invention of a delusion

In *Seminar III*, Lacan (1956a) differentiated "conformist" imaginary mechanisms employed by schizophrenic subjects from constructions such as President Schreber's delusional metaphor, a recurrent example of how a new "imaginary external world" can be created thanks to an elaboration of the symbolic (De Waelhens & Ver Eecke, 2001). The reader might have expected to find Schreber's self-cure in the previous section, but this was not so. Although narcissism was Freud's (1911c) emphasis on how the German judge achieved his temporary treatment, which Lacan explained through the mirror stage, in his case the symbolic was largely implicated too in knotting the imaginary. It was, moreover, for this reason that his invention is considered much more solid than treatments achieved by a stabilisation of the imaginary through the imaginary. His case is thus discussed in the present section.

In contrast to inventions that depend exclusively on the imaginary field, when emphasis is placed on the symbolic, the aim behind the mobilisation of this register is to impose order, its characteristic function, and stabilise the "vacillating imaginary world" (Miller, 2009a, p. 150). The composites and function of the symbolic were described in detail in Chapter Two. The imaginary cannot impose order itself, since its characteristic function is exactly specular: jumping from the one side to the other. The psychotic subject must find ways to treat the jouissance whose prey it can become by use of the signifier (Voruz & Wolf, 2007).

As was noted in Chapter Seven, one of Lacan's prominent students, Alfredo Zenoni, has suggested as the objective of work with schizophrenics to *find the connections between the symbolic and the body*, an alternative to the direct connections between the imaginary and the organ (2012) that are seen in the phenomena of the return of jouissance to the subject's body. In the same chapter I demonstrated how the signifier "Vizyenos" linked the imaginary to the real of the body through the mediation of the symbolic and not via a direct connection. Zenoni's (2012) suggestion, which translates into the clinic Lacan's reference to the schizophrenic in "L'Étourdit" (1973a), seems to be far from the objective of a mere "acquisition" of the body via the imaginary. The potential "secretary to the insane" also has the symbolic at his or her disposal.

Of course, to work exclusively with the symbolic in order to create a new imaginary world to anchor to the real does not seem easy, since the two registers are one in schizophrenia (Lacan, 1954). In fact, in the following investigation of the range of treatments through the symbolic, it is suggested that excluding the real is not simply impossible but might also be inadvisable. According to the existing—albeit limited—literature, utilising the real might be also a treatment orientation for schizophrenic subjects, since it is implicating the One in the place of the Other of the social bond.

As was concluded in *Part I*, paranoia and schizophrenia cannot coincide. A schizophrenic subject cannot become paranoiac in a reverse view of schizophrenia having been considered in the past as regression from paranoia (Freud, 1911c; Lacan, 1938).

However, the creation of a delusional metaphor to substitute for the failure of the paternal metaphor is referred to in the discussion of practices that can bring about a treatment with schizophrenic subjects. A schizophrenic's inclination toward paranoia, in the sense of the limitation of jouissance to the field of the Other, is sometimes described as progress (De Waelhens & Ver Eecke, 2001; Verhaeghe, 2008). It seems, however, that there is a demarcation line that must be drawn between paranoid structure and the attempts at a delusional metaphor. Let us return to Schreber, who was believed to have achieved a temporary treatment thanks to a delusional metaphor.

In *Part I*, I discussed the content and solidity of Schreber's construction in time. Based on Lacan's reference to paranoia in his later teaching (1975b), next to other contemporary psychoanalysts' perspectives (Laurent, 2007a; Miller, 1983) I suggested that it might be advisable to study Schreber from a schizophrenic rather than paranoid perspective, regardless of the theoretical lesson we draw from the function and content of his delusional metaphor.

As was suggested earlier, to consider a schizophrenic subject's attempt at treatment successful, it must tackle the effects of the detachment of the imaginary from the subjective constitution, that is, it must have hindered the return of jouissance to the corporeal aspect of the subject's body by anchoring the body image to language. In paranoia, this starts from establishing an identification with another's image.

Schreber's edifice did utilise figures of otherness (Flechsig, God, etc.). Yet the relation to those figures does not seem to have offered his body the effect of totality deriving from a solid specular identification. Schreber sees in the mirror a female torso. He also refers to his body as harbouring colonies of foreign nerves, as well as his being a leper's corpse leading other lepers' corpses (Schreber, 1903). These images do not point to a successful undergoing of the mirror stage. The position Schreber's invention guaranteed for his body does not seem to have safeguarded a solid narcissistic covering for it, dependent on the other's image; lepers' bodies are rather bodies in decay, dead bodies, which resemble the schizophrenic's fragmented body—in Georgios' case it reminds us of the corpses of his two dead sisters—rather than a body in whose totality the subject jubilates. Could this still be considered therefore as a paranoid construction that acts as treatment for a schizophrenic subject?

As was noted above, one might have been encouraged to discuss this case thus until the first half of the twentieth century, but thanks to Lacan's later teaching, Lacanian psychoanalysis has diverged from that direction. When Lacan says that a personality is the same as paranoia, equating it to the merging of the three registers, he points towards differentiating paranoia from its former "poor relation", schizophrenia. According to Zenoni (2012), when Lacan introduces his theory on knotting the three registers in absence of a Borromean knot, it is rather to schizophrenia that he will allude (p. 161).

Thus, the two directions in the treatment of the absence of a Borromean knot between the real, the symbolic, and the imaginary differ structurally. Therefore, if Schreber had indeed a schizophrenic rather than paranoid constitution, we can suggest that his treatment had a paranoid orientation, but did not establish a steady paranoid edifice, since, in the end, the three rings came apart in his final breakdown and death in the asylum, having a similar end to Georgios (see *Parts I & II*). What led to his temporary cure could have been, instead of identification of jouissance to the field of the Other based on a successful undergoing of the mirror stage, the elaboration of schizophrenic language that led to the creation of the neo-code (1958a) *Grundsprache* that gave him a feeling of a transsexual yet enjoyed body with a narcissistic covering.

The Lacanian focus therefore regarding working with schizophrenic subjects does not concern the establishment of a paranoid construction, but inventions that redistribute the jouissance of the real (attached to the symbolic) in anchoring the subject's body and its organs to their singular discourse, an orientation that comes directly from Freud (1911c; 1915e). Nothing guarantees that, for the schizophrenic, the paranoid solution is exceptionally solid, functional or therapeutic. What other way is there, therefore?

Similar to what I attempted to do in *Part II* to illustrate what clinicians might encounter and support in working with psychotic subjects, psychoanalysts frequently borrow examples from history, art, philosophy, and mathematics. The work of exceptional individuals from those fields can show how subjects have managed to channel a part of jouissance to the imaginary thanks to titanic and/or singular mobilisations of the symbolic. A clinician can use those cases, some of which are referred to below, as examples of conducting treatment with schizophrenic subjects other than via the exclusive use of the imaginary. However, the differentiation between the objective of paranoid and schizophrenic subjects must not be overlooked. For the description of those constructions the term *suppléance*, French for "replacement", is frequently used (Soler, 1992a).

This term was initially used by Lacan to talk about both psychosis and neurosis. First used in 1958 (Pellion, 2009), suppléance is used today more extensively and with a wider sense that in Lacan's time (Lysy-Stevens, 2002). It seems to encompass the variety of treatments that subjects generate in order to avoid the triggering of psychosis. In fact, imaginary constructions such as the "as-if" have been referred to as "imaginary suppléances" that can have a therapeutic effect (Galiana-Mingot, 2010). Suppléance may be an eligible candidate, against the delusional metaphor, for being held responsible for the particularities that appear in schizophrenic cases (Pellion, 2009). The word is therefore of "symbolic suppléances".

Soler (1988) comments on Joyce, whose relation to schizophrenia has been already discussed, as a suppléance encompassing the symbolic. His particular use of language helped him anchor the body that was falling "as easily as a fruit is divested of its soft ripe peel" (Joyce, 1916). Other well-known examples of psychotic subjects who achieved a treatment thanks to their laborious work in literature or art are Rousseau, Hölderlin, and Van Gogh (Soler, 1988).

The example of Jean-Jacques Rousseau's creation of a new symbolic (Soler, 1988) can help us designate further the appropriate treatment orientation for schizophrenia. If Schreber's case is suspended between schizophrenia and paranoia, Rousseau's falls unquestionably on the side of the second.

A psychotic subject, Rousseau was able to create through his writing a "prosthetic" or "compensatory symbolic order" (Leader, 2011, pp. 204, 207), triggering a "civilisation" of the Thing via the symbolic homogeneous to that of the delusional metaphor (Soler, 1988).

Miller (2012) sees Rousseau's endeavour as having succeeded in the objective of taming the real by channelling it to a figure of otherness. As is seen primarily in Rousseau's *Social Contract*, his work achieves the creation of a new Big Other. His subject's relation to an Other is established in an invention that bears "essentially" (Miller, 2012, p. 261) on the social bond. Its emergence dresses the subject with the narcissism that makes him an interlocutor of these new configurations of society.

A major difference between Rousseau and writers like Joyce or Luis Wolfson is the outcome of their writing concerning meaning. Rousseau's work on society, education and the sexual relationship via a multi-dimensional use of the symbolic does not entail Joyce or Wolfson's particular use of lalangue—which lies outside meaning—but generates a new meaning for those aspects of human experience. In contrast, the work of subjects like Joyce and Wolfson does not seem to have generated a universal meaning about what they write. They do not generate an Other, a field in which jouissance is identified.

Something of a similar nature seems to have occurred in Georgios' case. In *Part II*, Vizyenos' writing was discussed in light of the creation of a new discourse thanks to which his anchored body was dressed with a narcissistic covering. His pursuit of childhood created the invention that generated his name and his writing, which gave him a beautified body and established pseudo-quilting points. Yet this pursuit was never accomplished to the end, neither was it entirely based on meaning.

In fact, the subject of children's education, which occupied Rousseau's interest too, can demonstrate the difference between the two men. Vizyenos' advice on children's upbringing does not aim primarily at serving the social bond, but at defusing the child's "dark, intensive, and formless force" (1881b, p. 178). The first steps toward this direction, which is not Rousseau's service to the social bond (1762), were given in

Vizyenos' poetry. Athanasopoulos (1992) writes about Vizyenos' take on the meaning of childhood, which the former compares to Vizyenos' passion for mining, that maybe what the poet got from the abandoned mine of childhood was something common, worthless or of small value, like his children's poems and songs, which in Modern Greek Literature do not exist as bearers of some meaning.

Leader (2011) writes that psychotic inventions do not necessarily create meaning; they can empty it out too, as in Joyce and Wolfson. Zenoni, in fact, suggests corresponding what takes place in paranoia with regards to the Other and meaning, to what takes place in schizophrenia with regards to the body and language (2012).

Indeed, it seems that in the end Georgios did not serve meaning either. He did not generate a new world that would make him his Creator, like Rousseau. Neither did his poetry, short stories or scientific papers involve the discovery of a new aspect of childhood, in contrast to Rousseau, who generated a new perspective for society, love, and education (Miller, 2012). In other words, the "Other" to his name that his writing generated was a singular, self-made locus that was made first for personal consumption. The "new imaginary external world" created was not thus intended for the recognition and approval of the social Other. This is, probably, why he sarcastically calls one of his poetry collections *Rubbish*, to mock the Athenian literary establishment, the Other for whose approval he did not intend to sacrifice much.

Could we, therefore, use cases like Rousseau, Joyce, Wolfson—and Vizyenos—under the signifier of suppléance?

A number of significant figures in the Freudian Field (Laurent, 2012; Miller, 2012) avoid the use of suppléance, preferring instead the term "invention", whereas other psychoanalysts in the same institution (Maleval, 2015) use both terms, probably using suppléance in its more general meaning.

Accordingly, the psychotic subject must invent something to defend himself or herself against the real. Miller insists on the use of the term "invention" for a special reason: to contrast it to "discovery". "Invention" means that the subject is not required to find something new, but to improvise with what it has been given (Miller, 2012).

This reminds one directly of Freud's (1915e) remark that the first step towards a recovery is the schizophrenic's cathexis of the libido to word-presentations, which in Georgios' case I suggested as being the resonances of lalangue linked to the real signifier "child". What the person is given in schizophrenia is their direct relation to parts of the jouissance of language in the form of lalangue, the marks of the One. "Invention" seems to capture Freud's idea of generating something new out of what the schizophrenic is given better than suppléance, which is a signifier referring generally to replacement and could mean the introduction of a new entity.

To return to the question of differentiating between creations like those of Rousseau and Joyce, Miller (2012) takes a step further in his theory of psychotic inventions in creating a short catalogue. He differentiates the two forms that have been referred to above, the invention of a delusion and of an identification, and a third, the invention of a function for the language-organ.

An "invention of an identification" can be correlated to an "imaginary suppléance". "Invention of a delusion", on the other hand, can be a paranoid metaphor, which can be described as "symbolic suppléance". The latter could, therefore, be considered as a second option, next to the sole mobilisation of the imaginary, for schizophrenic subjects to channel jouissance to the image of their body. Both those types, however, describe inventions that pass through otherness. On the other hand, the invention of a function for the language-organ, for which I used Georgios as an example, might be worth the title of "real suppléance" (Hoffmann, 2004; Pellion, 2009).

In relation to schizophrenia, Miller (2012) stresses the importance of an instrumentalisation of language that will be the schizophrenic's invention of a discourse to act as his "own lines of recourse" (p. 261). It is exactly that instrumentalisation of language that can protect the subject from becoming the instrument of language himself, as we saw happening in Georgios' early forties.

It seems that the stress in this reference to language is on the side of the real. Therefore, this aspect of creations by schizophrenic subjects that can have an effect of treatment with the real of language in the first line, might have to be studied in a separate category. I believe that those indications show a different treatment direction to the ones presented above, which target otherness, and can link the schizophrenic's inventiveness with the sinthome, which elaborates upon the One.

Real suppléance/invention of a function for the language-organ/sinthome

In Chapter Seven, I discussed Georgios' case in light of the theory of knotting. I concluded that a treatment came from his invention neither due to a simple establishment of a relation to a specular other (imaginary suppléance) nor to a creation of a meaningful system about childhood (which could have had established an Other through a symbolic suppléance). At the basis of Georgios' writing lay the remnants of his first experiences with language: baby babbling, sounds from nature, Thracian exclamations, and words in Turkish. The subject Vizyenos subsisted thanks to the utilisation of the debris of the One (real) to create a consistency (imaginary) covering the hole in the concept of child (symbolic)—remember that ex-sistence, hole and consistency are Lacan's definitions for the real, the symbolic, and the imaginary in *Seminar XXIII* (see Chapter Three).

Based on Miller's (2012) differentiation of psychotic inventions, we can use this creation as an example of an invention of a function for the language-organ. Miller (2012) writes that in psychosis invention "is conditioned by [what is most essential]: the direct relation to language" (p. 266). Georgios elaborated on what he was given. He was not thus a discoverer, but a true inventor in the way Miller (2012) highlights the property of invention: to construct based on existing material.

This orientation, which, as above, seems to be better linked to Freud and Lacan's references to this psychotic type, can help us differentiate between inventions that emphasise the symbolic and those that emphasise the real. This may help us elaborate further on the relation between the sinthome and schizophrenia, discussed in Chapter Three.

Biagi-Chai (2011) has suggested differentiating between suppléance and sinthome, in relation to the options of the signifier and jouissance respectively. The schizophrenic's need to channel the jouissance inhabiting language might be better served by the second rather than the first, as we could, alternatively, argue for in cases like Rousseau's. In fact, even Soler, who at a first stage speaks generally about suppléance in the case of Joyce (1988), then discusses his case emphasising the real rather than the symbolic; she speaks of a "real operation on the real of language not caught within the network of language" (p. 190). She evokes, moreover, the same logic as Biagi-Chai (2011) when she writes that in Joyce the produced object imposes itself upon the real (Soler, 1988).

Lacan's (1975–1976) reading of Joyce, who also invented a use for the language-organ, shows in which cases it may be more appropriate to speak of sinthome rather than suppléance; the fourth knot Joyce creates based on an elaboration of the amalgamated real and symbolic, the ego, is not simply an imaginary construction, but a narcissistic pedestal that comes in the place of the object *a*, the condenser of jouissance

(Biagi-Chai, 2011). When therefore jouissance in the form of the real of language, which pertains to the mark of the One, is at the heart of that invention, this might have to be separated from a symbolic suppléance and could be called a sinthome.

Are we encouraged, however, to make such a claim by Lacan's own references to schizophrenia? Could a potential "secretary to the insane" envisage the creation of such a concept with schizophrenic subjects where the real comes first?

It is true that the ability to interconnect the real, the symbolic, and the imaginary thanks to a fourth knot, the sinthome, has not been largely discussed in relation to schizophrenia. Lacan, for his part, never did so. Moreover, in the more than three decades that have passed since his death and later teaching, minimal indications by influential scholars in the Lacanian orientation have not concurred on this issue.

Lacan's sporadic references to schizophrenia, which were discussed in the previous chapter, do not seem to be of help. His later teaching, where the theory of knotting and the paradigm of the sinthome were presented, is not an exception. He never says that Joyce was a schizophrenic, as was discussed repeatedly in the present—and he also never said it clearly about Schreber either. One could therefore quite naturally assume that schizophrenia is excluded from this field, especially when paranoia has been minimally, but quite clearly, referred to in the seminar on the sinthome as the merging of the real, the symbolic, and the imaginary. Is this the case, though?

As has been remarked already, Zenoni (2012) writes that when in his later teaching Lacan introduces the question of the knotting of the three registers with no reference to the notion of an Other, he alludes to schizophrenia. It has been already noted that the suggested Lacanian objective of treatment in schizophrenia is not to introduce a third, external factor of otherness, such as a specular other, Other or the object, but to create something to elaborate upon the subject's existing constitution—their unmediated relation to the real.

It seems that the emphasis on the real that characterises inventions by schizophrenic subjects might indeed call for a treatment direction separate from mere suppléance. In fact, returning to what was argued in the preceding chapter, which is that each schizophrenic subject's relation to the real is of utter importance, a treatment that focuses on it might be a suitable option for a schizophrenic subject. In fact, if schizophrenia is not referred to in the clinic of the sinthome, it might be because the two identify, as Miller (1993) has hinted with the theory of "generalised fore-closure" (see the preceding chapter). Allow me to return to Georgios' case for one last time.

As has been already discussed, Vizyenos' invention should be viewed as different to that of Rousseau because it allowed the use of elements from lalangue such as "ai-hak", "ding dang", "tra-la, la-la", etc., ele-ments circumscribing the subject's direct relation to the real. Psycho-analyst Barbara Bonneau (2011a) writes that schizophrenic subjects can create a sinthome, explaining, in her own terminology, that this comes from an elaboration upon what she calls the "icon" (the object having become one with an S_2 in schizophrenia). She compares this pre-existing status to the holophrase (2011a), Lacan's (1964a) term I have at some point parallelised to the signifier "child" in Georgios' case. Bonneau (2011b) suggests that the difference between autism—where holophrase prevails—and schizophrenia, is the schizophrenic's potential to form a discourse, a sinthome.

Yet although the relation of schizophrenia to the sinthome has been to some extent recognised, this might have to be rethought of according to the conclusions reached so far. Maybe the best way to put this is to argue that a schizophrenic subject is not excluded from the sinthomatic solution. The case of Georgios shows us a man keeping together the real, the symbolic, and the imaginary for a rather long time thanks to a writing that utilises units from lalangue, an activity allowing him to establish a marginal relation to a social bond rising on a pedestal. Why cannot this be an option for schizophrenic subjects? Soler (2014) puts, on the one side, sinthome and, on the other, schizophrenia as far as pure schizophrenia is concerned, adding "… if it exists" (p. 134). It seems to me that a pure schizophrenia would be exactly what I have suggested placing a bar on in Chapter Eight: it does not exist. The possibility for the creation of a sinthome should not be thus excluded from "impure" schizophrenics' options.

I believe that the etymology of the word symptom can act as support to this conclusion. To my lack, this comes once more from my mother tongue. "Symptom", from which the sinthome originates, comes from the Greek verb συμπίπτω (sympipto), which means "to coincide". If we adhere for a moment to the schizophrenic's propensity to take things lit-erally, we might expect and even encourage inventions like Vizyenos's, which helped what ex-sists (real), the hole (symbolic), and consistency (imaginary) coincide.

Summary to Part III

As was suggested in *Part II* on the occasion of the case example of Georgios Vizyenos, the contemporary psychoanalytic approach to schizophrenia cannot ignore the subject's relation to the real. The singular status of this relation can act as the cornerstone for both its psychoanalytic diagnosis and treatment.

Diagnosis can take place in two significant steps that revolve around it: differential diagnosis and the quest for the orientation of jouissance in the subject's discourse. Excluding the third factor that jouissance is channelled to crosses out the chance of paranoia and melancholia. Pursuing the jouissance at stake leads to the recognition of the presence of a single version of schizophrenia, since we have suggested striking this signifier with a bar: ~~schizophrenia~~.

Treatment cannot ignore the subject's direct relation to the real either. There is a range of treatment directions that aim at helping the schizophrenic subject assume its body. It seems that those who aim at establishing an imaginary constitution based on a specular relation, *a-a'*, overlook the schizophrenic's fundamental difficulty in establishing otherness, which Freud and Lacan highlighted in the first half of the twentieth century. The same happens partly with the encouragement of the establishment of a meaningful big Other. It seems that the attribution of a body image to the schizophrenic cannot go beyond what Freud had remarked about the cathexis of libido to word-presentations: that it is one of the subject's first attempts at a recovery. This direction of a recovery, with the sinthome among its potentials, can offer the subject's body a narcissistic covering different to that of the mirror stage. It does not pass through otherness, specular or related to discourse, which is also the paranoiac's orientation, but the One, as was shown in the preceding part on the occasion of the study of Georgios Vizyenos.

CONCLUSIONS

The reader might not be surprised to find the section of the conclusions starting with the putting forward of a paradox, one that characterises the series of chapters this book consists of. Further below they will find this not to be its only "paradoxical" quality, which, in my opinion, may not diminish its significance for psychoanalysis.

We started with reference to the introduction of the signifier "schizophrenia" into the psychiatric domain in the early twentieth century (*Part I*), and ended with its Lacanian diagnosis and treatment, in the second decade of the twenty-first century (*Part III*). However, the main case used for the argument concerning a specific orientation in the Lacanian conceptualisation of schizophrenia—the emphasis on the subject's relation to the real—was taken from the late nineteenth century (*Part II*). This might easily seem like a paradox. It is a reservation to be expected and is, to some extent, justified. However, it gives me the opportunity to highlight, for the last time, the distance between psychoanalytic discourse and the other discourses, with the former aiming at circumscribing the subject's singular relation to the real in light of the praxis of psychoanalysis.

The nineteenth-century Greek poet, writer, and scholar Georgios Vizyenos died, indeed, in an Athenian psychiatric hospital three years before Emil Kraepelin formed the separate category of dementia praecox in his *Textbook of Psychiatry* and twelve years before Eugen Bleuler first suggested replacing the term with schizophrenia. As was described in Chapter One, Freud formed his approach to schizophrenia (paraphrenia proper) a few years later, mainly in contrasting it to paranoia. He highlighted schizophrenics' inability to cure themselves in the way paranoiacs do, that is, through an establishment of otherness. Freud's main example was the famous President Schreber, who achieved such a thing by composing his memoirs. Jacques Lacan, who was born five years after Vizyenos' death, maintained this idea, at least in the first period in his teaching, when he studied Freud's reading of Schreber's memoirs. However, as time went by, Lacan made less use of the term "schizophrenia", having almost totally abandoned it in the period described as the "later Lacan". Nevertheless, as was concluded in Chapter Three, nothing prevents us from applying Lacan's teaching on knotting and the theory of the sinthome, which permeate the final period of his seminar, to the conceptualisation and treatment of schizophrenia. In fact, in the light of this approach, sinthome and schizophrenia seem to be found on the same side, and paranoia and neurosis are on the other.

The above-mentioned conclusion concerns Lacan's teaching of the mid-1970s, which took place one century after the beginning of Georgios Vizyenos' writing activity. Yet life itself, with its unexpected encounters, somehow linked Freud and Lacan's views on psychosis and subjectivity with Vizyenos. Research for *Part II* generated the following interesting finding: Vizyenos probably met both Kraepelin, who configured the precursor of schizophrenia, and Flechsig, Schreber's doctor, in 1870s Germany; the first as a fellow student at Wilhelm Wundt's academic lectures and the second as a professor of psychiatry at Leipzig. In addition, de Saussure, the Swiss linguist who formed the theory of the signifier that Lacan borrowed for his teaching on the symbolic, was another fellow student of Vizyenos's, apparently in both Leipzig and Berlin. Thus, we can form the hypothesis that if, like Schreber's doctor and the precursors of schizophrenia and the signifier, Freud or Lacan had had the chance to meet that bizarre-looking Greek student too, they would probably have had a glimpse into a first-class example of an edifice that is tackling the challenges that the lack of help from established discourse pose to the schizophrenic concerning his or her body.

In *Part II* it was suggested that the subjective elements in Vizyenos' writing are those in which he is utilising the primary form of language that precedes the subject's encounter with the discourse of the Other; what Lacan calls *lalangue*. Vizyenos does so in the form of children's babbling, sounds from nature, Thracian exclamations, and untranslated words in Turkish, which he uses in his poetry and fiction. By bringing those resonances of the real under the yoke of the signifier, Vizyenos is indeed projecting libido—or jouissance—not to some form of otherness, but to an image of the child's body covered with the narcissistic brightness of writers from classical literature. Thus, a different relation to the imaginary register is established; but not that of the mirror stage and identification, from which stems an enjoyment that comes from the totality of the body image that small others or the Other acknowledge. Vizyenos manages to enjoy the body by naming it himself alone. His case demonstrates that subjects who are not assisted by established discourse are not doomed, deprived as they are of the potential for the paranoiac's breakthrough. If schizophrenics do not believe in otherness, their breakthrough can come from their believing in themselves, not thanks to an external interlocutor, but to a discourse that knots the body to the amalgam of real and symbolic in a solitary manner. This knotting can be approached through Lacan's theory of the sinthome.

In trying to link those findings to the contemporary psychoanalytic approach to schizophrenia in Chapters Eight and Nine, it was concluded that the sinthomatic approach should not be excluded from the prospects for patients with this psychotic sub-type. In fact, the sinthome is contrasted to theories and techniques that approach the schizophrenic subject and attempt a treatment only through the imaginary or the symbolic, ignoring the significance of the real. Such approaches seem to rather suit other subjective constitutions, like paranoia. Trying to make the subject abandon an elaboration on the One to become the interlocutor of an other, specular or related to discourse, is similar to asking them to betray one of the few things they experience as true, as not being make-believe.

These conclusions seem topical today, more than thirty years after Lacan's death, and almost a hundred and twenty years after Vizyenos'. This is because, despite the time that has passed, people, schizophrenic or not, have not stopped being troubled by what Lacan called the real. The quality of Vizyenos' case is that, regardless of its time, it shows how a subject can elaborate upon a specific concept that touches on the real in avoiding, temporarily, the risks the schizophrenic is prone to in relation to having a body. This is a thread extending indeed for more than a hundred and twenty years. Yet, as was concluded in *Part III*, we can pick it up in the twenty-first century and apply it to the clinic of schizophrenia, as I have attempted to demonstrate also based on other examples from my own clinical experience.

In fact, from the first steps of the research that generated this book, it was my intention for its conclusions, summarised above, to be of assistance to clinicians seeing schizophrenic subjects. It remains to be shown whether this attempt was successful, which does not go without saying. A number of paradoxes may, indeed, arise from the approach attempted in the previous two hundred pages, next to the one already remarked a few pages above. These could be my suggesting a treatment orientation for an entire clinical entity stemming from a single case; praising a treatment—Vizyenos'—that was only temporary; using throughout the study a term that is later suggested "not to exist", etc.

Justified as those reservations might be concerning the study's objective and scientific character, I am not of the opinion that they necessarily lead to the work conducted, and the product generated, lacking value for psychoanalysis or even for its study in academic settings. In contrast, I believe the above-mentioned conclusions to be in accordance with the ethics of psychoanalysis, as these were established by Freud and further elaborated by Lacan.

Indeed, the methodology employed for the study and the relative generation of findings may seem paradoxical: "to treat a schizophrenic patient in the twenty-first century based on what an odd Greek poet born in 1849 did"? I would not be surprised to read or hear this. Yet, who ever said that psychoanalysis is hostile to paradoxes? Freud pointed to the unconscious knowing no negation. Where others see a contradiction, a psychoanalyst looks for an accord. Paradox, like a number of other signifiers starting with the preposition παρά (para, Greek for "contra-"), like parapraxis or paranoia, seems to me to be friends of psychoanalysis. I would not therefore exclude from them *para*phrenia, the term Freud suggested for schizophrenia.

In fact, it seems that the "mysterious" link among the contradicting coordinates of those paradoxes has been already described a few times throughout this book. It is, in fact, the same thing that makes parapraxis, paranoia, etc., work: the relation to the real. If one accepts that psychoanalysis' stress on the singular, which aims at circumscribing the subject's relation to the real, makes every case unique—and it is only from such cases that we can draw lessons for the clinic—then the obstacle of the paradox is overcome. If everyone's relation to the real is singular, then it is only from singular cases that we can harvest useful conclusions for clinical work. In the pages of the present book, I have attempted to approach what the subject's relation to the real is on the occasion of studying Vizyenos, and how we can draw lessons from him that can be applied to the clinic of psychosis. Others before me have, and probably many more after me will, demonstrate this by use of the same method I have employed: the paradigm of the psychoanalytic case history.

On the other hand, I would not like to leave the reader with the impression that by simply highlighting the contrast between psycho-analytic and scientific discourse, everything is welcome. Even when not applied clinically, psychoanalysis requires meticulous investiga-tion, analysis, and interpretation. President Schreber was not a patient whom Freud or Lacan ever saw, but their respective readings of his case can hardly be described as shallow or superficial. Therefore, simply believing that research for and the writing of the present book has been conducted in the service of the psychoanalytic, rather than the scien-tific, discourse does not mean that mistakes, omissions, or imprecisions have been automatically avoided. Stating that we attempt to function under the psychoanalytic discourse is not an excuse for failure.

Thus, allow me to express the hope that the present is not one more study ruminating Freud and Lacan's theoretical teaching and clinical observations and that it can prove useful to the clinician confronted with the schizophrenic subject, as well as the reader who is interested in the theoretical conception of this condition.

And, finally, one last word about the man whose case occupied the two thirds of the book: the tormented Thracian poet, writer, and scholar Georgios Vizyenos. I would like to express the wish that this book has paid the respect due to this man, who suffered so much, alive and dead. I would be very disappointed for the present to be one more piece that merely cannibalises the Greek writer's life and work, by stretching infor-mation and biographical data to fit the hypotheses put forward. In other words, I hope I have managed to apply the principles of the psychoana-lytic case history and the ethics of psychoanalysis by which Freud and Lacan approached Schreber: to pursue the fragments of subjectivity, instead of turning the person studied into an object of one's jouissance.

This danger, to which both the writer and the clinician runs the risk of succumbing to has, I hope, been resisted here.

.

REFERENCES

Aflalo, A. (2015). *The Failed Assassination of Psychoanalysis; the Rise and Fall of Cognitivism*. London: Karnac.

Akrivos, K., Armaos, D., Karageorgiou, T., Bella, Z., & Bechlikoudi, D. (2010). *Neoelliniki Logotechnia Eniaiou Lykeiou; Theoritiki Kateuthinsi* [Senior High School Modern Greek Literature; Theoretical Direction]. Athens: OEDB.

Alanen, Y. (2009a). Can we approach patients with schizophrenic psychoses from a psychological basis? In: Y. Alanen, M. González de Chávez, A. L. Silver, & B. Martindale (Eds.). *Psychotherapeutic Approaches to Schizophrenic Psychoses: Past, Present and Future* (pp. 3–9). London: Routledge.

Alanen, Y. (2009b). The Schreber case and Freud's double-edged influence on the psychoanalytic approach to psychosis. In: Y. Alanen, M. González de Chávez, A. L. Silver, & B. Martindale (Eds.). *Psychotherapeutic Approaches to Schizophrenic Psychoses: Past, Present and Future* (pp. 23–37). London: Routledge.

Alexiou, M. (1995). Why Vizyenos? *Journal of Modern Greek Studies, 13*(2): 289–298.

Allouch, J. (2015). Psychotic transference. In: P. Gherovici & M. Steinkoler (Eds.). *Lacan on Madness: Madness, yes you can't* (pp. 113–126). Hove: Routledge.

American Psychiatric Association (1952). *Diagnostic and Statistical Manual of Mental Disorders*. Arlington: American Psychiatric Publishing.

227

American Psychiatric Association (2000). *Diagnostic and Statistical Manual of Mental Disorders, 4th Edition, Text Revision.* Washington DC: American Psychiatric Publishing.

American Psychiatric Association (2013). *Diagnostic and Statistical Manual of Mental Disorders, 5th Edition.* Washington DC: American Psychiatric Publishing.

Arieti, S. (1974). *Interpretation of Schizophrenia.* New York: Basic.

Athanasopoulos, V. (1992). *Oi mythoi tis zois kai tou ergou tou Georgiou Vizyenou* [Myths of the life and work of Georgios Vizyenos]. Athens: Kardamitsa.

Barbeito, P. F. (1995). Altered States: Space, Gender, and the (Un) making of Identity in the Short Stories of Georgios M. Vizyenos. *Journal of Modern Greek Studies, 13*(2): 299–326.

Baud, P. (2003). Contribution à l'histoire du concept de schizophrenie [contribution to the history of the concept of schizophrenia]. Doctoral thesis at the University of Geneva, no 10339. Available at: www.archive-ouverte. unige.ch/unige:205.

Beaton, R. (1988). Foreword. In: G. Vizyenos, *My Mother's Sin and Other Stories* (pp. vii–xv). Hanover: Brown University Press.

Beck, B. J. (2008). Mental disorders due to a general medical condition. In: T. A. Stern, J. F. Rosenbaum, M. Fava, M., et al. (Eds.). *Massachusetts General Hospital Comprehensive Clinical Psychiatry.* Philadelphia: Elsevier Mosby.

Biagi-Chai, F. (2011). Sinthome ou suppléance comme réponses au vide [sinthome or suppléance as responses to the void]. UFORCA pour l'université populaire Jacques Lacan. Available at: www.lacan-universite. fr/wp-content/uploads/2011/01/Sinthome-ou-suppl%C3%A9ance-9.pdf.

Biagi-Chai, F. (2014). *Le cas Landru: A la lumière de la psychoanalyse* [The case Landru in light of psychoanalysis]. Paris: Érès.

Bleuler, E. ([1911] 1993). *Dementia Praecox ou Groupe des schizophrénies* [Dementia Praecox or the Group of Schizophrenias]. Paris: E.P.E.L.

Bleuler, E. (1934). *Textbook of Psychiatry.* New York: The MacMillan Company.

Bonneau, B. (2011a). Quelques notes différentielles concernant la schizophrénie, la névrose obsessionnelle et l'autisme [Some differential remarks about schizophrenia, obsessional neurosis and autism]. Available at: www.psychasoc.com/Textes/Quelques-notes-differentielles-concernant-la-schizophrenie-la-nevrose-obsessionnelle-et-l-autisme.

Bonneau, B. (2011b). Un jeu (je) de cheval: Une invention schizophréne [The eye(I) of the horse, a schizophrenic invention]. Available at: www. psychasoc.com/Textes/Un-jeu-je-de-cheval-une-invention-schizophrene.

Braunstein, N. (2003). Desire and jouissance in the teaching of Jacques Lacan. In: J. M. Rabaté (Ed.). *The Cambridge Companion to Lacan* (pp. 102–115). Cambridge: Cambridge University Press.

Braunstein, N. (2015). "You cannot choose to go crazy." In: P. Gherovici & M. Steinkoler (Eds.). *Lacan on Madness: Madness, yes you can't* (pp. 86–98). Hove: Routledge.

Breuer, J., & Freud, S. ([1893–1895] 2001). Studies on Hysteria. In: *The Standard Edition of the Complete Psychological Works of Sigmund Freud, Vol II*. London: Vintage Classics.

Briole, G. (2012). Kraepelin, the Fragility of a Colossal Oeuvre. *Hurly-Burly, 8*: 125–147.

Briole, M. H. (2003). Towards an "Existence of Discourse." *Mental Online, 13*: 64–68.

Brousse, M. H. (2009). Ordinary Psychosis in the Light of Lacan's Theory of Discourse. *Psychoanalytical Notebooks, 19*: 7–19.

Burns, J. (2007). *The Descent of Madness: Evolutionary Origins of Psychosis and the Social Brain*. London: Routledge.

Chrysanthopoulos, M. ([1994] 2006). *Georgios Vizyenos: Metaxy fantasias kai mnimis* [Georgios Vizyenos: Between imagination and memory]. Athens: Estia.

Clogg, R. (2013). *A Concise History of Greece*. Cambridge: Cambridge University Press.

Cordié, A. (1993). *Les cancres n'existent pas: Psychanalyses d'enfants en échec scolaire* [There are no dunces: psychoanalysis of children with school problems]. Paris: Seuil.

Dalle, B., & Weill, M. (1999). Psychanalyse et schizophrénie [Psychoanalysis and schizophrenia]. Encyclopedie Medico-Chirurgicale. *Psychiatrie, 37-291-A-10*: 1–10.

Dalzell, T. (2011). *Freud's Schreber: Between Psychiatry and Psychoanalysis. On Subjective Disposition to Psychosis*. London: Karnac.

Dana, G. (2015). From psychotic illness to psychotic existence. In: P. Gherovici & M. Steinkoler (Eds.). *Lacan on Madness: Madness, yes you can't* (pp. 47–55). Hove: Routledge.

De Waelhens, A. (2001a). Psychoanalytic interpretation of Psychosis. The Paternal Metaphor and Foreclosure. In: A. De Waelhens & W. Ver Eecke. *Phenomenology and Lacan on Schizophrenia, after the Decade of the Brain* (pp. 191–228). Leuven: Leuven University Press.

De Waelhens, A. (2001b). Concluding Reflections on the Problem of Psychosis. Psychoanalytic and Existential Criteria in Psychosis. In: A. De Waelhens & W. Ver Eecke. *Phenomenology and Lacan on Schizophrenia, after the Decade of the Brain* (pp. 229–249). Leuven: Leuven University Press.

De Waelhens, A., & Ver Eecke, W. (2001). *Phenomenology and Lacan on Schizophrenia, after the Decade of the Brain*. Leuven: Leuven University Press.

Deffieux, J. P. (2014). Parousiasi astheni [Presentation of patient]. *I Psychanalysi, 8*: 67–89.

Demaras, K. (1972). *A History of Modern Greek Literature*. New York: State University of New York Press.

Decker, H. S. (2007). How Kraepelinian are the Neo-Kraepelinians? From Emil Kraepelin to DSM-III. *History of Psychiatry, 18*: 337–360.

Deutsch, H. (1942). Some forms of emotional disturbance and their relationship to schizophrenia. *Psychoanalytic Quarterly, 11*: 301–321.

Dimasi, M. (2013). *Lexeis apo tin tourkiki glossa sta diigimata tou Georgiou Vizyenou kai i simeiotiki symvoli tous stin afigimatiki ploki* [Words from the Turkish language in the short stories of Georgios Vizyenos and their semantic contribution to narrative plot]. Thessaloniki: Kyriakides.

Dimiroulis, D. ([2009] 2012). O Vizyenos kai to ypokeimeno tis grafis [Vizyenos and the subject of writing]. In: N. Mavrelos (Ed.). *To evros tou ergou tou Georgiou Vizyenou; palaioteres anagnoseis kai nees proseggiseis* (pp. 58–70). Athens: Sokoli-Kouledaki.

Dravers, P. (2005). Joyce & the Sinthome: Aiming at the Fourth term of the Knot. *Psychoanalytical Notebooks*. Available at: http://londonsociety-nls. org.uk/Publications/013/Joyce-sinthome.pdf.

Ebert, A., & Bär, K. J. (2010). Emil Kraepelin: A pioneer of scientific understanding of psychiatry and psychopharmacology. *Indian Journal of Psychiatry, 52*(2): 191–192.

Ellenberger, H. (1970). *The Discovery of the Unconscious: The History and Evolution of Dynamic Psychiatry*. New York: Basic.

Ellmann, R. (1983). *James Joyce*. Oxford: Oxford University Press.

Evans, D. (1996). *An Introductory Dictionary of Lacanian Psychoanalysis*. London: Routledge.

Eysenck, H. J., Arnold, W., & Meili, R. (1975). *Encyclopedia of Psychology*. London: Fontana.

Feyaerts, J., & Vanheule, S. (2015). Madness, Subjectivity and the Mirror Stage: Lacan and Merleau-Ponty. In: P. Gherovici & M. Steinkoler (Eds.). *Lacan on Madness: Madness, yes you can't* (pp. 159–172). Hove: Routledge.

Fierens, C. (2002). *Lecture de L'Étourdit. Lacan 1972*. Paris: L'Harmattan.

Fink, B. (1995). *The Lacanian Subject. Between Language and Jouissance*. Princeton: Princeton University Press.

Fink, B. (1997). *A Clinical Introduction to Lacanian Psychoanalysis. Theory and Technique*. Cambridge: Harvard University Press.

Freud, A. ([1936] 1992). *The Ego and the Mechanisms of Defence*. London: Karnac.

Freud, S. ([1893f] 2001). Charcot. *S.E.*, 3: 11–23. London: Vintage Classics.

Freud, S. ([1894a] 2001). The Neuro-Psychoses of Defence. *S. E.*, 3: 41–68. London: Vintage Classics.

Freud, S. ([1895b] 2001). On the Grounds for Detaching a Particular Syndrome from Neurasthenia under the description "anxiety neuroses". *S. E.*, 3: 85–117. London: Vintage Classics.

Freud, S. ([1895f] 2001). A Reply to Criticisms of my Paper on Anxiety Neurosis. *S. E.*, 3: 118–139. London: Vintage Classics.

Freud, S. ([1896a] 2001). Heredity and the Aetiology of the Neuroses. *S. E.*, 3: 141–156. London: Vintage Classics.

Freud, S. ([1896b] 2001). Further Remarks on the Neuro-Psychoses of Defence. *S. E.*, 3: 157–185. London: Vintage Classics.

Freud, S. ([1900a] 2001). *The Interpretation of Dreams. S. E.*, 4 & 5. London: Vintage Classics.

Freud, S. ([1901b] 2001). *The Psychopathology of Everyday Life. S. E., 5.* London: Vintage Classics.

Freud, S. ([1905c] 2001). *Jokes and their Relation to the Unconscious. S. E., 8.* London: Vintage Classics.

Freud, S. ([1905d] 2001). *Three Essays on the Theory of Sexuality. S. E., 7:* 123–245. London: Vintage Classics.

Freud, S. ([1905e] 2001). Fragment of an Analysis of a Case of Hysteria. *S. E.*, 7: 1–122. London: Vintage Classics.

Freud, S. ([1908] 1994). Letter #70F. In: S. McGuire (Ed.). *The Freud/ Jung Letters: The Correspondence between Sigmund Freud and C. G. Jung* (pp. 97–98). London: Penguin.

Freud, S. ([1911c] 2001). The Psycho-Analytic Notes on an Autobiographical Account of a Case of Paranoia (Dementia Paranoides). *S. E.*, 12: 3–82. London: Vintage Classics.

Freud, S. ([1912–1913] 2001). *Totem and Taboo. S. E., 13:* 1–162. London: Vintage Classics.

Freud, S. ([1914c] 2001). On Narcissism: An Introduction. *S. E.*, 14: 67–105. London: Vintage Classics.

Freud, S. ([1914d] 2001). On the History of the Psycho-Analytic Movement. *S. E.*, 14: 7–66. London: Vintage Classics.

Freud, S. ([1915e] 2001). The Unconscious. *S. E.*, 14: 159–215. London: Vintage Classics.

Freud, S. ([1916–1917] 2001). *Introductory Lectures on Psycho-Analysis (Parts I and II). S. E., 15.* London: Vintage Classics.

Freud, S. ([1917e] 2001). Mourning and Melancholia. *S. E.*, 14: 237–260. London: Vintage Classics.

Freud, S. ([1918b] 2001). From the History of an Infantile Neurosis. *S. E.*, 17: 3–122. London: Vintage Classics.

REFERENCES

Freud, S. ([1920g] 2001). *Beyond the Pleasure Principle. S. E., 18*: 3–65. London: Vintage Classics.

Freud, S. ([1923b] 2001). *The Ego and the Id. S. E., 19*: 1–66. London: Vintage Classics.

Freud, S. ([1924b] 2001). Neurosis and Psychosis. *S. E., 19*: 147–153). London: Vintage Classics.

Freud, S. ([1924c] 2001). The Economic Problem of Masochism. *S. E., 19*: 157–171. London: Vintage Classics.

Freud, S. ([1924e] 2001). The Loss of Reality in Neurosis and Psychosis. *S. E., 19*: 181–187. London: Vintage Classics.

Freud, S. ([1926d] 2001). *Inhibitions, Symptoms and Anxiety. S. E., 20*: 77–175. London: Vintage Classics.

Frou-Frou (1882). *Mi Hanese, 292, May, 12th, 1882, pp. 2–3* [translated for this edition].

Galiana-Mingot, É. (2012). Quelques préalables théorico-cliniques à la conceptualisation lacanienne des suppléances [Some Preliminary Theoretical and Clinical Remarks for a Lacanian Conceptualization of Supplementary Devices]. *Recherches en psychanalyse, I 2010*(9): 132–156.

Gallagher, C. (2002). The New Tyranny of Knowledge: Seminar XVII (1969–1970)—Background and Overview. *The Letter. Lacanian Perspectives on Psychoanalysis, 24*: 1–22.

Gallagher, C. (2011). Psychological Object or Speaking Subject: from Diagnosis to Case Re-presentation. *The Letter. Lacanian Perspectives on Psychoanalysis, 46*: 21–38.

Gaudillière, J. M., & Davoine, F. (2009). The contribution of some French psychoanalysts to the clinical and theoretical approaches to transference in the psychodynamic treatment of psychosis. In: Y. Alanen, M. González de Chávez, A. L. Silver, & B. Martindale (Eds.). *Psychotherapeutic Approaches to Schizophrenic Psychoses: Past, Present and Future* (pp. 137–144). London: Routledge.

Gault, J. L. (2007). Two Statuses of the Symptom "Let Us Return to Finn Again." In: V. Voruz, & B. Wolf (Eds.). *The Later Lacan. An Introduction* (pp. 73–82). Albany: State University of New York Press.

Gherovici, P., & Steinkoler, M. (2015). *Lacan on Madness: Madness, yes you can't.* Hove: Routledge.

Glowinski, H. (2001). Alienation and Separation. In: H. Glowinski, Z. Marks, & S. Murphy (Eds.). *A Compendium of Lacanian Terms* (pp. 9–13). London: Free Association.

Grasser, F. (1998). Stabilizations in Psychosis. Texte présenté à la Xème Journée d'étude du GRAPP, à Marseille, le 7 mars 1998. *Ornicar? Digital; 20.* Available at: http://web.missouri.edu/~stonej/stab2.pdf.

Grigg, R. (1999). From the Mechanism of Psychosis to the Universal Condition of the Symptom: On Foreclosure. In: D. Nobus (Ed.). *Key Concepts of Lacanian Psychoanalysis* (pp. 48–74). New York: Other Press.

Grigg, R. (2001). Quilting Point (point de capiton). In: H. Glowinski, Z. Marks, & S. Murphy (Eds.). *A Compendium of Lacanian Terms* (pp. 144–147). London: Free Association.

Grigg, R. (2015). Melancholia and the unabandoned object. In: P. Gherovici & M. Steinkoler (Eds.). *Lacan on Madness: Madness, yes you can't* (pp. 139–58). Hove: Routledge.

Guéguen, P. G. (1992). On Fantasy: Lacan and Klein. *Newsletter for the Freudian Field, 1 & 2*: 66–75.

Guéguen, P. G. (2013). Who is mad and who is not? On Differential Diagnosis in Psychoanalysis. *Culture/Clinic: Applied Lacanian Psychoanalysis, 1*: 61–78.

Hare, E. H. (1959). The Origin and Spread of Dementia Paralytica. *British Journal of Psychiatry, 105*: 594–626.

Hassiotis, G. (1910). *Byzantinai selides, dimosieutheisai kata ta eti 1907–1908 en ti efimeridi o "Tachydromos" (Constantinoupoleos) ypo to pseudonymon Moutzoflos* [Byzantine pages published in the years 1907–1908 at the newspaper o "Tachydromos" {of Constantinople} under the pseudonym Moutzoflos]. Athens: Sakellariou.

Hemrich, G. (1985). Poios Iton o Foneus tou Adelfou mou; Paratiriseis pano sto diigimatiko tropo tou Georgiou Vizyenou [Who Was my Brother's Killer; remarks on the narrative of Georgios Vizyenos]. *Thrakika Chronika, 40*: 5–9.

Hinshelwood, R. D. (2001) *Thinking about Institutions: Milieux and Madness*. London: Jessica Kingsley.

Hoenig, J. (1995). Schizophrenia: clinical section. In: G. Berrios, E. German, & R. Porter (Eds.). *A History of Clinical Psychiatry: The Origin and History of Psychiatric Disorders*. (pp. 336–348). London: Athlone.

Hoffmann, C. (2004). Quelques réflexions à propos du déclenchement de la psychose et de ses suppléances dans le monde de l'adolescent contemporain [Some thoughts on the triggering of psychosis and its suppléances in the modern adolescent's world]. *Figures de la psychanalyse, 9*: 49–61.

Hoffmann, K. (2009). The Burghölzli School. Bleuler, Jung, Spielrein, Binswager and others. In: Y. Alanen, M. González de Chávez, A. L. Silver, & B. Martindale (Eds.). *Psychotherapeutic Approaches to Schizophrenic Psychoses: Past, Present and Future* (pp. 38–49). London: Routledge.

Homer (2014). *The Iliad and the Odyssey*. New York: Barnes & Noble.

Indianos, A. (1934). O Vizyenos stin Kypro [Vizyenos in Cyprus]. *Kypriaka Grammata; Etos A'; 1; September 15th*: 18a–20b.

Joyce, J. ([1916] 1992). *A Portrait of the Artist as a Young Man*. London: Penguin.

Joyce, J. ([1922] 1992). *Ulysses*. London: Penguin.

Joyce, J. ([1939] 2012). *Finnegans Wake*. London: Wordsworth Classics.

Jung, C. G. (1906 [1909]). *On the Psychology of Dementia Præcox*. New York: The Journal of Mental Disease Publishing Company.

Kaneis Allos ([1884] 1894). Attikai Imeres [Attic Days]. *Asty; 29.6.1886, 41*: 2.

Kantzia, E. ([2009] 2012). *To Onoma kai to Pragma. Platonikoi apoihoi sto diigima tou G. M. Vizyenou Diati i Milia den Egine Milea* [The Name and the Thing; Platonic Resonances in G. M. Vizyenos' Why the Apple-Tree did not become the Apple-Bearing-Tree]. Athens: Ermis.

Keridis, D. (2009). *Historical Dictionary of Modern Greece*. Maryland: Scarecrow Press.

Kiris (1895). To Dromokaiteion/Syndialexis me ton Vizyenon [Dromokaiteion/Discussion with Vizyenos]. *Estia, May 16th*: 2.

Klein, M. (1930). The psychotherapy of the psychoses. *British Journal of Medical Psychology, 10*(3): 242–244.

Klein, M. ([1932] 1960). *The Psycho-Analysis of Children*. London: The Hogarth Press and the Institute of Psycho-Analysis.

Klein, M. (1946). Notes on Some Schizoid Mechanisms. *International Journal of Psycho-analysis*, 27: 99–110.

Klein, M. (1961). *Narrative of a Child Analysis*. London: Hogarth.

Klotz, J. P. (2009). Ordinary Psychosis and Modern Symptoms. *Psychoanalytical Notebooks, 19*: 21–31.

Koshy, A., & Roos, K (2012). Infections of the nervous system. In: R. B. Daroff, R. G. M. Fenichel, J. Jankovic, & J. C. Mazziotta (Eds.). *Bradley's Neurology in Clinical Practice. 6th Edition* (pp. 1259–1267). Philadelphia: Elsevier Saunders.

Koutrianou, E. (2003). Introduction in *G. M. Vizyenou Ta Poiemata Tomos A'* [The poems of G. M. Vizyenos, Vol. 1]. Athens: MIET.

Koutrianou, E. (2012). "Espoudazon kata ton hronon ekeinon en Gotiggi …" Zitimata poietikis sto ergo tou G. Vizyenoy kai to heirografo "Lyrica"["That year I was studying at Göttingen …" Issues of poetics in the work of G. Vizyenos and his manuscript "Lyrics"]. In: N. Mavrelos (Ed.). *To evros tou ergou tou Georgiou Vizyenou; palaioteres anagnoseis kai nees proseggiseis* (pp. 20–26). Athens: Sokoli-Kouledaki.

Koutsaftis, F. (2000). *Mourning rock* [Motion picture]. Greece: New Hellenic Television, Greek Centre for Cinematography & Filippos Koutsaftis.

Kraepelin, E. (1899 [1902]). *Clinical Psychiatry, a Textbook for Students and Physicians, abstracted and adapted from the seventh edition of the German edition of "Lehrbuch der psychiatrie" by A. Ross. Diefendore*. New York: The Macmillan Company.

Kraepelin, E. ([1904] 1968). *Lectures on Clinical Psychiatry*. New York: Hafnr Publishing Company.

Kraepelin, E. (1913). *General Paresis*. New York: The Journal of Mental Disease Publishing Company.

Küchenhoff, B. (2008). Bleuler, Jung and Freud on Dementia Praecox (Schizophrenia) in 1908. *The Letter, 40*: 69–82.

Kyriakos, K. ([2009] 2012). Skinikes kai kinimatographikes diaskeves ton ergon tou Georgiou Vizyenou [Theatrical and cinematographic adaptations of the works of Georgios Vizyenos]. In: N. Mavrelos (Ed.). *To evros tou ergou tou Georgiou Vizyenou; palaioteres anagnoseis kai nees proseggiseis* (pp. 180–197). Athens: Sokoli-Kouledaki.

Lacan, J. ([1932] 1975). *De la psychose paranoïaque dans ses rapports avec la personnalité*. Paris: Seuil.

Lacan, J. ([1933] 1975). Motifs du crime paranoïaque: Le Crime des soeurs Papin. In: J. Lacan. *De la psychose paranoïaque dans ses rapports avec la personnalité* (pp. 389–398). Paris: Seuil.

Lacan, J. ([1938] 2003). *Family Complexes in the Formation of the Individual*. London: Karnac.

Lacan, J. ([1946] 2006). Presentation on Psychical Causality. In: B. Fink (Ed.). *Jacques Lacan Écrits* (pp. 123–158). London: W. W. Norton and Company.

Lacan, J. ([1949] 2006). The Mirror Stage as Formative of the *I* Function as Revealed in Psychoanalytic Experience. In: B. Fink (Ed.) *Jacques Lacan Écrits* (pp. 75–81). London: W. W. Norton and Company.

Lacan, J. ([1951] 2006). Presentation on Transference. In: B. Fink (Ed.). *Jacques Lacan Écrits* (pp. 176–85). London: W. W. Norton and Company.

Lacan, J. ([1953a] 2006). The Function and Field of Speech and Language in Psychoanalysis. In: B. Fink (Ed.). *Jacques Lacan Écrits* (pp. 197–268). London: W. W. Norton and Company.

Lacan, J. ([1953b] 1991). *The Seminar of Jacques Lacan. Book I: Freud's Papers on Technique*. London: W. W. Norton and Company.

Lacan, J. ([1954] 2006). Response to Jean Hyppolite's commentary on Freud's "Verneinung". In: B. Fink (Ed.). *Jacques Lacan Écrits* (pp. 318–333). London: W. W. Norton and Company.

Lacan, J. ([1955a–1956a] 1993). *The Seminar of Jacques Lacan. Book III: The Psychoses*. London: Routledge.

Lacan, J. ([1955b] 1988). *The Seminar of Jacques Lacan. Book II: The Ego in Freud's Theory and in the Technique of Psychoanalysis*. Cambridge: Cambridge University Press.

Lacan, J. ([1957a] 2006). The Instance of the Letter in the Unconscious, or Reason Since Freud. In: B. Fink (Ed.). *Jacques Lacan Écrits* (pp. 412–441). London: W. W. Norton and Company.

Lacan, J. ([1957b] 1998). *Le Séminaire. Livre V: Les formations de l' Inconscient*. Paris: Seuil.

Lacan, J. ([1958a] 2006). On a Question Prior to Any Possible Treatment of Psychosis. In: B. Fink (Ed.). *Jacques Lacan Écrits* (pp. 445–88). London: W. W. Norton and Company.

Lacan, J. ([1958b] 2006). The Direction of the Treatment and the Principles of its Power. In: B. Fink (Ed.). *Jacques Lacan Écrits* (pp. 489–542). London: W. W. Norton and Company.

Lacan, J. ([1958c] 2013). *Le Séminaire. Livre VI: Le désir et son interprétation*. Paris: Martinière.

Lacan, J. ([1960a] 2006). The Subversion of the Subject and the Dialectic of Desire in the Freudian Unconscious. In: B. Fink (Ed.). *Jacques Lacan Écrits* (pp. 671–702). London: W. W. Norton and Company.

Lacan, J. ([1960b] 1992). *The Seminar of Jacques Lacan. Book VII: The Ethics of Psychoanalysis*. London: Routledge.

Lacan, J. ([1960–1961] 2001). *Le Séminaire. Livre VIII: Le transfert*. Paris: Seuil.

Lacan, J. ([1962–1963] 2014). *The Seminar of Jacques Lacan. Book X: Anxiety*. Cambridge & Malden: Polity Press.

Lacan, J. ([1963] 2005). *Des noms-du-père* [The Names-of-the-Father]. Paris: Seuil.

Lacan, J. ([1964a] 1998). *The Seminar of Jacques Lacan. Book XI: The Four Fundamental Concepts of Psychoanalysis*. New York: W. W. Norton & Company.

Lacan, J. ([1964b] 2006). On Freud's "Trieb" and the Psychoanalyst's Desire. In: B. Fink, (Ed.) *Jacques Lacan Écrits* (pp. 722–725). London: W. W. Norton and Company.

Lacan, J. ([1964c] 2006). Position of the Unconscious. In: B. Fink (Ed.). *Jacques Lacan Écrits* (pp. 703–721). London: W. W. Norton and Company.

Lacan, J. ([1964–1965] 2000). *Le Seminaire: Problèmes crouciaux pour la psychoanalyse*. Paris: Broché.

Lacan, J. ([1966a] 2001). Présentation des Mémoires d'un névropathe. In: J.-A. Miller (Ed.). *Autres écrits* (pp. 213–217). Paris: Seuil.

Lacan, J. ([1966b] 2001). Réponses à des étudiants en philosophie [Answers to students of philosophy]. In: J.-A. Miller (Ed.). *Autres écrits* (pp. 203–206). Paris: Seuil.

Lacan, J. (1967a). Petit discours aux psychiatres de Saint-Anne [Brief lecture to psychiatrists of Saint-Anne]. *Unpublished*.

Lacan, J. ([1967b] 2012). Address on Child Psychoses. *Hurly-Burly, 8*: 269–277.

Lacan, J. ([1969–1970] 2007). *The Seminar of Jacques Lacan. Book XVII: The Other Side of Psychoanalysis*. New York: W. W. Norton & Company.

Lacan, J. ([1971] 2007). *Le Séminaire. Livre XVIII: D'un discours qui ne serait pas du semblant*. Paris: Seuil.

Lacan, J. ([1971–1972] 2011). *Le Séminaire. Livre XIX: … ou pire*. Paris: Seuil.

Lacan, J. ([1972–1973] 1999). *The Seminar of Jacques Lacan. Book XX: On Feminine Sexuality, the Limits of Love and Knowledge*. New York: W. W. Norton & Company.

Lacan, J. ([1972] 1978). Du discours psychanalytique [On psychoanalytic discourse]. In: G. B. Contri (Ed.). *Lacan in Italia, 1953–1978. En Italie Lacan* (pp. 27–39). Milan: La Salamandra.

Lacan, J. ([1973a] 2001). L'Étourdit. In: J.-A. Miller (Ed.). *Autres écrits* (pp. 449–495). Paris: Seuil.

Lacan, J. ([1973b] 2001). Introduction à l'édition allemande d'un premier volume des Écrits. In: J.-A. Miller (Ed.). *Autres écrits* (pp. 553–559). Paris: Seuil.

Lacan, J. (1973–1974). *Le Séminaire. Livre XXI. Les Non-Dupes Errent*. Paris: Seuil.

Lacan, J. ([1975–1976] 2005). *Le Séminaire. Livre XXIII: Le sinthome*. Paris: Seuil.

Lacan, J. ([1975a] 2001). Joyce le symptôme. In: J.-A. Miller (Ed.). *Autres écrits* (pp. 565–570). Paris: Seuil.

Lacan, J. ([1975b] 2001). Présentation des Mémoirs d'un névropathe. In: J. Lacan *Autres écrits* (pp. 213–217). Paris: Seuil.

Lacan, J. ([1976a] 1989). Geneva lecture on the symptom. *Analysis*, 1: 7–25.

Lacan, J. ([1976b] 2013). Yale University: Lecture on the Body. *Culture/Clinic: Applied Lacanian Psychoanalysis*, 1: 5–7.

Lacan, J. ([1976c] 2013). Columbia University: Lecture on the symptom. *Culture/Clinic: Applied Lacanian Psychoanalysis*, 1: 8–16.

Lacan, J. ([1979] 2013). There are Four Discourses. *Culture/Clinic: Applied Lacanian Psychoanalysis*, 1: 3–4.

Laing, R. D. (1990). *The Politics of Experience and the Bird of Paradise*. New York: Penguin.

Laplanche, J., & Pontalis, J.-B. (1973). *The Language of Psycho-Analysis*. London: The Hogarth Press and the Institute of Psycho-Analysis.

Laurent, É (2003). Relieve Anxiety? *Mental Online, 13*: 6–14.

Laurent, É. (2007a). Three Enigmas: Meaning, Signification, Jouissance. In: V. Voruz & B. Wolf (Eds.). *The Later Lacan. An Introduction* (pp. 116–127). Albany: State University of New York Press.

Laurent, É. (2007b). The Purloined Letter and the Tao of the Psychoanalyst. In: V. Voruz & B. Wolf (Eds.). *The Later Lacan. An Introduction* (pp. 25–52). Albany: State University of New York Press.

Laurent, É. (2012). Psychosis or Radical Belief in the Symptom. *Hurly-Burly, 8*: 243–251.

Laurent, É. (2015a). The Stepladder (Escabeau) and Freudian Sublimation. *Lacanian Studies at the ECF: «Speaking lalangue of the body»; 04. II. 2015.*

Laurent, É. (2015b). Psychoanalysis and the post-DSM crisis. *Hurly-Burly, 12*: 41–56.

Leader, D. (2011). *What is Madness?* London: Penguin.

Leader, D. (2015). The specificity of manic-depressive psychosis. In: P. Gherovici & M. Steinkoler (Eds.). *Lacan on Madness: Madness, yes you can't* (pp. 127–38). Hove: Routledge.

Leucht, S., Corves, C., Arbter, D., Engel, R., Li, C., & Davis, J. (2009). Second-generation versus first-generation antipsychotic drugs for schizophrenia: a meta-analysis. *The Lancet, 373*(9657): 31–41.

Lysy–Stevens, A. (2002). What One Calls "Untriggered" Psychoses. *Courtil Papers*. Available at: www.ch-freudien-be.org/Papers/Txt/lysy-fc12.pdf.

MacCannell, J. F. (2015). The Open Ego. Woolf, Joyce and the "mad" subject. In: P. Gherovici & M. Steinkoler (Eds.). *Lacan on Madness: Madness, yes you can't* (pp. 205–218). Hove: Routledge.

Mackridge, P. (2009). *Language and National Identity in Greece.* Oxford: Oxford University Press.

Malengreau, P. (2003). The Psychotic's Partner and the Psychotic's Secretary. *Mental Online, 13*: 69–74.

Maleval, J. C. (2000). *La forclusion du nom-du-père. Le concept et sa Clinique* [The foreclosure of the Name-of-the-Father. The concept and its clinic]. Paris: Seuil.

Maleval, J. C. (2015). Treatment of the psychoses and contemporary psychoanalysis. In: P. Gherovici & M. Steinkoler (Eds.). *Lacan on Madness: Madness, yes you can't* (pp. 99–111). Hove: Routledge.

Mansell, P. (1995). *Constantinople: City of the World's Desire 1453–1924.* London: Murray.

Mavrelos, N. ([2009] 2012). *To evros tou ergou tou Georgiou Vizyenou; palaioteres anagnoseis kai nees proseggiseis* [The variety of Georgios Vizyenos's work: older readings and new approaches]. Athens: Sokoli-Kouledaki.

McGuire, S. (1994). *The Freud/Jung Letters: The Correspondence between Sigmund Freud and C. G. Jung.* New Jersey: Princeton University Press.

Menard, A. (2009). *Du symptôme au sinthome, le paradigme psychotique et son échec.* Extrait de la Conférence donnée le 17 octobre 2009, à la Section Clinique de Clermont-Ferrand. Available at: www.sectionclinique-clermont-ferrand.fr/FR/data/fichiers/file/a-menard-sc-clermont-ferrand.pdf.

Merry, B. (2004). *Encyclopedia of Modern Greek Literature.* Westport: Greenwood.

Miller, D. (2006). The Father and Invention. *Scilicet of the Name-of-the-Father-English version*: 62–63.

Miller, J.-A. ([1979] 2003). Jacques Lacan. In: N. Linardou-Blanchet (Ed.) *O Lacan kai I Psychanalysi* (pp. 13–23). Athens: Ekkremes.

Miller, J.-A. (1983). Schizophrénie et paranoïa [Schizophrenia and paranoia]. *Quarto, 10*: 18–38.

Miller, J.-A. ([1986] 2007). Paratiriseis gia tin ennoia tou perasmatos stin praxi sti didaskalia tou Jacques Lacan [Remarks on the concept of the passage à l'acte in Jacques Lacan's teaching]. In: N. Linardou-Blanchet & R. Blanchet (Eds.). *Theoria tis psychanalytikis therapeias* (pp. 152–161). Athens: Ekkremes.

Miller, J.-A. ([1987] 2003). Lacan kai psychosi [Lacan and psychosis]. In: N. Linardou-Blanchet (Ed.). *O Lacan kai I Psychanalysi* (pp. 59–78). Athens: Ekkremes.

Miller, J.-A. (1993). Forclusion généralisée [Generalised Foreclosure]. *Cahier/ Association de la Cause freudienne VLB*, 1: 4–8.

Miller, J.-A. (1997). *Les Conversations du Champ Freudien* [The Conversations of the Freudian Field]. Paris: Agalma.

Miller, J.-A. (2001). Ironic Clinic. *Psychoanalytical Notebooks*, 7: 9–24.

Miller, J.-A. (2003a). Lacan's later teaching. *Lacanian Ink; 21*. Available at: http://www.lacan.com/frameXXI2.htm.

Miller, J.-A. (2003b). The Incidence of the Subject in the Psychoses. *(Re)-turn: A Journal of Lacanian Studies*, 1: 35–60.

Miller, J.-A. (2006). Le tout dernier Lacan [The final Lacan]. *Orientation Lacanienne III*, Année 2006.

Miller, J.-A. (2007). The Sinthome, a Mixture of Symptom and Fantasy. In: V. Voruz & B. Wolf (Eds.). *The Later Lacan. An Introduction* (pp. 55–72). Albany: State University of New York Press.

Miller, J.-A. (2008). Everyone is mad. *Culture/Clinic*, 1: 17–42.

Miller, J.-A. (2009a). Ordinary psychosis revisited. *Psychoanalytical Notebooks*, 19: 139–167.

Miller, J.-A. (2009b). *I Aitiogenesi tou ypokeimenou* [The Causation of the subject]. *I Psychanalysi*, 6: 28–67.

Miller, J.-A. (2010). *L'Autre Méchant: Six cas cliniques commentés* [The bad Other: Six commented clinical cases]. Paris: Navarin.

Miller, J.-A. (2011). L'un tout seul [The one all alone]. *Orientation Lacanienne III*, Année 2011.

Miller, J.-A. (2012). Psychotic Invention. *Hurly-Burly*, 8: 253–268.

Miller, J.-A. (2013). The Other without Other. *Hurly-Burly*, 10: 15–29.

Miller, J.-A. (2015). The Unconscious and the speaking body. *Hurly-Burly*, 12: 119–132.

Mooers, C. (1991). *The Making of Bourgeois Europe*. London: Verso.

Morel, G. (2003). A Young Man without an Ego: A Study of James Joyce and the Mirror Stage. In: P. Adams (Ed.). *Art: Sublimation or Symptom* (pp. 123–146). London: Karnac.

Morel, G. (2011). *Sexual Ambiguities*. London: Karnac.

Morel, G. (2015). Ilse or the law of the mother. In: P. Gherovici & M. Steinkoler (Eds.). *Lacan on Madness: Madness, yes you can't* (pp. 33–46). Hove: Routledge.

Moscowitz, A., & Heim, G. (2011). Eugen Bleuler's Dementia Praecox or the Group of Schizophrenias (1911): A Centenary Appreciation and Reconsideration. *Schizophrenia Bulletin, 37*(3): 471–479.

Moulas, P. ([1980] 1994). O Georgios Vizyenos kai to Neoelliniko Diigima [Georgios Vizyenos and the Modern Greek Short Story]. In: G. Vizyenos. *Neoellinika Diigimata*. Athens: Ermis.

Moulas, P. (2013). *G. M. Vizyenos. Stous dromous tis logiosynis* [G. M. Vizyenos. In the roads of scholarship]. Athens: Cultural Foundation of the National Bank.

Nicolle, D., & Hook, C. (1995). *The Janissaries*. Oxford: Osprey Publishing.

Nobus, D. (1999). Life and Death in the Glass: A New Look at the Mirror Stage. In: D. Nobus (Ed.). *Key Concepts of Lacanian Psychoanalysis* (pp. 101–138). New York: Other Press.

Palamas, K. (1994). *Apanta*, Vol. VIII [Complete works]. Athens: Kostis Palamas Foundation.

Pankow, G. ([1958] 2011). À propos de l'expérience du miroir dans la névrose et dans la psychose [About the mirror experience in neurosis and psychosis]. *L'évolution psychiatrique, 76*: 373–390.

Papadopoulou, I. ([2009] 2012). I kalogeri kai i latreia tou Dionysou en Thrakei: O G. Vizyenos, i "martyria" tou gia tin epiviosi enos "archaiou" dromenou sti Thraki kai I schesi tou syggrafea me to archaio drama [Monks and the worship of Dionysus in Thrace: G. Vizyenos, his "testimony" on the survival of an "ancient" event in Thrace and the write's relation to acient drama]. In: N. Mavrelos (Ed.). *To evros tou ergou tou Georgiou Vizyenou; palaioteres anagnoseis kai nees proseggiseis* (pp. 199–214). Athens: Sokoli-Kouledaki.

Papakostas, Y. (2004). *Georgiou Vizyenou Epistoles* [Letters by Georgios Vizyenos]. Athens: Pataki.

Paschalis, M. ([2009] 2012). O Latinikos vios (vita) tou Georgiou Vizyenou: logotechnika protypa kai ideologia [The Latin life (vita) of Georgios Vizyenos: literary patterns and ideology]. In: N. Mavrellos (Ed.). *To evros tou ergou tou Georgiou Vizyenou; palaioteres anagnoseis kai nees proseggiseis* (pp. 215–227). Athens: Sokoli-Kouledaki.

Pellion, F. (2009). Quelques réflexions sur la pertinence clinique et psychopathologique de la notion de «suppléance» [Some reflections upon the clinical pertinence and psychopathology of the notion of "suppléance"]. *Recherces en psychanalyse, 1 2009*(7): 92–101.

Redmond, J. D. (2013). Contemporary perspectives on Lacan's theories of psychosis. *Frontiers in Psychology, 4*: 350. Available at: www.ncbi.nlm.nih.gov/pmc/articles/PMC3695380/.

Ribolspi, M., Feyaerts, J., & Vanheule, S. (2015). Metaphor in psychosis: on the possible convergence of Lacanian theory and neuro-scientific

research. *Frontiers in Psychology, 6: 664.* Available at: www.ncbi.nlm.nih.
gov/pmc/articles/PMC4452801/.

Rodriguez, L. (2001). Autism and Childhood Psychosis. In: H. Glowinski,
Z. Marks, & S. Murphy (Eds.). *A Compendium of Lacanian Terms* (19–32).
London: Free Association.

Roudinesco, E. (1997). *Jacques Lacan: An Outline of a Life and History of a
System of Thought.* Cambridge: Polity Press.

Rousseau, J. J. ([1762] 2007). *Emile; or On Education.* Sioux Falls: Nuvision.

Sauvagnat, F. (2000). On the specificity of elementary phenomena. *Psychoanalytical Notebooks, 4:* 95–110.

Scharfetter, C. (2001). Eugen Bleuler's schizophrenia's–synthesis of various
concepts. *Schweizer Archiv fur Neurologie und Psychiatrie, 152:* 34–37.

Schreber, D. P. ([1903] 2000). *Memoirs of My Nervous Illness.* New York: New
York Reviews Books Classics.

Sideras, A., & Sideras-Lytra, P. (2009). Introduction in *Vizyenos, G.
To Paidiko Paichnidi se Schesi me tin Psychologia kai tin Pedagogiki*
[Children's play in terms of psychology and pedagogy]. Thessaloniki:
Kyriakides.

Skriabine, P. (2009). Ordinary Psychosis with a Borromean Approach. *Psychoanalytical Notebooks, 19:* 45–55.

Sledge, W. (1992). Classic Article: Introduction to Victor Tausk's On the
Origin of the "Influencing Machine" in Schizophrenia. *Journal of Psychotherapy Practice and Research, 1*(2): 184–206.

Solano Suarez, E. (2006). Jouissance and the Name-of-the-Father. *Scilicet of
the Name-of-the-Father-English version:* 65–67.

Soler, C. ([1988] 2012). Le travail de la psychose [Work with psychosis]. In:
C. Soler (Ed.) *L'inconscient à ciel ouvert de la psychose* (pp. 187–193). Toulouse: Presses Universitaires du Mirail.

Soler, C. ([1992a] 2012). Stabilization de la psychose [Stabilization of psycho-
sis]. In: C. Soler (Ed.). *L'inconscient à ciel ouvert de la psychose* (pp. 195–210).
Toulouse: Presses Universitaires du Mirail.

Soler, C. ([1992b] 2012). L' expérience énigmatique du psychotique, de
Schreber à Joyce [The enigmatic experience of the psychotic, from
Schreber to Joyce]. In: C. Soler (Ed.). *L'inconscient à ciel ouvert de la psy-
chose* (pp. 97–114). Toulouse: Presses Universitaires du Mirail.

Soler, C. ([1999] 2012). Le dit schizophrène [The so-called schizophrenic].
In: C. Soler (Ed.). *L'inconscient à ciel ouvert de la psychose* (pp. 115–123).
Toulouse: Presses Universitaires du Mirail.

Soler, C. (2003). The paradoxes of the symptom in psychoanalysis. In: J. M.
Rabaté (Ed.). *The Cambridge Companion to Lacan* (pp. 86–101). Cambridge:
Cambridge University Press.

Soler, C. (2014). *Lacan—The Unconscious Reinvented.* London: Karnac.

Stefanou, S. (1936). Torina kai Perasmena/Georgios Vizyenos/Philologikai Anamniseis [Current and Past/George Vizyenos/Philological Memories]. *Athinaika Nea, March 14th*: 3.

Stevens, A. (2009). Mono-symptoms and Hints of Ordinary Psychosis. *Psychoanalytical Notebooks, 19*: 57–66.

Szasz, T. (1974). *Schizophrenia: The Sacred Symbol of Psychiatry*. New York: Basic.

Tandon, R., Keshavan, M., & Nasrallah, H. (2008a). Schizophrenia, "Just the facts": What we know in 2008: Part 1: Overview. *Schizophrenia Research, 100*(1–3): 4–19.

Tandon, R., Belmakerc, R. H., Gattazd, W., Lopez-Ibor J., Okashaf, A., Singhg, B., Steinh, D., Oliei, J. P., Fleischhackerj, W., & Moellerb, H. J. (2008b). World Psychiatric Association Pharmacopsychiatry Section statement on comparative effectiveness of antipsychotics in the treatment of schizophrenia. *Schizophrenia Research, 100*(1–3): 20–38.

Tandon, R., Gaebel, W., Barch, D., Bustillo, J., Gur, R., Heckers, S., Malaspina, D., Owen, M., Schultz, S., Tsuang, M., Van Os, J., & Carpenter, W. (2013). Definition and description of schizophrenia in the DSM-5. *Schizophrenia Research, 150*: 3–10.

Tausk, V. ([1919] 1992). On the Origin of the "Influencing Machine" in Schizophrenia. *Journal of Psychotherapy Practice and Research, 1*(2): 185–206.

Thurston, L. (1999). Ineluctable Nodalities: On the Borromean Knot. In: D. Nobus (Ed.). *Key Concepts of Lacanian Psychoanalysis* (pp. 139–63). New York: Other Press.

Valéttas, G. (1892 [1937]). Philologika sto Vizyeno [Philological in Vizyenos]. *Thrakika, 8*: 266.

Vanheule, S. (2011a). *The Subject of Psychosis: A Lacanian Perspective*. London: Palgrave MacMillan.

Vanheule, S. (2011b). A Lacanian perspective on psychotic hallucinations. *Theory & Psychology, 21*(1): 86–106.

Vanheule, S. (2012). Diagnosis in the field of psychotherapy: a plea for an alternative to the DSM-5. *Psychology and Psychotherapy: Theory, Research and Practice, 85*: 128–142.

Vanheule, S. (2014). *Diagnosis and the DSM. A Critical Review*. Basingstoke: Palgrave Macmillan.

Vanheule, S., & Geldhof, A. (2012). Knotted subjectivity: On Lacan's use of knot theory in building a non-universalist theory of the subject. In: A. Gülerce (Ed.). *Re (con) figuring psychoanalysis: Critical Juxtapositions of the Philosophical, the Socio-historical and the Political* (pp. 114–128). London: Palgrave MacMillan.

Varelas, L. (2014). *Meta tharrous anisihian empneontos: I kritiki proslipsi toy Vizyenou* [Courageously inspiring anxiety: The critical reception of Vizyenos]. Thessaloniki: University Studio Press.

Vasiliadis, N. (1910). *Eikones Konstantinoupoleos kai Athinon* [Images from Constantinople and Athens]. Athens: Estia [translated for this edition].

Ver Eecke, W. (2001a). Situating the Contribution of A. De Waelhens. In: A. De Waelhens & W. Ver Eecke. *Phenomenology and Lacan on Schizophrenia, after the Decade of the Brain* (pp. 15–36). Leuven: Leuven University Press.

Ver Eecke, W. (2001b). The usefulness of the theory of De Waelhens/Lacan as an effective approach to schizophrenia, after the decade of the brain. In: A. De Waelhens & W. Ver Eecke. *Phenomenology and Lacan on Schizophrenia, after the Decade of the Brain* (pp. 37–121). Leuven: Leuven University Press.

Ver Eecke, W. (2009). Philosophical Questions about the Theory of Psychosis in the Early Lacan. *Psychoanalytical Notebooks, 19*: 233–239.

Verhaeghe, P. (1994). From Impossibility to Inability: Lacan's theory of the Four Discourses. *The Letter, 3*: 76–99.

Verhaeghe, P. (1999). Causation and Destitution of a Pre-ontological Non-entity: On the Lacanian Subject. In: D. Nobus (Ed.). *Key Concepts of Lacanian Psychoanalysis* (pp. 164–189). New York: Other Press.

Verhaeghe, P. (2008). *On Being Normal and Other Disorders. A Manual for Clinical Psychodiagnostics*. London: Karnac.

Verhaeghe, P. (2015). Today's madness does not make sense. In: P. Gherovici & M. Steinkoler (Eds.). *Lacan on Madness: Madness, yes you can't* (pp. 68–81). Hove: Routledge.

Vizyenos, G. ([1873] 1996). Poiitika Protoleia [Poetic Juvenilia]. In: E. Koutrianou (Ed.). *G. M. Vizyenos Ta Poiimata* (pp. 233–263). Athens: Kostas & Eleni Ourani Foundation.

Vizyenos, G. ([1881a] 2004). Curriculum Vitæ. In: Y. Papakostas (Ed.). *Georgiou Vizyenou Epistoles* (pp. 42–45). Athens: Pataki.

Vizyenos, G. ([1881b] 2009). *To Paidiko Paichnidi se Schesi me tin Psychologia kai tin Pedagogiki* [Children's play in terms of psychology and pedagogy]. Thessaloniki: Kyriakides [translated for this edition].

Vizyenos, G. ([1883a] 1988). My Mother's Sin. In: G. Vizyenos. *My Mother's Sin and Other Short Stories by Georgios Vizyenos* (pp. 4–23). Hanover: Brown University Press.

Vizyenos, G. ([1883b] 1988). Who was my Brother's Killer? In: G. Vizyenos. *My Mother's Sin and Other Stories by Georgios Vizyenos* (pp. 56–94). Hanover: Brown University Press.

Vizyenos, G. ([1883c] 1988). Between Piraeus and Naples. In: G. Vizyenos. *My Mother's Sin and Other Stories by Georgios Vizyenos* (pp. 24–52). Hanover: Brown University Press.

Vizyenos, G. ([1883–1884] 2014). *Thracian Tales*. Athens: Aiora.

Vizyenos, G. ([1884a] 1988). The Consequences of the Old Story. In: G. Vizyenos. *My Mother's Sin and Other Stories by Georgios Vizyenos* (pp. 99–152). Hanover: Brown University Press.

Vizyenos, G. ([1884b] 1988). The Only Journey of His Life. In: G. Vizyenos. *My Mother's Sin and Other Stories by Georgios Vizyenos* pp. 155–183). Hanover: Brown University Press.

Vizyenos, G. ([1885a] 2001). Why the Apple Tree Did Not Become the Apple-Bearing Tree. *Modern Greek Studies Yearbook, 16–17*: 155–157.

Vizyenos, G. ([1885b] 2013). Stoicheia Logikis [Elements of Logic]. In: P. Moulas (Ed.). *G. M. Vizyenos. Stous dromous tis logiosynis* (pp. 159–282). Athens: Cultural Foundation of the National Bank.

Vizyenos, G. ([1888a] 2013). Oi Kalogeroi kaii latreia tou Dionyssou en Thrakei [Monks and the worship of Dionysus in Thrace] In: P. Moulas (Ed.). *G. M. Vizyenos. Stous dromous tis logiosynis* (pp. 283–329). Athens: Cultural Foundation of the National Bank.

Vizyenos, G. ([1888b] 2013). Stoicheia Psychologias [Elements of Psychology]. In: *G. M. Vizyenos. Stous dromous tis logiosynis* (pp. 331–470). Athens: Cultural Foundation of the National Bank.

Vizyenos, G. ([1888c] 2013). Ai eikastikai technai kata tin a' eikosipentaetirida tis vasileias Georgiou A' [Fine arts during the first quarter century of the reign of George I]. In: P. Moulas (Ed.). *G. M. Vizyenos. Stous dromous tis logiosynis* (pp. 475–528): Athens: Cultural Foundation of the National Bank.

Vizyenos, G. ([1889–1892] 2013). Epilogi limmaton tou G. M. Vizyenou apo to Egkyklopaidikon Lexicon ton Bart & Hirst [Chosen entries by G. M. Vizyenos from the Encyclopedic Dictionary by Bart & Hirst]. In: P. Moulas (Ed.). *G. M. Vizyenos. Stous dromous tis logiosynis* (pp. 529–597). Athens: Cultural Foundation of the National Bank.

Vizyenos, G. ([1890] 2004). Epistoli #14. In: Y. Papakostas (Ed.). *Georgiou Vizyenou Epistoles* [Letters by Georgios Vizyenos] (pp. 73–76). Athens: Pataki [translated for this edition].

Vizyenos, G. ([1892] 2013). Errikos Ibsen [Henrik Ibsen]. In: P. Moullas (Ed.). *G. M. Vizyenos. Stous dromous tis logiosynis* (pp. 581–597). Athens: Cultural Foundation of the National Bank.

Vizyenos, G. (1894). Ana ton Elikona: Ballísmata [On Helicon: Ballads]. In: P. Moulas (Ed.). *G. M. Vizyenos. Stous dromous tis logiosynis* (pp. 599–710). Athens: Cultural Foundation of the National Bank.

Vizyenos, G. ([1895] 1988). Moscóv-Selím. In: G. Vizyenos. *My Mother's Sin and Other Stories by Georgios Vizyenos* (pp. 186–229). Hanover: Brown University Press.

Vizyenos, G. (1997). *Georgios Vizyenos Paidikai Poiiseis* [Georgios Vizyenos. Children's Poems]. Thesaloniki: Zitros [translated for this edition].

Vizyenos, G. (2003). *G. M. Vizyenos. Ta Poiimata* [G. M. Vizyenos. The Poems]. Athens: Kostas & Eleni Ourani Foundation [translated for this edition].

Voruz, V., & Wolf, B. (2007). *The Later Lacan. An Introduction*. Albany: State University of New York Press.

Wachsberger, H. (2007). From the Elementary Phenomenon to the Enigmatic Experience. In: V. Voruz & B. Wolf (Eds.). *The Later Lacan. An Introduction* (pp. 107–115). Albany: State University of New York Press.

Warner, R. (1994). *Recovery from Schizophrenia: Psychiatry and Political Economy*. London: Routledge.

Wundt, W. ([1896] 2013). *Lectures On Human And Animal Psychology*. London: Forgotten Books.

Wyatt, W. (1988a). Introduction to My Mother's Sin. In: G. Vizyenos. *My Mother's Sin and Other Stories by Georgios Vizyenos* (pp. 1–3). Hanover: Brown University Press.

Wyatt, W. (1988b). Introduction to Who Was My Brother's Killer? In: G. Vizyenos. *My Mother's Sin and Other Stories by Georgios Vizyenos* (pp. 53–94). Hanover: Brown University Press.

Xireas, M. (1949). *Agnosta Viografika Stoiheia kai Kataloipa tou Vizyenou* [Unknown Biographical Elements and Remnants of Vizyenos]. Nicosia, Cyprus.

Zenoni, A. (2008). The Psychoanalytic Clinic in Institution: Psychosis. *Courtil Papers*. Available at: www.ch-freudien-be.org/Papers.

Zenoni, A. (2012). La mesure de la psychose: Note sur ladite schizophré-nie [The measure of psychosis: Notes on so-called schizophrenia]. In: A. Zenoni (Ed.). *L'Autre pratique clinique: Psychanalyse et institution thérapeutique* (pp. 158–176). Toulouse: Érès.

INDEX

affective psychosis, 9
Aflalo, A., 12, 27, 65, 66, 77, 184, 185,
        188, 191, 198
Akrivos, K., 128
Alanen, Y., 9, 21, 29
Alexiou, M., 117, 128
alienation and separation, 67, 69, 73
        and psychotic subject, 179
Allouch, J., 60, 61, 200
analyst as other, 59
Arbter, D., 196
Arieti, S., 173
Armaos, D., 128
Arnold, W., 8
artificial personalities, 56
as-if personality, 55–56, 203–204
Athanasopoulos, V., 96, 97, 101,
        110, 115, 116, 117, 119, 121,
        122, 124, 133, 134, 135, 140,
        141, 142, 143, 144, 147,
        149, 213
autism, 17, 107, 217
auto-eroticism

absence of capacity to establish
        otherness, 168
cathexis of libido to
        word-presentations, 29
Lacan on, 42
libido, 23

Bär, K. J., 8
Barbeito, P. F., 117
Barch, D., 189
Baud, P., 18
Beaton, R., 134
Bechlikoudi, D., 128
Beck, B. J., 146
being and having, 159
Bella, Z., 128
Belmakerc, R. H., 196
Biagi-Chai, F., 80, 94, 112, 148, 157,
        161, 182, 183, 215, 216
big Other, 47–49, 51, 55, 64, 65–66,
        72, 167, 177, 179, 212, 219
Bleuler, E., xii, 3, 7, 25, 27, 30, 48,
        175, 189

247

For Product Safety Concerns and Information please contact our EU
representative GPSR@taylorandfrancis.com
Taylor & Francis Verlag GmbH, Kaufingerstraße 24, 80331 München, Germany

www.ingramcontent.com/pod-product-compliance
Lightning Source LLC
Chambersburg PA
CBHW050704280326
41926CB00088B/2517